CW00539051

GERMAN
SENTENCE BUILDERS

A lexicogrammar approach

Pre-intermediate to Intermediate

THE LANGUAGE GYM

Copyright © G. Conti and D. Viñales

All rights reserved
ISBN: 9783949651298

Imprint: Independently Published

Edited by Alice Wallner

About the authors

Gianfranco Conti taught for 25 years at schools in Italy, the UK and in Kuala Lumpur, Malaysia. He has also been a university lecturer, holds a Master's degree in Applied Linguistics and a PhD in metacognitive strategies as applied to second language writing. He is now an author, a popular independent educational consultant and professional development provider. He has written around 2,000 resources for the TES website, which have awarded him the Best Resources Contributor in 2015. He has co-authored the best-selling and influential book for world languages teachers, "The Language Teacher Toolkit", "Breaking the sound barrier: Teaching learners how to listen", in which he puts forth his Listening As Modelling methodology and "Memory:what every language teacher should know". Gianfranco writes an influential blog on second language acquisition called The Language Gym, co-founded the interactive website language-gym.com and the Facebook professional group Global Innovative Language Teachers (GILT). Last but not least, Gianfranco has created the instructional approach known as E.P.I. (Extensive Processing Instruction) which underpins the content and structure of this book.

Dylan Viñales has taught for 15 years, in schools in Bath, Beijing and Kuala Lumpur in state, independent and international settings. He lives in Kuala Lumpur. He is fluent in five languages, and gets by in several more. Dylan is, besides a teacher, a professional development provider, specialising in E.P.I., metacognition, teaching languages through music (especially ukulele) and cognitive science. In the last five years, together with Dr Conti, he has driven the implementation of E.P.I. in one of the top international schools in the world: Garden International School. This has allowed him to test, on a daily basis, the sequences and activities included in this book with excellent results (his students have won language competitions both locally and internationally).

Sonja Fedrizzi graduated from the University of Vienna in 2007. In the 15 years since, she has taught all levels of German, Spanish, French and EAL in both the state and private sector in Austria, Australia and since 2016 in Scotland. Sonja is an involved member of the Scottish and UK modern language teachers' community, with regular appearances on language teaching webinars and conferences where she shares her expertise in blended and digital teaching. One focus area has been the implementation of the E.P.I. method in the digitally assisted classroom, which she has been refining in her classrooms for more than two years. Gianfranco Conti's approach to engagement has measurably improved learning outcomes for her students, and Sonja views E.P.I. as an inclusive game-changing method, capable of nurturing student confidence, self-efficacy and achievement. A native speaker of German, Sonja became lead author for German content on the Language Gym in 2021.

DEDICATION

For Catrina
- Gianfranco

For Ariella and Leonard
- Dylan

For E & P
- Sonja

Acknowledgements

Writing a book is a time-consuming yet rewarding endeavour, although it's a bit easier the third time round. Dylan would like to thank his wife, Natasha, again for her help and support, for being an amazing mother and partner; and for generally holding the fort while he worked away at his part of the book. He would also like to thank his parents, John and Angie, for their unconditional and unwavering support and love.

Gian would like to thank his long-time partner, Corynn, for her unconditional support during the creation of this volume.

Sonja would like to thank her husband for his ongoing support and her mother-in-law for cooking her meals whilst she was busy writing this book. Alice, Sandi, Sarah, Nicola, Simona, Elena, Silvia and Dannielle, thank you for your encouragement. Klaudia, thank you for the finishing touches. Dylan and Gianfranco, thank you for this opportunity, your patience and wisdom. I have been fortunate to learn from the best. Herzlichen Dank.

Secondly, a huge thanks to our editor:

Alice Wallner graduated from the University of Vienna in 2008. She has been teaching German as a foreign language at the University of Vienna in Austria, the Metropolitan University of Educational Sciences in Chile, and at King's College London. She also worked at London's Goethe Institut. Since 2019, she has been teaching German and English as foreign languages at the University Preparation Programme of the Vienna Universities. Her contributions to this book have gone far beyond editing and proofreading.

Thirdly, heartfelt thanks to our designer Jean for the superb work carried out designing the book cover and the other illustrations and graphics within this book.

Finally, thanks to all the wonderful, supportive and passionate educators on Twitter who have helped enhance our book with their suggestions and comments, and to the members of the Global Innovative Language Teachers (GILT) Facebook group for their engagement and input into our polls. We consider ourselves very lucky to have such colleagues to inspire and spur us on.

Vielen Dank an euch alle.

Introduction

Hello and welcome to the first 'text' book designed to be an accompaniment to a German, Extensive Processing Instruction course. The book has come about out of necessity, because such a resource did not previously exist.

How to use this book if you have bought into our E.P.I. approach

This book was originally designed as a resource to use in conjunction with our E.P.I. approach and teaching strategies. Our course favours flooding comprehensible input, organising content by communicative functions and related constructions, and has a big focus on reading and listening as modelling. The aim of this book is to empower the pre-intermediate to intermediate learner with linguistic tools - high-frequency structures and vocabulary - useful for real-life communication. Since, in a typical E.P.I. unit of work, aural and oral work play a huge role, this book should not be viewed as the ultimate E.P.I. coursebook, but rather as a **useful resource** to **complement** your Listening-As-Modelling and Speaking activities.

Sentence Builders – Online Resources

Please note that all the content from these units also exist inside the Vocab Trainer, Boxing Game and Audio Boxing Game on the Language Gym website (available via subscription), inside a designated Book level, which match, unit by unit, the content of this book. There are also downloadable sentence builders which will be available in bilingual and German only versions on the Locker Room section, also on the Language Gym.

How to use this book if you don't know or have NOT yet bought into our approach

Alternatively, you may use this book to dip in and out of as a source of printable material for your lessons. Whilst our curriculum is driven by communicative functions rather than topics, we have deliberately embedded the target constructions in topics which are popular with teachers and commonly found in published coursebooks.

If you would like to learn about E.P.I. you could read one of the authors' blogs. The definitive guide is Dr Conti's "Patterns First – How I Teach Lexicogrammar" which can be found on his blog (www.gianfrancoconti.com). There are also blogs on Dylan's wordpress site (mrvinalesmfl.wordpress.com) such as "Using sentence builders to reduce (everyone's) workload and create more fluent linguists" which can be read to get teaching ideas and to learn how to structure a course, through all the stages of E.P.I.

The book "Breaking the Sound Barrier: Teaching Learners how to Listen" by Gianfranco Conti and Steve Smith, provides a detailed description of the approach and of the listening and speaking activities you can use in synergy with the present book.

The basic structure of the book

The book contains 19 macro-units which concern themselves with a specific communicative function, such as '**Saying where I live**', '**Talking about my daily routine and activities**', '**Making after-school plans with a friend**' or '**Talking about a recent day trip**'. You can find a note of each communicative function in the Table of Contents. Each unit includes:

- a sentence builder modelling the target constructions;
- a set of vocabulary building activities which reinforce the material in the sentence builder;
- a set of narrow reading texts exploited through a range of tasks focusing on both the meaning and structural levels of the text;
- a set of translation tasks aimed at consolidation through retrieval practice;
- a set of writing tasks targeting essential writing micro-skills such as spelling, functional and positional processing, editing and communication of meaning.

Each sentence builder at the beginning of a unit contains one or more constructions which have been selected with real-life communication in mind. Each unit is built around that construction but not solely on it. Based on the principle that each E.P.I instructional sequence must move from modelling to production in a seamless and organic way, each unit expands on the material in each sentence builder by embedding it in texts and graded tasks which contain both familiar and unfamiliar (but comprehensible and learnable) vocabulary and structures. Through lots of careful recycling and thorough and extensive processing of the input, by the end of each unit the student has many opportunities to encounter and process the new vocabulary and patterns with material from the previous units.

Alongside the macro-units you will find:

- **Question-skills units**: two pages on understanding and creating questions. These micro-units occur after **every** unit in the book, so as to recycle the same question patterns in different linguistic contexts;
- **Revision workouts**: these are retrieval practice tasks aimed at keeping the previously learnt vocabulary alive. These too occur at regular intervals, after **every other** unit.

The point of all the above micro-units is to implement lots of systematic recycling and interleaving, two techniques that allow for stronger retention and transfer of learning.

It should be noted that, unlike the first book in this series, this volume does not contain grammar sections. The key grammar points will be explained and drilled extensively in a dedicated booklet which will be published over the next few months.

Important *caveat*

1) This is a '**no frills**' book. This means that there are a limited number of illustrations (only on unit title pages). This is because we want every single little thing in this book to be useful. Consequently, we have packed a substantive amount of content at the detriment of its outlook. In particular, we have given serious thought to both **recycling** and **interleaving**, in order to allow for key constructions, words and grammar items to be revisited regularly so as to enhance exponentially their retention.

2) **Listening** as modelling is an essential part of E.P.I. There will be an accompanying listening booklet released shortly which will contain narrow listening exercises for all 15 units, following the same content as this book.

3) **All content** in this book matches the content on the **Language Gym** website. For best results, we recommend a mixture of communicative, retrieval practice games, combined with Language Gym games and workouts, and then this book as the follow-up, either in class or for homework.

4) An **answer booklet** is also available, for those that would like it. We have produced it separately to stop this book from being excessively long.

5) This book is suitable for **pre-intermediate** to **intermediate** learners. This equates to a **CEFR A1-A2** level, or a pre-intermediate to intermediate level **Y8-Y9** class. You do not need to start at the beginning, although you may want to dip in to certain units for revision/recycling. You do not need to follow the book in order, although many of you will, and if you do, you will benefit from the specific recycling/interleaving strategies. Either way, all topics are repeated frequently throughout the book.

We do hope that you and your students will find this book useful and enjoyable.

Gianfranco, Dylan & Sonja

Table of Contents

Unit 1

Saying where I live

In this unit you will learn:

- To say where you live
- To say where your town, neighbourhood and home are located

Key sentence patterns:

- *Ich wohne in/Ich lebe in* + location
- *Mir gefällt meine Nachbarschaft* + *weil* + adjective/noun phrase/infinitive

Grammar:

- causal clause with *weil*
- negation with *kein*

UNIT 1: Saying where I live

Ich lebe **Ich wohne** *[I live in]* **Wir leben** **Wir wohnen** *[We live in]*	**in Berlin** **in Brisbane** **in Cardiff** **in Dublin** **in Edinburgh** **in London** **in Wien**	**Das** *[It]*	**ist** *[is]* **liegt** *[is located]*	**im Norden von** **im Nordwesten von** **im Osten von** **im Süden von** **im Südwesten von** **im Westen von** **im Zentrum von**	**Australien** **Deutschland** **England** **Irland** **Österreich** **Schottland** **Wales**

***In der Nähe von meinem Haus** *[Near my house]* **In meiner Gegend** *[In my area]* **In meiner Nachbarschaft** *[In my neighbourhood]* **In meiner Stadt** *[In my city]* **In meiner Straße** *[In my street]* **Im Zentrum** *[In the centre]*	**gibt es** *[there is/are]* **haben wir** *[we have]*	**einen** *[a]* **keinen** *[no]*	**Jugendklub** *[youth club]* **großen Park** *[big park]* **botanischen Garten** *[botanical garden]* **Fußballplatz** *[football pitch]*	
		eine *[a]* **keine** *[no]*	**Bibliothek** *[library]* **Fußgängerzone** *[pedestrian street]*	**Kirche***[church]* **Schule** *[school]*
		ein *[a]* **kein** *[no]*	**Aquarium** **Einkaufszentrum** *[shopping centre]* **Kino** *[cinema]* **Sportzentrum** *[sports centre]*	
		viele *[a lot of]* **nicht viele** *[not a lot of]*	**junge Leute** *[young people]* **alte Gebäude** *[old buildings]* **schöne Straßen** *[beautiful streets]*	**Sporteinrichtungen** *[sports facilities]* **Geschäfte** *[shops]* **Restaurants** *[restaurants]*
	gibt es *[there is/are]*	**viel** *[a lot]* **nicht viel** *[not a lot]*	**Kriminalität** *[of crime]* **zu sehen** *[to see]* **zu tun** *[to do]*	
		viele *[a lot]* **nicht viele** *[not a lot]*	**Angebote für** *[on offer for]*	**Jugendliche** **junge Leute** *[young people]*

Mir gefällt meine Nachbarschaft (nicht), weil *[I do/don't like my neighbourhood because]*	**sie** *[it]*	**gefährlich** *[dangerous]* **ruhig** *[quiet]* **sauber***[clean]* **sicher** *[safe]* **sympathisch** *[friendly]* **schmutzig** *[dirty]*	**ist** *[is]*
	es *[it]*	**keine Umweltverschmutzung** *[not polluted]* **eine gute Infrastruktur** *[good infrastructure]* **viel Verkehr** *[a lot of traffic]*	**gibt** *[is]*
	man (nicht) *[one]*	**gut essen gehen** *[eat well]* **schön spazieren gehen** *[go for walks]* **Sport machen** *[do sports]*	**kann** *[can/ cannot]*

***Author's note: "In der Nähe... " formally requires the genitive case, e.g. "in der Nähe meines Hauses". However, "In der Nähe von + [dative case]" has become more common in general.**

1. Match

In meiner Stadt... *[In my town...]*	
gibt es keine Bibliothek.	there is a big park.
haben wir ein Einkaufszentrum.	there is no youth club.
haben wir ein Kino.	there is a pedestrian street.
gibt es viel Kriminalität.	there is no library.
gibt es eine Fußgängerzone.	we have a shopping centre.
haben wir viele Restaurants.	we have a cinema.
gibt es nicht viele Angebote für junge Leute.	there is a lot of crime.
gibt es nicht viele alte Gebäude.	there is not a lot on offer for young people.
haben wir nicht viele Geschäfte.	we have many restaurants.
gibt es einen großen Park.	there are not many old buildings.
gibt es keinen Jugendklub.	we don't have many shops.

2. Break the flow

a. InderNähevonmeinemHausgibteseine nbotanischenGarten.

b. InmeinerStadthabenwireinSportzentrum.

c. ImZentrumgibteseinKino.

d. InmeinerStraßegibtesnichtvielzutun.

e. InmeinerNachbarschafthabenwireinEinka ufszentrum.

f. InmeinerStadtgibteseineBibliothek.

g. ImZentrumgibteseineFußgängerzone.

3. Missing letters

a. Mir gef__llt mein__ Nachbarschaft nicht, weil sie gefä__rlich ist.

b. I__ Zentrum hab__n wir ei__ Aquarium.

c. Ich leb__ in P__ris.

d. In meine__ Stadt gibt es nicht viel__ schön__ Straße__.

e. In meine__ Gegend gibt es nicht viel__ junge Mensche__.

f. In meine__ Straße gibt es ei__ Kino.

4. Translate into English

a. ...gibt es einen Jugendklub.

b. ...haben wir keine Kirche.

c. ...gibt es nicht viele Angebote.

d. Es gibt alte Gebäude.

e. Wir haben viele Sporteinrichtungen.

f. Es gibt kein Kino.

g. Wir haben eine Bibliothek.

5. Complete

In meiner Stadt…

a. gibt es viele alte G______________.

b. haben wir viele S_______________ *[sports facilities]*.

c. gibt es kein K___________.

d. haben wir einen J_____________.

e. gibt es ein A______________.

f. gibt es nicht viele Angebote für J_____________.

g. haben wir einen botanischen G_________.

h. gibt es nicht viele G______________.

6. Faulty translation: correct the wrong English translation. PLEASE NOTE: not all the translations are incorrect

a. Ich lebe in Berlin. Das liegt im Osten von Deutschland.
I live in Berlin. It is located in the west of Germany.

b. Mir gefällt meine Nachbarschaft, weil sie sauber ist.
I like my neighbourhood because it is clean.

c. Wir wohnen in Wien. Das ist in Österreich.
I live in Vienna. It is in Austria.

d. In meiner Nachbarschaft gibt es ein Sportzentrum.
In my city there is a sports centre.

e. Mir gefällt meine Nachbarschaft nicht, weil es viel Verkehr gibt.
I don't like my neighbourhood because there is a lot of pollution.

f. In meiner Straße gibt es viele Geschäfte.
In my street there are many old buildings.

g. Im Zentrum haben wir einen botanischen Garten.
In the centre we have a pedestrian street.

h. Mir gefällt meine Stadt, weil sie modern ist.
I like my city because it's old-fashioned.

7. Complete the table

English	Deutsch
old buildings	
neighbourhood	
	viele Angebote
	viel Verkehr
it is in the north	
	im Zentrum von
	Kriminalität

8. Complete the table

English	Deutsch
	es gibt einen botanischen Garten
good infrastructure	
	schöne Straßen
because it is friendly (the neighbourhood)	
	gefährlich
	in meiner Stadt

9. Complete the translation

a. Im Zentrum haben wir ein Kino. — *We have a ___________ in the centre.*

b. In der Nähe von meinem Haus gibt es eine Fußgängerzone. — *Near my _________ there is a pedestrian street.*

c. In meiner Straße gibt es viele Cafés. — *In my street ______________ many cafes.*

d. In meiner Gegend gibt es nicht viele Angebote für junge Leute. — *In my area there is not a lot ______________ for young people.*

e. In meiner Stadt haben wir viele Restaurants. — *In my city _______________ restaurants.*

f. In meiner Nachbarschaft gibt es keine Geschäfte. — *In my neighbourhood there are no __________.*

g. In meiner Stadt gibt es alte Gebäude. — *In my city there are ________ buildings.*

10. Translate into English

a. In der Nähe von meinem Haus gibt es einen botanischen Garten.

b. Im Zentrum haben wir einen großen Park.

c. In meiner Stadt gibt es kein Aquarium.

d. In meiner Stadt gibt es nicht viele Angebote für Jugendliche.

e. Mir gefällt meine Nachbarschaft, weil es keine Umweltverschmutzung gibt.

f. In meiner Gegend gibt es eine Fußgängerzone.

g. Wir leben in Edinburgh. Das liegt im Südosten von Schottland.

11. Correct the grammar and/or spelling errors

a. viel alte Gebäude

b. es gibt kein Kirche

c. ich leben in Genf

d. im Centrum von Wien

e. in meins Straße

f. in der Näher meines Hauses

g. mir gefellt meine Gegend

h. in meine Nachbarnschaft

i. kein Fußgängerzone

12. Sentence puzzle: rewrite the sentences in the correct order

a. gibt es In meiner Gegend viele Angebote.	*In my area there is a lot on offer.*
b. Köln Ich lebe in.	*I live in Cologne.*
c. gibt viele es Geschäfte In meiner Straße.	*In my street there are many shops.*
d. In viele meiner gibt es junge Leute Stadt.	*In my city there are a lot of young people.*
e. Im wir kein haben Zentrum Kino.	*In the centre we have no cinema.*
f. Cardiff. Wir in liegt Das in wohnenWales.	*We live in Cardiff. It is located in Wales.*

13. Match

gefährlich	dangerous
sicher	good infrastructure
sauber	safe
schmutzig	very quiet
gut essen gehen	clean
gute Infrastruktur	eat well
sehr ruhig	lots of traffic
viel Verkehr	dirty

14. Multiple choice: choose the grammatically correct answer

1	2	3
alte Gebäude	alt Gebäude	alteren Gebäude
in den Nähe von meines Hauses	in der Nähe von meinem Haus	in dem Nähe vom mein Haus
im Zentrum	in Zentrum	ims Zentrum
viel zu sehen	vieler zu sehen	vielem zu sehen
in meiner Nachbarschaft	in meinen Nachbarschaft	in meines Nachbarschaft.
in meiner Stadt	in meinen Stadt	ins meiner Stadt
wir habe	wir hab	wir haben

15. Complete with the correct option

a. In meiner Stadt _______ es einen botanischen Garten.

b. Ich _________ in Nizza. Das liegt im ________ von Frankreich.

c. Im ____________ haben wir ein neues Einkaufszentrum.

d. In meiner Nachbarschaft, gibt es nicht _______________ für Jugendliche.

e. In der ________ meines _________ gibt es einen Jugendklub.

f. In meiner Straße gibt es eine ___________.

gibt	Nähe	Bibliothek	viele Angebote
Zentrum	lebe/wohne	Süden	Hauses

16. Match

eine Fußgängerzone	a lot on offer for young people
kein Einkaufszentrum	a pedestrian street
sympathisch	old buildings
viel Verkehr	lots to see
viel zu sehen	friendly
Angebote für Jugendliche	no shopping centre
alte Gebäude	eat well
Sport machen	a lot of traffic
gut essen gehen	because it's quiet
…weil sie ruhig ist	do sports

17. Spot the intruders: read the translations and spot the extra words in the German sentences.

a. Mir gefällt meine Nachbarschaft, weil sie extrem sauber ist.

I like my neighbourhood because it is clean.

b. In meiner Straße gibt es viele moderne Geschäfte.

In my street there are a lot of shops.

c. Ich lebe nicht im Norden von England.

I live in the north of England.

d. Was mir an meiner Nachbarschaft nicht gefällt, ist die starke Umweltverschmutzung.

What I don't like about my neighbourhood is the pollution.

e. In meiner Nachbarschaft gibt es einen großen beeindruckenden botanischen Garten.

In my neighbourhood there is a big botanical garden.

f. In meiner Gegend haben wir eine Kirche und eine neue Schule.

In my area we have a church and a school.

g. Mir gefällt meine Nachbarschaft nicht, weil man schön spazieren gehen kann.

I like my neighbourhood because you can go for walks.

h. Mir gefällt meine Stadt, weil es super Cafés und Restaurants gibt.

I like my city because there are cafes and restaurants.

Ich heiße Sabine. Ich wohne in Wien, komme aber aus Salzburg. Wien liegt im Osten von Österreich. Mir gefällt meine Nachbarschaft, weil sie sehr sicher und sauber ist. Sie liegt im Zentrum der Stadt und hat eine gute Infrastruktur.
In meiner Straße gibt es viele alte Gebäude und Cafés, aber keine Sporteinrichtungen. Trotzdem gibt es viele Angebote für junge Leute. In meiner Gegend gibt es einen Jugendklub, ein Kino und ein Einkaufszentrum. Der botanische Garten ist auch toll. In der Nähe von meinem Haus gibt es eine Fußgängerzone mit vielen Geschäften.
Generell ist meine Nachbarschaft sehr lebendig *[lively]* und multikulturell. Was mir nicht gefällt, ist, dass es manchmal viel Verkehr gibt.
(Sabine, 14 Jahre. Salzburg)

18. Find the German equivalent in Sabine's text

a. I live in
b. is located
c. a good infrastructure
d. old buildings
e. sports facilities
f. there is, however, …
g. near my house
h. a lot of traffic
i. in my area
j. shopping centre

Ich heiße Ewen und bin sechzehn Jahre alt. Ich wohne in München, komme aber ursprünglich aus Glasgow. München liegt im Süden von Deutschland. Ich wohne am Stadtrand *[on the outskirts]* von München. Meine Nachbarschaft gefällt mir nicht, weil es viel Verkehr gibt und es in meiner Gegend daher *[therefore]* sehr schmutzig ist.
In meiner Straße gibt es nicht viele Angebote für junge Leute. Es gibt weder *[neither]* einen Jugendklub noch *[nor]* ein Einkaufszentrum. Wir haben nur zwei kleine Geschäfte: ein Blumengeschäft und ein Lampengeschäft. Wie langweilig!
In der Nähe von meinem Haus gibt es ein Aquarium. Leider *[unfortunately]* gibt es keinen Park, wo man Fußball spielen kann.
(Ewen, 16 Jahre. Glasgow)

19. Complete the translation of Ewen's text.

My name is Ewen and I am _________ years old. I live in Munich but am originally from Glasgow. Munich is in the _________________ of Germany. I _______ on the outskirts of Munich.
I don't like my _______________ because there is a lot of ___________ and therefore my area is very _____________.
In my street there is not a lot _____________ for young people. There is neither a ____________ nor a ________________. We only have two _______ shops: a flower shop and a lamp _______. How boring!
________________ there is an aquarium. Unfortunately, there is no ___________ where you can play football.

20. Answer the following questions on Ewen's text in German.

a. Wie alt ist Ewen?
b. Wo wohnt er?
c. Woher kommt er?
d. Wo befindet sich Ewens Nachbarschaft?
e. Warum gefällt ihm seine Nachbarschaft nicht?
f. Was gibt es nicht in Ewens Straße?
g. Was gibt es in Ewens Straße?
h. Wie findet er das?
i. Was liegt in der Nähe von seinem Haus?
j. Was gibt es leider nicht?

Ich heiße Daniela und bin fünfzehn Jahre alt. Ich komme aus Bern in der Schweiz, lebe aber in Hamburg mit meiner Familie, weil mein Vater hier arbeitet. Hamburg liegt im Norden von Deutschland. Ich lebe im Zentrum von Hamburg, was sehr touristisch und deshalb sehr laut ist. In der Nähe von meinem Haus gibt es eine Fußgängerzone, wo es viele schöne Geschäfte gibt. In meiner Straße gibt es auch viele Cafés und Restaurants, wo junge Leute gerne essen gehen.

Mir gefällt meine Nachbarschaft, weil sie sauber ist und es eine gute Infrastruktur gibt. Im Zentrum gibt es auch einen großen Park, wo ich Freunde treffen kann. Außerdem gibt es auch einen Jugendklub und ein Kino in der Nähe von meinem Haus. Das finde ich super! Manchmal stört *[bothers]* mich der Verkehr. Meine Nachbarschaft ist durch die vielen Autos nicht sehr ruhig. Dennoch ist das Angebot für Jugendliche groß und es gibt immer viel zu tun.

(Daniela, 15 Jahre. Bern)

21. Find the German equivalent in Daniela's text

a. because my dad works here

b. is located

c. in the north of

d. touristy

e. therefore

f. noisy

g. like to eat out

h. pedestrian street

i. to meet friends

j. furthermore

k. that's great

l. sometimes

m. the traffic

n. however

o. the offer for young people

p. always

q. a lot to do

Ich heiße Andrea und lebe in Berlin. Eigentlich komme ich aber aus Graz in Österreich. Ich wohne in einer ländlichen *[rural]* Gegend, wo es viel Natur gibt, ich viel Rad fahren und mit dem Hund spazieren gehen kann.
In meiner Nachbarschaft gibt es viele Angebote für junge Leute. Mir gefallen vor allem die vielen Fußballplätze und die Jugendklubs, die ich nach der Schule besuchen kann. Auch der botanische Garten ist ein Hit!
Ich finde es gut, dass es auch ein Einkaufszentrum gibt und ein großes Sportzentrum. Dort treffe ich mich mit Freunden aus der Schule.
Am Wochenende fahre ich oft mit meiner Familie ins Zentrum von Berlin. Dort gehen wir alle gemeinsam in Cafés und Restaurants. Das ist super. Mir gefällt Berlin, weil die Infrastruktur gut ist und man super spazieren gehen kann.
Generell bin ich sehr glücklich *[happy]* in Berlin.
(Andrea, 11 Jahre. Graz)

22. Comprehension questions

a. In what kind of area does Andrea live?

b. What activities can she do in that area?

c. What makes her neighbourhood attractive for young people?

d. Where does she meet with her school friends?

e. Where does Andrea go on the weekends?

f. Does anyone accompany her?

g. What activities does she do when she gets there?

h. Is she happy about where she lives?

23. Complete the sentences with the missing words

a. Die _ _ _ _ _ in meiner Nachbarschaft sind _ _ _ _ _ _ _ _ _ _ _ _.

The people in my neighbourhood are very friendly.

b. In meiner Nachbarschaft _ _ _ _ _ _ viel _ .

In my neighbourhood there is a lot of pollution.

c. In meiner Stadt _ _ _ _ _ _ viel _ _ _ _ _ _ _ _ .

In my town there is a lot of traffic.

d. Im Zentrum gibt es _ _ _ _ _ _ _ _ _ _ _ und deshalb ist es sehr _ _ _ _ _ _ _ _ _ _.

There are a lot of cars and therefore it is very dirty.

e. Mir gefällt meine Nachbarschaft, weil es viele _ _ _ _ _ _ _ _ _ _.

I like my neighbourhood because there are many cafés.

f. In meiner _ _ _ _ _ gibt es _ _ _ _ _ _ _ _ _ _ _ _ _ _ _ _ _.

In my town there are many shops.

g. In meiner Straße _ _ _ _ _ _ nicht viel _ _ _ _ _ _.

In my street there are not many things to do.

h. In der Nähe _ _ _ _ _ _ _ _ _ _ _ _ _ _ _ _ _ gibt es einen _ _ _ _ _ _ _ _ _ _ _ _.

Near my house there is a big park.

24. Translate into English

a. Jugendliche
b. Bibliothek
c. Geschäfte
d. Nachbarschaft
e. Stadt
f. Autos
g. Infrastruktur
h. Cafés
i. Straße
j. Park
k. Leute
l. Haus

25. Find in the wordsearch the German translation of the phrases below, then write it next to each of them as shown in the example

M	D	F	L	C	R	Y	G	G	N	Z	H	L	B	D	E	A	G
J	X	H	J	F	I	R	I	E	G	X	E	F	R	A	T	I	Q
P	D	V	C	Q	X	U	Y	K	I	T	H	Z	C	S	F	F	T
D	S	R	V	I	T	F	M	S	H	Y	U	C	Y	B	Ä	A	Q
A	K	Z	Z	K	L	N	M	L	A	V	R	U	L	E	H	A	H
S	I	U	C	P	T	K	C	R	I	U	D	A	T	S	C	I	D
P	T	N	Q	A	J	F	C	E	A	Y	B	E	A	T	S	S	I
L	J	R	B	S	L	W	L	Ü	Y	C	I	E	N	E	E	I	L
N	E	F	A	V	E	V	F	H	L	E	C	B	R	I	G	M	X
R	Z	G	X	ß	E	J	Y	B	A	G	R	D	H	S	E	N	Y
S	S	E	A	R	E	K	T	B	V	C	R	G	E	T	L	O	X
A	K	K	K	M	X	A	A	A	Z	F	S	H	I	A	L	R	L
W	O	E	H	W	U	Q	G	H	I	Q	L	I	E	J	O	D	M
R	H	J	M	I	E	T	O	J	R	E	T	K	O	S	T	E	S
R	T	D	A	T	S	R	E	D	N	I	P	B	L	A	Z	N	U
E	T	Z	D	W	T	U	C	D	Q	B	B	V	H	S	O	H	R
M	E	I	N	E	N	A	C	H	B	A	R	S	C	H	A	F	T
O	S	E	K	X	I	I	R	A	D	N	M	L	M	R	K	G	G

e.g. the best thing is — ***das Beste ist***

a. street

b. in the north

c. too much traffic

d. in the city

e. very happy

f. great shops

g. my neighbourhood

h. clean

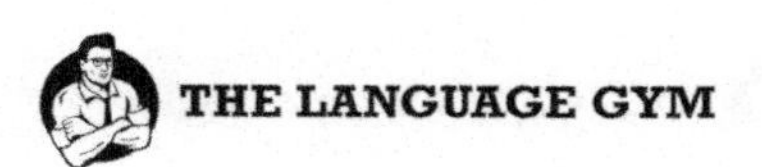

26. Complete with suitable words

a. Ich lebe in einer Stadt im Norden von __________________.

b. Mein Straße liegt im ____________ der Stadt.

c. Mir gefällt meine Gegend nicht, weil sie zu ____________ ist.

d. In meiner Straße gibt es viele _____________.

e. Es gibt viel Kriminalität und daher ist es hier nicht sehr _____________.

f. Mir gefällt meine Nachbarschaft nicht, weil es zu viel ______________ gibt.

g. In meiner Gegend gibt es viele ____________ für junge Leute.

27. Form logical phrases joining bits from each column

Ich wohne	weil es eine gute Infrastruktur gibt.
In meiner Stadt	der Verkehr.
Es gibt	Fußballplätze.
Manchmal stört mich	gibt es eine Kirche.
Im Zentrum gibt es einen	großen Park.
Mir gefallen die	im Süden von Wien.
Wir haben keinen	viele Angebote für junge Leute.
Mir gefällt meine Gegend,	Jugendklub.

28. Guided translation

a. I_____ m________ N__________________ g______ e___ v____ V___________.

In my neighbourhood there is a lot of traffic.

b. M___ g______ m_______ G___________ n______, w_____ s___ g_____________ i____.

I don't like my area because it is dangerous.

c. I___ m_______ S____________ g_____ e___ v________ G________________.

In my street there are many shops.

d. I____ l_____ i____ B_____________ i____ S___________ v_____ E___________.

I live in Brighton, in the south of England.

e. I___ l_____ i____ B_________. D_____ l______ i___ W________ v___ Ö____________.

I live in Bregenz. It is in the west of Austria.

f. I___ m__________ S______ g____ e___ v_____ A____________ f___ j_______ L_________.

In my city there is a lot on offer for young people.

g. I___ m__________ G___________ g_____ e__ e________ b____________ G________.

In my area there is a botanical garden.

h. M____ g__________ m_________ N_______________, w_____ s____ s________ i____.

I like my neighbourhood because it is safe.

i. G__________ s______ d____ L_________ i___ m__________ N________________ s____ s___________.

In general, the people of my neighbourhood are very friendly.

29. Spot the missing word: there is a missing word in each line, spot it and add it in

a. In Nachbarschaft gibt es einen großen Park.

b. In meiner Straße es viele Geschäfte.

c. Generell sind die Leute in meiner sehr nett.

d. Im Zentrum es eine Fußgängerzone.

e. Ich lebe Berlin. Das liegt im Osten von Deutschland.

f. Ich lebe Norden von Kanada.

g. Gefällt meine Gegend sehr gut.

h. Es gibt viele für Jugendliche in meiner Stadt.

i. In der Nähe von Haus gibt es einen Jugendklub.

j. Meine Gegend sehr sauber.

30. Tangled translation: rewrite in German

a. Meine Stadt **is in** Süden **of Italy.**

b. In meiner **area there is** ein großes **shopping centre** mit vielen **great shops**.

c. In der Nähe **of my house** gibt es keinen botanischen Garten.

d. Mir gefällt **my neighbourhood**, weil es viele **on offer for young people** gibt.

e. Im Zentrum **have we** eine große **pedestrian street.**

f. Meine **neighbourhood** liegt am Stadtrand von **Vienna**.

g. In meiner Stadt **there are many** alte Gebäude **and restaurants**.

h. In meiner **city there are** nicht viele **beautiful streets**, aber viele Cafés **and libraries**.

31. Translate into German:

a. to live in a town

b. my neighbourhood is

c. near my house

d. a big park

e. a shopping centre

f. in my street

g. not far from

h. to walk the dog

i. to ride a bike

j. in the north of Germany

k. on the outskirts

l. my neighbourhood

m. the best thing is

n. a lot on offer for young people

32. Translate into German:

I live in a town in the north of Germany. My neighbourhood is on the outskirts of the town. My area is clean and modern. There are many parks and sports facilities. There are not many shops but there is a shopping centre near my house. In my street there is a sports centre, a small supermarket and a bar. Near my house there is a big park where I ride a bike and walk my dog. What I like about my neighbourhood is that the people are friendly. What I don't like is that there is not much to do for young people.

33. Complete the sentences creatively

a. Meine Stadt liegt…

b. Meine Gegend ist…

c. In der Nähe von meinem Haus…

d. Mir gefällt meine Nachbarschaft, weil…

e. Das Beste an meiner Stadt ist…

f. Im Zentrum von London gibt es…

g. In der Nähe vom Park gibt es…

h. Mir gefällt meine Gegend nicht, weil...

34. Write a sentence for each of the following words. Do not repeat any of the sentences in exercise 33!

a. Gegend

b. Beste

c. Straße

d. Infrakstruktur

e. Verkehr

f. Gebäude

35. Spot and correct the spelling/grammar mistakes (there are many!)

a. In meine Gegend gibt es viel Geschafte.

b. In mene Straße gisbt es einen Jungenkluft.

c. Das Schlimmste an meine Nachbarschoft ist der viele Verkehr.

d. Wir lebe in Paros. Da liegt in Frankenreich.

e. Wo ist dein Nachbarschaft?

f. Die Leute in meinem Straß ist freundlich.

36. Write a paragraph in German about Sandra in the first person singular (I) and one about Thomas in the third (he)

	Sandra	Thomas
Location of town	north of Germany	south of Basel
Location of neighbourhood	town centre	outskirts
Sports facilities	two sports centres and a tennis club	a swimming pool, a stadium and a football pitch
Green spaces	a botanical garden	one small park
Environment	a lot of pollution	no pollution but a bit *[etwas]* noisy
Amenities for young people	many restaurants, youth clubs and theatres	a shopping centre and the park
Best thing	safety	the pedestrian street
Worst thing	too many tourists; noisy	crime
People in their neighbourhood	very friendly	unfriendly and rude

Question Skills Unit 1

English	Deutsch
Where do you live?	**Wo wohnst du?**
In what part of Germany is your city?	**In welchem Teil von Deutschland liegt deine Stadt?**
What is on offer for young people in your city?	**Welche Angebote gibt es für junge Leute in deiner Stadt?**
What sights are there in your city?	**Welche Sehenswürdigkeiten gibt es in deiner Stadt?**
Describe your town/city.	**Beschreib deine Stadt.**
Describe your village (very small town).	**Beschreib dein Dorf.**
Do you like your neighbourhood/area? *Why? Why not?*	**Gefällt dir deine Nachbarschaft/deine Gegend?** **Warum? Warum nicht?**
What is the best thing about your town/city?	**Was gefällt dir am besten an deiner Stadt?**
What is the worst thing about your town/city?	**Was gefällt dir am wenigsten an deiner Stadt?**
What are the shops like in your neighbourhood?	**Wie sind die Geschäfte in deiner Nachbarschaft?**
Do you have a favourite shop? Which is it?	**Hast du ein Lieblingsgeschäft? Welches ist es?**
What are the people like in your neighbourhood?	**Wie sind die Leute in deiner Gegend?**
Are there many green zones?	**Gibt es viele Grünflächen?**

1. Split questions

Wo	am besten an deiner Stadt?
Hast du	deine Nachbarschaft?
Wie sind	ein Lieblingsgeschäft?
Welche Sehenswürdigkeiten	wohnst du?
Was gefällt dir	die Leute in deiner Gegend?
Gefällt dir	gibt es in deiner Stadt?

2. Find and write in the missing words

a. Hast du Lieblingsgeschäft?

b. Gefällt deine Stadt?

c. Wo wohnst?

d. In welchem von Deutschland liegt deine Stadt?

e. Was gefällt dir besten an deiner Stadt?

f. Beschreib Nachbarschaft.

g. Wie die Leute in deiner Gegend?

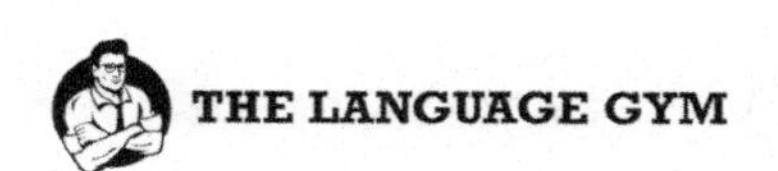

3. Match questions and answers

Wo liegt deine Stadt?	Sie heißt „das Weinviertel".
Wo genau liegt deine Nachbarschaft?	Es gibt einen Jugendklub und ein Schwimmbad.
Wie heißt deine Gegend?	Der Verkehr natürlich.
Welche Angebote gibt es für junge Leute in deiner Gegend?	Im Osten von Österreich.
Wie ist das Nachtleben?	Ja, gibt es. Es gibt hier viele Parks.
Was gefällt dir an deiner Gegend nicht?	Spitze. Es gibt viele Nachtklubs.
Was gefällt dir am besten an deiner Gegend?	Ja. Es ist sehr modern und hat einen Lift.
Gibt es viele Grünflächen?	Am Stadtrand.
Gefällt dir dein Gebäude?	Die Angebote für junge Leute.
Wie heißt du?	Ich fahre Rad und gehe mit dem Hund spazieren.
Was machst du in deiner Freizeit?	Ich heiße Margot.
Wie sind die Leute in deiner Stadt?	Sie sind sehr nett und offen.

4. Guided translation

a. W_ _ _ _ g_ _ _ _ _ _ _ d_ _ d_ _ _ D_ _ _ n_ _ _ _? *Why don't you like your village?*

b. G_ _ _ e_ v_ _ _ _ G_ _ _ _ _ _ _ _ _ _ _? *Are there many green zones?*

c. G_ _ _ _ _ _ _ d_ _ d_ _ _ G_ _ _ _ _ _ _? *Do you like your building?*

d. W_ l_ _ _ _ d_ _ _ _ N_ _ _ _ _ _ _ _ _ _ _ _ _ _ ? *Where is your neighbourhood?*

e. W_ _ i_ _ d_ _ N_ _ _ _ _ _ _ _ _ _? *What is the nightlife like?*

f. W_ _ _ _ _ S_ _ _ _ _ _ _ _ _ _ _ _ _ _ _ _ _ _ _ g_ _ _ e_? *What sights are there?*

g. W_ l_ _ _ _ d_ _ _ _ S_ _ _ _? *Where is the city located?*

h. W_ _ g_ _ _ _ _ _ _ d_ _ n_ _ _ _ a_ d_ _ _ _ _ S_ _ _ _? *What do you not like about your city?*

5. Translate

a. Why don't you like…? ____________________

b. Where is Mainz located…? ____________________

c. What is there in…? ____________________

d. How is…? ____________________

e. In which part…? ____________________

f. What is the worst thing? ____________________

g. What is the best thing? ____________________

h. Are there…? ____________________

i. What shops are there? ____________________

6. Answer the following questions in your own words, using full sentences

Wo wohnst du?

Wo genau liegt deine Stadt?

Welche Angebote gibt es für junge Leute?

Welche Sehenswürdigkeiten gibt es in deiner Stadt?

Beschreib deine Stadt.

Gefällt dir deine Gegend?

Warum? Warum nicht?

Unit 2

Saying what I can do in my neighbourhood

In this unit you will learn:

- To say what you usually do and where you do it, using a variety of key verbs
- To talk about what you did recently in your neighbourhood

Key sentence patterns:

- *Man kann* + infinitive
- *Man kann* + noun/prepositional phrase
- *bin ich/habe ich* + Past Participle

Grammar:

- Modal verb *können* + the infinitive
- Perfect tense with *haben* and *sein* + Past Participle

UNIT 2: Saying what I can do in my neighbourhood

<table>
<tr><td>In meiner Nachbarschaft kann man viele Dinge unternehmen
[In my neighbourhood one can do many things]</td></tr>
</table>

<table>
<tr>
<td rowspan="4">Man kann zum Beispiel
[One can..., for example,]</td>
<td rowspan="4">im Einkaufszentrum
[in the shopping centre]
im Park [in the park]
im Sportzentrum
[in the sports centre]
im Stadion [in the stadium]
im Stadtzentrum [in the city centre]
im Tennisklub [in the tennis club]
im Wald [in the woods]
im Schwimmbad
[at the swimming pool]
im Fitnessstudio [in the gym]
im historischen Viertel der Stadt
[in the historic quarter of the city]
in der Fußgängerzone
[in the pedestrian street]</td>
<td>historische Gebäude
[historic buildings]
Kunstgalerien [art galleries]
Museen [museums]
Schlösser [castles]</td>
<td>besichtigen
[...visit]
besuchen
[...visit]</td>
</tr>
<tr>
<td>auf Konzerte [concerts]
einkaufen [shopping]
feiern [partying]
*Rad fahren [ride a bicycle]
reiten [horseriding]
schwimmen [swimming]
spazieren [for a walk]
wandern [hiking]</td>
<td>gehen
[...go]</td>
</tr>
<tr>
<td>**Sightseeing [sightseeing]
Sport [sports]</td>
<td>machen
[...do]</td>
</tr>
<tr>
<td>Fußball [football]
Golf [golf]
Tennis [tennis]</td>
<td>spielen
[...play]</td>
</tr>
<tr>
<td>Man kann sich zum Beispiel</td>
<td>in der Altstadt [in the old town]
im Kino [in the cinema]
am Fußballplatz in der Nähe von meinem Haus
[on the football pitch near my house]</td>
<td>römische Ruinen [Roman ruins]
Filme [films]
Fußballspiele
[football matches]</td>
<td>ansehen
[...see / watch]</td>
</tr>
</table>

<table>
<tr>
<td rowspan="5">Vorgestern
[The day before yesterday]
Gestern
[Yesterday]
Vor drei Tagen
[Three days ago]
Letztes Wochenende
[Last weekend]
Letzten Freitag
[Last Friday]</td>
<td>bin ich
[I...]</td>
<td>auf ein Konzert meiner Lieblingsband
[to see a concert of my favourite band]
ins Fußballstadion [to the football stadium]
mit meinem Freund/meiner Freundin im Park spazieren
[for a walk in the park with my boyfriend/girlfriend]</td>
<td>gegangen
[...went]</td>
</tr>
<tr>
<td rowspan="4">habe ich
[I]</td>
<td>mir einen Film im Kino [a film in the cinema]</td>
<td>angesehen
[...watched]</td>
</tr>
<tr>
<td>das Stadtmuseum [city museum]
eine Kunstgalerie [art gallery]</td>
<td>besichtigt
besucht
[...visited]</td>
</tr>
<tr>
<td>Sightseeing</td>
<td>gemacht
[...did]</td>
</tr>
<tr>
<td>im Sportzentrum Tennis [tennis in the sports centre]</td>
<td>gespielt
[...played]</td>
</tr>
<tr>
<td colspan="4">Author's notes: 1) The word order in German sentences is more flexible than in English. Reordering a sentence can subtly change the emphasis, but the meaning typically remains the same.
2) * "Fahrrad" is typically abbreviated to "Rad".
3) **The word sightseeing has been adopted into German. You can use it in different phrases such as "Sightseeing gehen" or "Sightseeing machen" or "Ich war Sightseeing".</td>
</tr>
</table>

1. Match

Man kann Sport machen.	One can go to the stadium.
Man kann spazieren gehen.	One can go hiking.
Man kann ins Stadion gehen.	One can play football.
Man kann ins Schwimmbad gehen.	One can party.
Man kann ins Kino gehen.	One can do sports.
Man kann feiern gehen.	One can go to the cinema.
Man kann Fußball spielen.	One can go to concerts.
Man kann wandern gehen.	One can go for a walk.
Man kann einkaufen gehen.	One can visit art galleries.
Man kann auf Konzerte gehen.	One can go shopping.
Man kann sich Fußballspiele ansehen.	One can see football matches.
Man kann Kunstgalerien besuchen.	One can go to the swimming pool.

2. Complete with *gehen*, *machen*, *spielen* or *besuchen*

a. Man kann Sport __________.

b. Man kann Sightseeing _________.

c. Man kann Fußball ___________.

d. Man kann ins Stadion ____________.

e. Man kann Schlösser ____________.

f. Man kann nicht feiern __________.

g. Man kann spazieren _________.

h. Man kann Konzerte __________.

3. Break the flow

a. MankanninderAltstadtGalerienbesichtigen.

b. MankannamStrandspazierengehen.

c. MankannimParkFußballspielen.

d. MankannimStadionaufKonzertegehen.

e. MankannsichimStadionFußballspieleansehen.

f. MankanninderAltstadtSchlösserbesichtigen.

g. MankanninderFußgängerzoneeinkaufengehen.

h. MankannimSportzentrumTennisspielen.

4. Sentence puzzle: rewrite the German

a. kann Man ansehen Fußballspiele sich.

One can see football matches.

b. Man spazieren kann Park im gehen.

One can go for a walk in the park.

c. kann im feiern Stadtzentrum gehen Man.

One can party in the town centre.

d. kann im besichtigen Viertel ein Schloss der Man historischen Stadt.

One can visit a castle in the historic part of town.

e. kann machen Man Sport Sportzentrum im.

One can do sports in the sports centre.

5. Translate into English

a. Man kann spazieren gehen.

b. Man kann feiern gehen.

c. Man kann ins Schwimmbad gehen.

d. Man kann einkaufen gehen.

e. Man kann in der Fußgängerzone Kleidung kaufen.

f. Man kann Rad fahren gehen.

g. Man kann ins Kino gehen.

h. Man kann sich Fußballspiele ansehen.

i. Man kann im Park Fußball spielen.

6. Match

Man kann im botanischen Garten	Pflanzen und Bäume sehen.
Man kann im Schwimmbad	gut essen.
Man kann sich im Stadion	schwimmen gehen.
Man kann in den Geschäften im Stadtzentrum	schöne Kleidung kaufen.
Man kann sich im Kino	Rad fahren gehen.
Man kann in der Altstadt	historische Gebäude und Schlösser besichtigen.
Man kann im Restaurant	Filme ansehen.
Man kann im Park	Fußballspiele ansehen.

7. Split sentences: form logical sentences

Man kann sich Filme	ansehen.
Man kann historische Gebäude	essen gehen.
Man kann sich Fußballspiele	ansehen.
Man kann in Restaurants	machen.
Man kann in Geschäften	gehen.
Man kann Sport	besichtigen.
Man kann Rad fahren	einkaufen gehen.

8. Translate into English

a. einkaufen gehen

b. die Altstadt

c. sich Fußballspiele ansehen

d. sich Filme ansehen

e. ins Stadion gehen

f. die Geschäfte

g. die Fußgängerzone

h. Rad fahren

i. feiern gehen

j. Sightseeing machen

k. im Wald

9. Faulty translation
Please note: not all translations are wrong

a. das historische Viertel: *the industrial area*

b. im Einkaufszentrum: *in the pedestrian street*

c. alte Gebäude: *historic buildings*

d. ins Stadion gehen: *to go to the park*

e. schwimmen gehen: *to go horse riding*

f. einkaufen gehen: *to go shopping*

g. die Fußgängerzone: *the main square*

h. Rad fahren gehen: *to go running*

i. Schlösser besichtigen: *to see monuments*

j. feiern gehen: *to go sightseeing*

k. Sightseeing gehen: *to see tourists*

l. an den Strand gehen: *to go to the beach*

10. Spot and correct the grammar/spelling errors

a. Man kann im Park spaziren gehen.

b. Man kann historishe Gebeude besichtigen.

c. Man kann gehen schwimmen.

d. Man kann eine Schloss besichtigen.

e. Man kann Rad faren gehen.

f. Man kann Fusball spilen.

g. Man kann besuchen die Altstadt.

h. Man kann sich Fußbalspiele ansehn.

i. Man kann gehen ins Kino.

j. Man kann Tenis spilen.

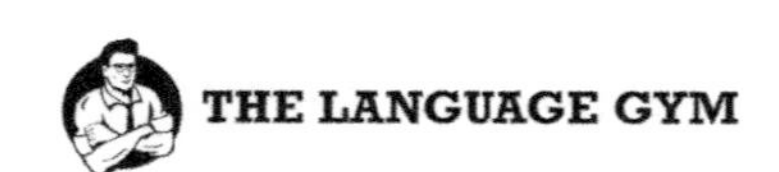

11. Match

Ich habe einen Palast besucht.	I visited a palace.
Vorgestern bin ich an den Strand gegangen.	I went bike riding.
Ich bin Rad fahren gegangen.	Yesterday I went shopping.
Ich bin ins Kino gegangen.	I went to the cinema.
Gestern bin ich einkaufen gegangen.	I took many photos.
Letztes Wochenende habe ich Sport gemacht.	The day before yesterday I went to the beach.
Ich habe viele Fotos gemacht.	Last weekend I did sports.

12. Complete with the missing letters

a. Ich bin Rad fahren g _ _ _ _ _ _ _ _.

b. Ich habe Sport ge _ _ _ _ _.

c. Man kann z_ _B _ _ _ _ _ _ _ _ im Park Fußball spielen.

d. Ich habe Sightseeing ge _ _ _ _ _.

e. Ich bin an den S _ _ _ _ _ gegangen.

f. Ich habe viel _ Fotos ge _ _ _ _ _.

g. L _ _ _ _ _ _ Wochen _ _ _ _ bin ich im Wald wandern gegangen.

h. Ich bin ins Kino ge _ _ _ _ _ _.

13. Translate into English

a. Vorgestern habe ich ein Schloss in der Altstadt besichtigt.

b. Letzten Freitag bin ich mit meiner Familie in den Park gegangen.

c. Vor drei Tagen habe ich mir im Stadion ein Fußballspiel angesehen.

d. Letzten Samstag bin ich im Park Rad fahren gegangen.

e. Letzen Sonntag bin ich schwimmen gegangen.

f. Gestern habe ich im Tennisklub Tennis gespielt.

g. Letzte Woche bin ich mit meinem Freund ins Kino gegangen.

h. Gestern Nachmittag habe ich mir einen Actionfilm im Fernsehen angesehen.

14. Spot and add in the missing words

a. Gestern habe ich Schloss besucht.

b. Vorgestern ich mit meiner Schwester einkaufen gegangen.

c. Letzen Freitag bin ich Stadion gegangen.

d. Vor drei Tagen ich Sightseeing in Wien gemacht.

e. Ich mag meine Gegend, weil viele Dinge unternehmen kann.

f. Letzte Woche habe ich Stadtmuseum besucht.

15. Fill in the gaps

a. Ich habe mir einen Film _ _ _ _ _ _ _ _ _ _.

b. Ich _ _ _ _ Sport gemacht.

c. Ich habe T _ _ _ _ _ gespielt.

d. Ich habe viele Fotos _ _ _ _ _ _ _ _.

e. Ich bin s _ _ _ _ _ _ _ _ _ gegangen.

f. Ich habe das Stadtmuseum mit meiner Freundin _ _ _ _ _ _ _ _.

g. Gestern habe ich mit Freunden Fußball _ _ _ _ _ _ _ _.

h. Vorgestern bin ich in zwei M _ _ _ _ _ gegangen und habe mir Werke von Paul Klee _ _ _ _ _ _ _ _ _ _ _.

i. Vor drei Tagen bin ich im Park _ _ _ gefahren.

j. Gestern _ _ _ _ ich ein Schloss in der Altstadt besichtigt.

Hallo. Ich bin Stefan. Ich wohne am Stadtrand in der Nähe von den Bergen. Meine Nachbarschaft ist sehr hässlich. Es gibt viele alte und schmutzige Gebäude. Für junge Leute gibt es nicht viele Angebote. Es gibt jedoch einige Sporteinrichtungen wie zum Beispiel Golfplätze, einen Tennisklub und ein Fitnessstudio. Es gibt auch einen kleinen Park. Gestern habe ich dort viel Sport gemacht. Am Morgen bin ich im Park Rad fahren gegangen und habe Tennis gespielt. Am Nachmittag bin ich im Sportzentrum mit meinem besten Freund schwimmen gegangen.

(Stefan, 13 Jahre. Rosenheim)

16. Find and correct the mistakes in the translation of Stefan's text

Hi. I am Stefan. I live on the outskirts of the city, near the sea. My neighbourhood is very beautiful. There are many old and historic buildings. There is not much on offer for young people. Fortunately, there are some sports facilities such as tennis courts, a table-tennis club and a gym. Also, there is a big park. Therefore, one can go shopping. Yesterday, I did a lot of walking, In the morning I rode my motorbike in the park and played handball. In the afternoon I went horse-riding in the countryside with my best friend.

17. Find the German equivalent of the following phrases in Lisa's text

a. the old town

b. near the port

c. in my neighbourhood

d. very beautiful

e. historic buildings

f. a flea market

g. there isn't a lot on offer

h. one can go for a walk

i. I went shopping

j. I bought

k. I went sailing

l. it was a lot of fun

m. went to the cinema

n. watched a romantic film

Hallo, ich bin Lisa. Ich wohne in der Altstadt von Hamburg in der Nähe vom Hafen. In meiner Gegend ist es sehr schön. Es gibt ein Schloss und viele historische Gebäude.

Es gibt keine Einkaufszentren, aber viele sehr nette kleine Geschäfte und einen Flohmarkt. Daher kann man viele interessante Dinge und schöne Kleidung kaufen. Darüber hinaus gibt es viele Restaurants und Straßencafés. Das Nachtleben ist sehr gut.

Ich liebe meine Gegend, aber für junge Leute gibt es nicht viele Angebote. Zum Beispiel gibt es nicht viele Sporteinrichtungen.

Zum Glück gibt es einen kleinen Park, in dem man Frisbee spielen, Fahrrad fahren und spazieren gehen kann. Es gibt auch einen Tennisklub und einen Segelklub.

Gestern bin ich mit meiner Mutter einkaufen gegangen und habe ein rosa Kleid und weiße Schuhe gekauft. Dann bin ich mit meinem Vater segeln gegangen. Das hat echt Spaß gemacht! Dann bin ich mit meinem Freund ins Kino gegangen. Wir haben uns einen romantischen Film angesehen. Ich hatte eine fantastische Zeit.

(Lisa, 12 Jahre. Hamburg)

18. Read Lisa's text and tick the words not mentioned

a. Schwimmbad	f. Stadtrand
b. Spaß	g. Flohmarkt
c. Kleid	h. Sporteinrichtungen
d. Nachtleben	i. Bräutigam
e. Kleinigkeiten	j. Mutter

Hallo. Ich bin Robert. In meiner Stadt gibt es viel zu tun. Deshalb liebe ich sie. Es gibt viele Bars und Restaurants, viele schöne Geschäfte, viele Sporteinrichtungen, Grünflächen und historische Plätze. Im Sommer gibt es viele Shows auf dem Rathausplatz und im Stadion. Ich liebe es, auf Konzerte zu gehen, weil mir Live-Musik gut gefällt.

Meine Wohnung ist am Stadtrand nahe der Donau. Es gibt viele Angebote für junge Leute. Man kann im Park in der Nähe von meiner Schule Rad fahren gehen, sich im Stadion Fußballspiele ansehen, im Schwimmbad schwimmen gehen, ins Kino gehen und vieles mehr.

Gestern Morgen war ich mit meinen Freunden im Sportzentrum. Ich war schwimmen und dann Gewichte heben. Dann bin ich mit meiner Mutter im Einkaufszentrum in der Nähe von meinem Haus einkaufen gegangen. Dann bin ich mit meinen Freunden im Park Skateboard gefahren. Schließlich bin ich zu meinem Freund Philip gegangen, um mir ein Fußballspiel anzuschauen.

(Robert, 15 Jahre. Wien)

19. True, False or Not mentioned?

a. Robert loves his town.

b. There is a big theatre.

c. He lives on the outskirts.

d. He lives far from the river Danube.

e. He goes to the stadium often.

f. Yesterday morning he lifted weights.

g. He watched a football match with his girlfriend.

20. Find the German equivalent in Robert's text

a. there is a lot to do

b. therefore

c. many beautiful shops

d. historic places

e. near the river Danube

f. one can go bike riding

g. one can watch football matches

h. much more

i. yesterday morning

j. I went swimming

k. lift weights

l. I went shopping

m. went skateboarding in the park

n. to my friend's house

21. Do the tasks below

a. List in English all the places mentioned in the first paragraph.

b. List in English the 5 things one can do in Robert's area, mentioned in the second paragraph.

c. List in English the 5 things Robert did, mentioned in the third paragraph.

22. Read Robert's text: translate the words you can find in the text and cross out the rest

a. die Altstadt	h. gestern	o. das Fußballspiel
b. Rad gefahren	i. am Morgen	p. die Leute
c. schwimmen	j. spät	q. mit Freunden
d. einkaufen	k. nahe	r. die Jugendlichen
e. sofort	l. weit	s. die alten Leute
f. danach	m. ich bin gegangen	t. die Gewichte
g. bald	n. ich habe mir angesehen	u. mit uns

Hallo. Ich bin Markus. Meine Stadt heißt Konstanz. Sie liegt im Süden von Deutschlands nahe der Grenze zur Schweiz. Sie ist eine historische Stadt mit einer sehr schönen Altstadt.

Es gibt viele Touristen, also viel Verkehr und Lärm, aber für junge Leute gibt es viele Angebote. Am besten gefällt mir der Bodensee. Ich wohne ganz in der Nähe. Ich liebe es, am See spazieren zu gehen.

Meine Nachbarschaft ist ziemlich modern. Es gibt viele sehr schöne Geschäfte, Bars und Restaurants, drei Einkaufszentren, zwei Kinos und viele Sporteinrichtungen wie Schwimmbäder, Fitnessstudios und Sportzentren. Es gibt auch viele Grünflächen. Das Nachtleben ist toll.

Daher kann man viele Dinge tun: gut essen, in den Park gehen, draußen laufen und Sport treiben, am See spazieren gehen und vieles mehr.

Gestern Morgen war ich mit meinen Freunden am See. Wir sind geschwommen, haben uns gesonnt und haben Volleyball gespielt. Dann bin ich mit meiner Mutter im Einkaufszentrum in der Nähe von meinem Haus einkaufen gegangen. Danach bin ich mit meinem Freund Paul bis fünf Uhr nachmittags im Park Rad gefahren. Schließlich bin ich zu meinem Freund Philip gegangen, um Videospiele zu spielen.

Dieses Wochenende werde ich mir eine sehr interessante Dokumentation ansehen. Sie handelt von Katzen, meinen Lieblingstieren. Ich mag, wie sie sich bewegen. **(Markus, 12 Jahre. Konstanz)**

24. Correct any wrong statements about Markus' text

a. His town is far from Switzerland.

b. He lives close to the Bodensee.

c. He loves going for a walk in the park.

d. His neighbourhood has an ok nightlife.

e. His neighbourhood has no green spaces.

f. Yesterday he went for a walk with his mother.

g. He played videogames with Paul.

23. Translate into German

a. old town: A________________

b. noise: L________________

c. young people (2): j________________

d. near the border (3): n________________

e. to go for a walk (2): s________________

f. sports facilities S________________

g. green spaces: G________________

h. therefore: d________________

i. many things (2): v________________

j. one can eat well (4): m________________

k. much more (2): v________________

l. yesterday morning (2): g________________

m. I sunbathed (4): i________________

n. I went shopping (4): i________________

o. to play videogames (2): V________________

25. Complete the sentences in German based on Markus' text

a. Er heißt ________________.

b. Seine Heimatstadt heißt ________________.

c. Die Altstadt ist sehr ________________.

d. Wegen der vielen Touristen gibt es ________________.

e. Er wohnt ganz ________________ vom Bodensee.

f. Die Geschäfte sind ________________.

g. In Konstanz gibt es viele Angebote für ________________.

h. Gestern hat er mit seinem Freund Philip ________________.

i. Dieses Wochenende wird sich Markus eine Dokumentation über ____________ ansehen.

26. Complete with the missing letters

a. I _ _ w _ _ _ _ a _ S _ _ _ _ _ _ _ _ _.	*I live on the outskirts.*
b. M _ _ k _ _ _ v _ _ _ _ D _ _ _ _ m _ _ _ _ _ _.	*One can do many things.*
c. M _ _ k _ _ _ g _ _ _ _ e _ _ _ _.	*One can eat well.*
d. M _ _ k _ _ _ e _ _ _ _ _ _ _ _ _ _ g _ _ _ _.	*One can go shopping.*
e. M _ _ k _ _ _ S _ _ _ _ m _ _ _ _ _ _.	*One can do sports.*
f. G _ _ _ _ _ _ _ w _ _ i _ _ i _ E _ _ _ _ _ _ _ _ _ _ _ _ _ _ _ _ _	*Yesterday I went to the shopping centre.*
g. V _ _ d _ _ _ T _ _ _ _ h _ _ _ i _ _ e _ _ _ _ F _ _ _ a _ _ _ _ _ _ _ _ _ _.	*Three days ago I watched a film.*
h. V _ _ _ _ _ _ _ _ _ _ _ b _ _ i _ _ i _ _ S _ _ _ _ _ _ _ g _ _ _ _ _ _ _ _.	*The day before yesterday I went to the stadium.*

27. Sentence puzzle: write the sentences below in the correct order

a. Ich angesehen Film Kino einen im mir habe.

b. bin Park Vorgestern fahren im gegangen Rad ich.

c. man kann In machen Sport meiner Nachbarschaft.

d. drei bin gegangen Tagen ich Einkaufszentrum Vor ins.

e. viele Nachbarschaft In gibt es meiner schöne Geschäfte.

f. In man kann meiner tun Nachbarschaft viele Dinge.

g. kann im Fußball Man spielen Park.

29. Translate into German

a. the park

b. my neighbourhood

c. three days ago

d. yesterday

e. the day before yesterday

f. last week

g. near my house

h. one can eat

28. Complete with a suitable word

a. Gestern _______ ich mir im Kino einen Action_______ _______________.

b. Vorgestern _____ ich mit meiner Mutter ___ Einkaufszentrum _________________ ___________________.

c. In meiner ___________ kann man viele Dinge ____________.

d. Letzte Woche _____ ich in der Nähe von meinem Haus Rad _____________.

e. Ich lebe in einer ____________ Stadt, das historische __________ gefällt ______ sehr.

f. In meiner Gegend ______ es ein tolles Nachtleben. Man kann in ___________ und Restaurants gut ______________.

g. _____________ Wochenende ____ ich _____ Einkaufszentrum in der Nähe von _________ Haus gegangen. Danach ____ ich mit _______ Freunden schwimmen ______________.

30. Spot and correct the mistakes. HINT: not all sentences are wrong

a. In meiner Gegend kann man viele Dinge unternehmen.

b. Man kann viele Sehenswürdigkeiten besichtigen.

c. Man kann Museums und Schlösse besuchen.

d. Ich wohne im Stadtrand.

e. Gestern ich habe ins Einkaufszentrum in der Nähe von meinem Haus gegangen.

f. Vorgestern habe ich Kleid in einem Geschäft im Stadtzentrum gekauft.

g. Vor drei Tagen bin ich mit meinem besten Freund feiern gegangen.

h. Man kann im Stadion gehen.

33. Write two paragraphs in the first person singular (I) about Emma and Luke. NOTE: you cannot repeat the same information twice

Emma (12 years old from Germany)	**Luke** (17 years old from England)
• say your name, age and nationality • describe your physique and personality (4 details) • say you live in the south of Germany, near Switzerland • describe your neighbourhood, what is there to see and do (4 details minimum) • say one thing you like and one that you dislike about your neighbourhood • say 4 things that you did last weekend in your neighbourhood	• say your name, age and nationality • describe your physique and personality (4 details) • say you live in the south of England, near London, in the countryside • describe your town: size, what is there to see and do (4 details minimum) • say one thing you like and one that you dislike about your town • say 4 things that you did last weekend in your neighbourhood and 4 things you are going to do next weekend

31. Complete

a. Ich bin _ *I went swimming*

b. Ich habe mir einen Film _ _ _ _ _ _ _ _ _ _ *I saw a film*

c. Ich bin _ _ _ _ _ _ _ _ _ *I went*

d. Ich habe _ _ _ _ _ _ _ _ *I visited*

e. Ich habe _ _ _ _ _ _ _ _ _ *I played*

32. Translate into German

a. In my neighbourhood there is a lot on offer.

b. In my town there are many shops and a flea market.

c. There is a big park near my house.

d. In the old town there are many historic buildings and a medieval palace.

e. The nightlife is excellent. There are many bars and restaurants.

f. One can do many sports because there is a big sports centre.

g. Yesterday I went sailing with my father.

h. Two days ago I rode a bike in the park with my best friend.

i. Last weekend I went for a walk on the beach with my girlfriend.

j. Last week I went sightseeing in Vienna. I took a lot of photos.

k. There is a castle in my town.

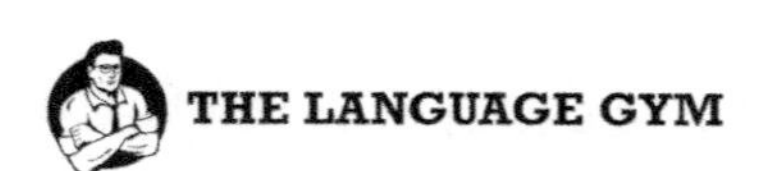

Question Skills Unit 2

English	German
What can you do in your neighbourhood to stay in shape?	**Was kann man in deiner Gegend unternehmen, um in Form zu bleiben?**
What sports can you do?	**Welche Sportarten kann man ausüben?**
Which sights can one visit?	**Welche Sehenswürdigkeiten kann man besuchen?**
What did you do in your neighbourhood recently?	**Was hast du kürzlich in deiner Nachbarschaft unternommen?**
Where did you go last weekend?	**Wo warst du letztes Wochenende?**
Did you do any sports last week?	**Hast du letzte Woche Sport gemacht?**
What did you do last weekend?	**Was hast du letztes Wochenende unternommen / gemacht?**

1. Match questions and answers

Was kann man machen, um in Form zu bleiben?	Man kann Fußball und Tennis spielen.
Welche Sportarten kann man ausüben?	Ich habe Fußball und Golf gespielt.
Welche Sehenswürdigkeiten kann man besuchen?	Ja. Es gibt eine Galerie, die ich oft besuche.
Wie ist deine Nachbarschaft?	Man kann im Fitnessstudio Sport machen.
Gibt es in deiner Gegend Kunstgalerien?	Sie ist sehr groß, modern und ruhig.
Was hast du letztes Wochenende gemacht?	Es gibt ein barockes Schloss und eine Kathedrale.

2. Complete the questions with: *Wie, Wo, Was, Wem oder Welche*

a. ______ liegt deine Gegend?

b. ______ ist das Beste an deiner Gegend?

c. ______ lange lebst du schon dort?

d. ______ warst du?

e. Mit ______ bist du ausgegangen?

f. ______ Sportarten kann man ausüben?

g. ______ hast du gestern unternommen?

h. ______ hast du letztes Wochenende gemacht?

i. ______ machst du normalerweise Sport?

j. ______ war das Beste, das du am Wochenende gemacht hast?

k. ______ Sehenswürdigkeiten kann man besuchen?

3. Sentence puzzle: rewrite the sentences

a. kann man Stadt unternehmen Was in deiner?

b. können Was junge unternehmen Gegend in deiner Leute?

c. lange lebst Wie schon in Straße du dieser?

d. Welche es deiner Stadt Sehenswürdigkeiten in gibt?

e. letztes in hast Wochenende deiner du Was unternommen Nachbarschaft?

f. gibt von deine Welche Nähe Sporteinrichtungen der es in Haus?

g. deiner hast Was Gegend du gestern in gemacht?

4. Complete with a suitable word

a. Was ______ man in deiner Stadt unternehmen?

b. Was _____ du letzte Woche ________________?

c. Wie ist deine ________________?

d. Wie lange __________ du schon dort?

e. Wo _________ deine Gegend?

f. _________ Sehenswürdigkeiten gibt es in deiner Gegend?

5. Write a question for each answer

a.	Sie liegt im Norden von Deutschland.
b.	Meine Stadt heißt Bremen.
c.	Meine Gegend heißt Donaustadt.
d.	Meine Gegend liegt am Stadtrand.
e.	Es gibt Sportzentren und ein Schwimmbad.
f.	Ich habe nicht viel gemacht.
g.	Ich bin mit meinem Freund ausgegangen.
h.	Das Beste war das Wetter. Es war sonnig.
i.	Das Schlimmste war, dass ich meine Hausaufgaben machen musste.

6. Guided translation

a. Where is your area located? W _ l _ _ _ _ d _ _ _ _ G _ _ _ _ _ ?

b. What is there to do for young people? W _ _ k _ _ _ _ _ j _ _ _ _ L _ _ _ _ u _ _ _ _ _ _ _ _ _ _ _ ?

c. Who did you go out with? M _ _ w _ _ b _ _ _ d _ a _ _ _ _ _ _ _ _ _ _ _ ?

d. How was it? W _ _ w _ _ e _ ?

e. Did you do any sports? H _ _ _ d _ S _ _ _ _ _ g _ _ _ _ _ _ _ ?

7. Translate into German

a. What tourist attractions are there?

b. What can one do to stay fit?

c. What did you do last weekend?

d. What is your neighbourhood like?

e. Who did you go out with?

f. Did you do any sports last week?

Vocab Revision Workout 1

1. Match

die Stadt	the climbing wall
der Süden	the country
das Land	the old town
die Gegend	the outskirts
die Kletterwand	the green spaces
die Altstadt	the south
die Gebäude	the nightlife
der Stadtrand	the buildings
die Grünflächen	the neighbourhood
das Nachtleben	the stadium
das Stadion	the city

2. Complete with *spielen*, *gehen*, *ansehen* or *besuchen / besichtigen*

a. Man kann schwimmen ____________.

b. Man kann Fußball ____________.

c. Man kann einkaufen ____________.

d. Man kann auf Konzerte ____________.

e. Man kann historische Schlösser ____________.

f. Man kann Golf ____________.

g. Man kann sich Filme ____________.

h. Man kann nicht feiern ____________.

i. Man kann nicht im Park Fußball ____________.

3. Sentence puzzle: rewrite the sentences in the correct order

a. Nähe eine von gibt meinem es In der Fußgängerzone Haus. *Near my house there is a pedestrian street.*

b. der gibt viele es In Geschäfte Fußgängerzone. *In the pedestrian street there are many shops.*

c. es Straßen schöne In viele Altstadt gibt der. *In the old town there are many beautiful streets.*

d. meinem gibt es Haus der In von eine Kletterwand Nähe. *Near my house there is a climbing wall.*

e. Sportzentrum Sport machen kann Im man. *One can do sports in the sports centre.*

f. ansehen kann alte Ruinen man In Altstadt sich der römische. *One can see Roman ruins in the old town.*

g. Nähe altes gibt Hafen In es ein Schloss der vom sehr. *Near the port there is a very old castle.*

h. gehen örtlichen kann Schwimmbad im schwimmen Man. *One can go swimming in the local pool.*

4. Missing letters

a. ge _ _ _ _ _ *yesterday*

b. ich ha_ _ ge_ _ _ _ _ _ *I did*

c. man ka _ _ *one can*

d. ich ha _ _ ge _ _ _ _ _ _ _ _ *I played*

e. ich ha _ _ ge _ _ _ _ _ _ *I saw*

f. die Str _ _ _ *street*

g. meine Ge _ _ _ _ _ *my area*

h. meine St _ _ _ *my city*

i. sich an _ _ _ _ _ _ *to watch*

j. die Fu_ _ _ _ _ _ _ _ _ _ _ _ *pedestrian street*

5. Spot and correct the (many) spelling errors

a. Edinburgh isst in Schotland.

b. In der Nehe von meinem Haus giebt es eine Fußgengerzone.

c. In meiner Stadt gibt es einen großen Parc.

d. Mir gefellt meine Gegend, weil sie sicher ist.

e. Meine Nachbarschaft ist sauba und guht gepflegt.

f. In meiner Gegend giebt es viel Verker.

g. In meiner Straße kann man im Park Fusball spilen.

h. Gestern habe ich Tennis im Tennisklub gespilt.

i. Ich leben am Stadtrand.

6. Categories: write the numbers into the best fitting category

1. Norden	2. Tennis	3. Boxen	4. Konzert	5. Osten	6. Stadt
7. Haus	8. Süden	9. Film	10. Klettern	11. Kino	12. Buch
13. Fußball	14. Museum	15. Westen	16. Schloss	17. Wohnung	18. Gewichte heben

Gebäude *[Buildings]*	**Sportarten** *[Sports]*	**Unterhaltung** *[Entertainment]*	**Geografie** *[Geography]*

7. Match activity and place

sich ein Fußballspiel ansehen	im Einkaufszentrum
sich einen Film ansehen	in der Altstadt
klettern gehen	im Stadion
schwimmen gehen	im Fitnessstudio
einkaufen gehen	im Kino
Sightseeing machen	im Schwimmbad
Gewichte heben	im botanischen Garten
sich exotische Pflanzen ansehen	in der Kletterhalle

8. Complete with a suitable word

a. Ich bin ins Einkaufs_______________ gegangen.

b. Ich habe die ______________ besichtigt.

c. Ich bin ins ______________ gegangen.

d. Ich habe _______________ gespielt.

e. Ich bin ins _____________________ schwimmen gegangen.

f. Ich habe mir im ____________ einen Film angesehen.

g. Ich habe im Park _______________ gespielt.

9. Guided translation

a. I___ l_________ i___ L_______________.

I live in London.

b. E_ g___ e__ K____ i__ d___ N____ v___ m_____ H____.

There is a cinema near my house.

c. I___ m_________ G_________ g____ e___ v________ j_______ L_________.

In my neighbourhood there are many young people.

d. E__ g______ e___ s_________ F___________________.

There is a beautiful pedestrian street.

e. M___ k_______ j_________ g__________.

One can go jogging.

f. M___ k_______ s_____ F_________ a______________.

One can watch films.

10. Translate into German

a. I went to the shopping centre.

b. I went to watch a concert.

c. I watched a film at the cinema.

d. I swam at the swimming pool.

e. I visited an ancient castle.

f. Last week I played tennis.

g. Last weekend I went shopping in the pedestrian area.

h. Yesterday I went hiking with my brother in the woods near my house.

i. I played football in the park.

Unit 3

Describing my street

In this unit you will learn:

- To say what places there are in my street
- To describe where things are located

Key sentence patterns:

- *In meiner Straße gibt es* + noun phrase
- Noun + locative adverbial/prepositions + prepositional phrase
- *Mein Haus* + *ist/befindet sich* + location
- *Es gibt* + *kein/keine* + noun + adverbial

Grammar:

- Using locative adverbials and prepositions
- *Kein/keine*
- masculine/neuter/feminine/plural: *von dem (*contraction: *vom)/von der/von den*

UNIT 3: Describing my street

	Masculine nouns	Feminine nouns	Neuter nouns
In meiner Straße gibt es *[In my street there is]* **In der Nähe von meinem Haus gibt es** *[Near my house there is]*	**einen Bahnhof** *[a train station]* **einen Fußballplatz** *[a football pitch]* **einen kleinen Park** *[a small park]* **einen Supermarkt**	**eine Bäckerei** *[a bakery]* **eine Buchhandlung** *[a book shop]* **eine Fleischerei** *[a butcher's]* **eine Kirche** *[a church]* **eine Moschee** *[a mosque]*	**ein chinesisches Restaurant** *[a Chinese restaurant]* **ein Einkaufszentrum** *[a shopping centre]* **ein Gebäude** *[a building]* **ein Schwimmbad** *[a pool]* **ein Sportzentrum** *[a sports centre]* **ein Kleider/Schuh/-geschäft** *[a clothes/shoe shop]*

Das Kino *[The cinema]* **Mein Haus** *[My house]* **Mein Gebäude** *[My building]* **Meine Wohnung** *[My flat]*	**befindet sich** *[is located]* **ist** *[is]*	**vor** *[in front of]* **nahe** *[near]* **neben** *[next to]* **hinter** *[behind]* **gegenüber** *[opposite]*	**der** *[the]*	**Bäckerei** *[the bakery]* **Bibliothek** *[the library]* **Fleischerei** *[the butcher's]*
			dem *[the]*	**Fußballplatz** **Parkplatz** *[the parking lot]*
			den *[the]*	**Tennisplätzen** *[the tennis courts]*
		in der Nähe *[near]* **links** *[to the left of]* **rechts** *[to the right of]* **weit entfernt** *[far from]* **zehn Minuten mit dem Auto entfernt** *[a 10 minute car ride from]* **zehn Minuten zu Fuß entfernt** *[a 10 minute walk from]*	**von der** *[the]*	**Kirche** *[the church]*
			vom *[the]*	**Haus** *[house]* **Musikgeschäft** *[music shop]*
			von den *[the]*	**Geschäften** *[the shops]*
		am Ende der Straße *[at the end of the street]* **an der Ecke** *[on the corner]*		

Mein Haus **Meine Wohnung**	**liegt**	**zwischen** *[between]*	**der Bäckerei (fem.)** **dem Park (masc.)** **dem Kino (ntr.)**	**und**	**der Bibliothek (fem.)** **dem Supermarkt (masc.)** **dem Schwimmbad (ntr.)**

Es gibt *[There is]*	**keinen** *[no – sg. masc]*	**Park**	**in der Nähe von meinem Haus** *[near my house]* **in meiner Nachbarschaft** *[in my neighbourhood]* **in der Nähe** *[nearby]*
	keine *[no – sg. fem]*	**Kirche**	
	kein *[no – sg. ntr.]*	**Schwimmbad**	
***Author's note: You can add "-geschäft" to many types of goods to describe a specific shop, e.g. "Schuhgeschäft"** *[shoe shop]* **or "Sportgeschäft"** *[sports shop]*			

1. Match

rechts von	near
links von	in my street
hinter	in front of
gegenüber	behind
neben	far from
in der Nähe von	next to
weit von	my house is
in meiner Straße	to the left of
mein Haus liegt/ist	100 metres away from
in meiner Gegend	opposite
mein Gebäude liegt/ist	ten minutes away by car
zehn Minuten mit dem Auto entfernt von	in my neighbourhood
hundert Meter entfernt von	to the right of
vor	my building is

2. Complete the translations

a. in meiner Straße: *in my* _________

b. weit von: __________ *from*

c. hundert Meter entfernt von:
__________ *metres away from*

d. in meiner Gegend:
in my _____________

e. mein Haus ist: *my* ___________ *is*

f. nicht weit von: *not* ________ *from*

g. gegenüber meinem Gebäude:

opposite ___ _______________

3. Richtig (true) oder falsch (false). Write R for *richtig* or F for *falsch* next to each statement below, based on the map.

Golfklub			Park			
Fleischerei	**Antons Haus**	**Bibliothek**	**Musikgeschäft**	**Bäckerei**	**Supermarkt**	**Kleidergeschäft**
			Hauptstraße			
Lauras Haus	**Fitnessstudio**	**Bar**	**indisches Restaurant**	**chinesisches Restaurante**	**Kino**	**Laden an der Ecke**
Supermarkt	**Schwimmbad**	**ialienisches Restaurant**	**Gastgarten**		**Parkplatz**	

a. Antons Haus ist neben der Bibliothek. ____

b. Die Bäckerei befindet sich gegenüber dem chinesischen Restaurant. ____

c. Das Musikgeschäft ist vor dem Park. ____

d. Es gibt ein Einkaufszentrum in der Hauptstraße. ____

e. Das Kino ist in der Nähe von Lauras Haus. ____

f. Es gibt einen Supermarkt in der Hauptstraße. ____

g. Der Golfklub ist hinter Antons Haus. ____

4. Faulty translation: spot the mistakes in the English translations and correct them. Please note: not all translations have a mistake

a. In meiner Straße gibt es viele Geschäfte.	*In my street there are not many shops.*
b. In der Nähe von meinem Haus gibt es ein Fitnessstudio und ein Schwimmbad.	*Near my house there are a gym and pool.*
c. Der Tennisklub ist vor der Schule.	*The tennis club is behind the school.*
d. Es gibt keine Kleidergeschäfte in meiner Straße.	*There are no clothes shops in my area.*
e. Gibt es hier eine Bibliothek?	*Is there a library near here?*
f. Der Park ist hinter dem Bahnhof.	*The park is behind the bus station.*
g. Es gibt einen Supermarkt neben dem Kino.	*There's a supermarket next to the sports centre.*

5. Break the flow

a.InmeinerStraßegibteskeineKleidergeschäfte.

b.EsgibteinRestaurantzehnMinutenzuFußentferntvonhier.

c.DieBäckereibefindetsichnebenderFleischerei.

d. WoistdieBibliothek?

e. DaschinesischeRestaurantistgegenübervonderKirche.

6. Complete with the missing letters

a. Es gibt eine Ki _ _ _ _ in der Nähe von meinem Ha _ _.

b. Ne _ _ _ dem Supermarkt gibt es ein Ki _ _.

c. Es gibt einen Park hi _ _ _ _ dem Restaurant.

d. Es gibt keine Kleiderg _ _ _ _ _ _ _ _ _ in meiner Straße.

e. W _ ist d _ _ Bibliothek?

f. Mein Haus ist gegen _ _ _ _ vom Par _.

g. D _ _ Gesch _ _ _ ist rechts v _ _ Kino.

7. Multiple choice: choose the correct translation

	1	2	3
a. behind	vor	hinter	innerhalb
b. next to	an der Ecke	weit entfernt von	neben
c. opposite	gegenüber	in der Nähe von	unter
d. in front of	über	vor dem	innerhalb
e. to the right of	rechts von	links von	an der Ecke
f. to the left of	innerhalb	rechts von	links von
g. Where is…?	Wer ist…?	Wo ist...?	Ist hier…?
h. in between	neben	innerhalb	zwischen
i. on the corner	vor	an der Ecke	in meiner Gegend
j. far from	weit entfernt von	in der Nähe von	hinter
k. there is	da sind	es gibt	daher ist
l. in my street	in meiner Gegend	in meinem Haus	in meiner Straße

8. Location puzzle: complete the street map with the 10 missing names of places below, using the words in BOLD in the text below

a. Peters Haus ist gegenüber Martas Haus.
b. Zwischen Martas Haus und dem örtlichen Schwimmbad ist ein kleiner Supermarkt.
c. Zwischen dem Kleidergeschäft und dem Friseur ist die Bibliothek.
d. Rechts vom Golfklub gibt es einen sehr großen Parkplatz.
e. Hinter dem Kino gibt es eine Fleischerei.
f. Links neben dem Kino ist ein Basketballplatz.
g. Links von der Loos Bar gibt es ein italienisches Restaurant.
h. Hinter dem Café Korb ist ein Spielzeuggeschäft.
i. Hinter Peters Haus ist ein Fußballplatz.
j. Rechts vom Spielzeuggeschäft gibt es ein Eisgeschäft.

<table>
<tr><td colspan="3">Golfklub</td><td colspan="4"></td></tr>
<tr><td>Martas Haus</td><td></td><td>Schwimm-bad</td><td>Kleider-geschäft</td><td colspan="2"></td><td>Friseur</td></tr>
<tr><td colspan="7">Kärntnerstraße</td></tr>
<tr><td></td><td>Café Korb</td><td></td><td>Loos Bar</td><td></td><td colspan="2">Opernkino</td></tr>
<tr><td></td><td></td><td></td><td colspan="2">Garten</td><td colspan="2"></td></tr>
</table>

9. Translate into English

a. Marcels Haus ist gegenüber dem Bahnhof.

b. Das städtische Schwimmbad liegt zwischen dem Sportzentrum und dem Supermarkt.

c. Die Bibliothek befindet sich am Ende der Straße.

d. Rechts vom Golfklub befindet sich eine riesige Bibliothek.

e. Hinter dem Kino befindet sich eine Laufstrecke.

f. Links neben dem Kino befindet sich eine Bushaltestelle.

g. Links von meiner Schule gibt es ein chinesisches Restaurant.

h. Hinter der Polizeistation befindet sich ein Spielzeuggeschäft.

i. Neben Ralfs Haus gibt es einen Fußballplatz und einen Basketballplatz.

j. In der Nähe von meinem Haus befindet sich eine sehr große Sporthalle mit einem olympischen Schwimmbecken.

k. Das Stadion ist weit entfernt von meinem Haus.

Mein Name ist Luise, ich komme aus Jena, lebe aber in Bremen. Ich liebe meine Nachbarschaft, weil es so viele Angebote gibt. Es gibt viele Sportmöglichkeiten, so dass man viel Sport treiben kann. In meiner Straße gibt es zum Beispiel ein Fitnessstudio, einen Park mit Eislaufplatz und ein Sportzentrum mit einem olympischen Schwimm-becken. Gestern habe ich im Fitnessstudio Gewichte gehoben. Es war sehr anstrengend, hat aber viel Spaß gemacht.
In meiner Nachbarschaft sind viele Geschäfte. In der Nähe von meinem Haus, zirka fünf Minuten zu Fuß entfernt, ist ein riesiges Einkaufszentrum, wo man alles Mögliche kaufen kann. Hundert Meter von meinem Haus ist mein Lieblings-kleidergeschäft und am Ende der Straße ist ein sehr cooles Sportgeschäft. Ich habe mir gestern ein neues Paar Sneaker gekauft.
In meiner Nachbarschaft gibt es Restaurants, wo man gut essen kann. Neben meinem Haus ist links ein chinesisches und auf der anderen Seite ein indisches Restaurant. Letzten Samstag habe ich im chinesischen Restaurant gegessen. Das Essen war köstlich. **(Luise, 15 Jahre. Jena)**

10. Find the German equivalent in Luise's text

a. ...but I live

b. there is a lot on offer

c. sports facilities

d. on my street there are

e. an ice rink

f. I lifted weights

g. it was very tiring

h. there are many shops

i. five minutes away on foot

j. 100 metres from my house

k. at the end of the street

l. very cool

m. a pair of sneakers

n. one can eat well

o. next to my house

p. on the left

q. at the Chinese restaurant

11. Tick the items that you can find in Luise's text and cross out the ones you can't

a. in my neighbourhood

b. a lot of sports

c. music shop

d. on the left

e. the food was very tasty

f. yesterday

g. tomorrow

h. very funny

i. to go jogging

j. clothes shop

k. Olympic-size swimming pool

l. sports shoes/trainers

m. a skirt

n. near

o. my house

12. Answer the questions below in English

a. Why does Luise like her neighbourhood?

b. What four sports facilities does Luise mention?

c. What was tiring but fun?

d. How far is the shopping centre from her house?

e. What can one buy there?

f. Where is her favourite clothes shop?

g. How does she describe the sports shop?

h. What is next to her house, on the left?

i. Where did she eat last Saturday?

j. How was the food?

Mein Name ist Marcel. Ich komme aus Linz, lebe aber in Salzburg, einer sehr schönen und historischen Stadt im Westen von Österreich. Ich wohne in einer Gegend am Stadtrand. Es gefällt mir nicht, weil es nicht viele Sporteinrichtungen gibt, daher kann man nicht viel Sport machen. Es gibt ein sehr altes und schlecht ausgestattetes Fitnessstudio, einen sehr kleinen, hässlichen und schlecht gepflegten Park und eine sehr schlechte Sporthalle: Es gibt weder ein Schwimmbad noch Tennisplätze. In meiner Gegend gibt es auch keinen Fußballplatz. Gestern bin ich im Park joggen und im Wald in der Nähe von meinem Haus Rad fahren gegangen. Es war sehr anstrengend, aber sehr lustig.

Nicht weit von meinem Haus gibt es ein riesiges Einkaufszentrum, zehn Minuten mit dem Auto entfernt. Es gibt viele schöne Geschäfte und man kann alles Mögliche kaufen. Mein Lieblingsgeschäft ist das Videospielegeschäft.

Was ich an meiner Nachbarschaft am meisten mag, ist, dass ich hier viele Freunde habe. Mein bester Freund Mario wohnt fünf Minuten zu Fuß von meinem Haus entfernt, daher sehen wir uns oft.

In meiner Gegend sind viele nette Restaurants, wo man sehr gut essen kann. Neben meinem Haus ist links ein italienisches und rechts ein mexikanisches Restaurant. Letzten Samstag war ich im mexikanischen Restaurant. Das Essen war sehr lecker und scharf.

(Marcel, 16 Jahre. Linz)

15. Tick the words / phrases that you can find in Marcel's text

a. zu Fuß	h. bester
b. Rad fahren	i. selten
c. rechts	j. lecker
d. in der Nähe	k. fettig
e. alles Mögliche	l. anstrengend
f. wenig	m. man kann
g. viele	n. Gerichte

13. Find the German equivalent in Marcel's text

a. I live in
b. a very beautiful town
c. on the outskirts
d. sports facilities
e. therefore
f. a very old gym
g. small, ugly
h. neither a swimming pool
i. yesterday I went jogging
j. exhausting
k. near my house
l. not very far from my house
m. ten minutes away by car
n. one can buy all sorts of things
o. I have many friends here
p. where one can eat very well
q. next to my house
r. on the left
s. on the right

14. Answer providing as many details as possible.

a. What does Marcel say about Salzburg?
b. Why does he not like his neighbourhood?
c. What does he say about the gym, the park and the sports centre?
d. What did he do yesterday?
e. Where is the shopping centre?
f. What can you buy there?
g. What is his favourite shop?
h. What does he like the most about his neighbourhood?
i. What is there to the left of his house?
j. What is there to the right?
k. Where did he eat last Saturday?
l. How was the food?

16. Translate into English

a. rechts von der Schule

b. in der Nähe von meinem Haus

c. gegenüber dem Kino

d. vor dem Supermarkt

e. am Ende der Straße

f. nicht weit von meinem Haus

g. neben dem Schwimmbad

h. fünf Minuten zu Fuß

i. hundert Meter von meinem Haus entfernt

17. Sentence puzzle: rewrite the sentences in the correct order

a. meiner In gibt viele Gegend Geschäfte es.
In my neighbourhood there are many shops.

b. neben Fitnessstudio gibt meinem ein Es Haus.
There is a gym next to my house.

c. am Das ist der Ende Schwimmbad Straße.
The swimming pool is at the end of the street.

d. weit nicht von Meine ist Schule Haus meinem entfernt.
My school is not far from my house.

18. Find in the wordsearch the German translation of the phrases below, then write it next to each of them, as shown in the example

D	L	T	T	T	H	A	D	G	O	B	T	G	Q	I
H	L	I	Y	F	C	A	E	U	N	X	E	T	M	N
U	J	A	N	V	W	G	C	V	T	B	S	T	G	D
C	I	E	W	K	E	K	Y	K	Ä	Y	F	Z	L	E
K	N	C	H	N	S	E	O	U	S	Ä	G	B	F	R
W	T	S	Ü	N	Z	V	D	X	H	V	V	L	O	N
F	F	B	X	W	T	E	O	C	U	J	Q	N	H	Ä
K	E	E	U	I	J	L	S	N	P	U	N	W	N	H
R	N	O	V	T	I	E	W	T	H	C	I	N	H	E
Q	R	K	Q	W	G	Y	F	X	X	F	I	Z	A	V
W	N	G	C	S	B	K	A	K	S	E	Q	L	B	Z
A	Y	R	A	T	X	B	C	M	U	E	C	I	D	B
S	F	D	T	N	I	K	F	X	Q	I	N	I	J	D
I	N	M	E	I	N	E	R	S	T	R	A	ß	E	R
I	X	O	Y	J	D	S	H	Y	ß	U	F	U	Z	G

e.g. not far from — ***nicht weit von***

a. opposite

b. wood

c. train station

d. the shop

e. in my street

f. to the left of

g. nearby

h. building

i. by foot

19. Tick the words below which are names of shops

a. die Fleischerei

b. der Wald

c. der Park

d. die Bäckerei

e. der Supermarkt

f. der Apfel

g. das Gebäude

20. Complete with the missing letters

a. die Bäc _ _ _ _ _ — *the bakery*

b. die Fle _ _ _ _ _ _ _ _ _ — *the butcher's*

c. der Par _ — *the park*

d. die Bi_lio _ _ _ _ — *the library*

e. das Mu _ _ _ ges_ _ _ _ _ _ — *the music shop*

f. das Ge _ _ _ _ _ — *the building*

g. die K_ _ _ _ _ — *the church*

21. Complete with the missing words

a. In meiner Straße gibt es viele ____________.	*In my street there are many shops.*
b. Die Bäckerei ist fünf Minuten zu _____ entfernt.	*The bakery is five minutes away on foot.*
c. Die Bibliothek ist _________ meiner Schule.	*The library in next to my school.*
d. Die ____________ ist dort _____________.	*The butcher's is there, on the right.*
e. Mein Auto ist _____ _____ Supermarkt.	*The car is in front of the supermarket.*
f. Das Stadion ist sehr _______ entfernt von meinem Haus.	*The stadium is very far from my house.*
g. Das Schwimmbad ist am _________ der Straße.	*The swimming pool is at the end of the road.*
h. In meiner _________ gibt es nicht viele _____________.	*In my street there aren't many shops*
i. __________ meinem Haus gibt es einen Park.	*Behind my building there is a park.*

22. Translate into German

a. *next to my house*	n__________ m___________ H___________
b. *opposite my building*	g_____________ m__________ G_______________
c. *far from here*	w_________ v________ h___________
d. *on the right*	r____________ v_____
e. *on the left*	l____________ v_____
f. *near my house*	I____ d______ N_______ v____ m_________ H___________
g. *behind the butcher's*	h_____________ d______ F_______________________
h. *next to the bakery*	n________ d_____ B______________________

23. Write a paragraph in which you:

1. Say where in Germany your town is located, and whether like it or not (*aim for 20 words*)
2. Say where your neighbourhood is located, what shops and other places there are, what there is to do and how much you like it (*aim for 40 words*)
3. Describe the street below as if it were the street where you live (*aim for 40 words*)

Tennisklub			**Park**		
mein Haus	**Supermarkt**	**Schwimm-bad**	**Kleider-geschäft**	**Bibliothek**	**Friseur**
Lindenstraße					
meine Schule	**Café Kult**	**Musik-geschäft**	**Bar Papageno**	**Fitnessstudio**	**Stadtkino**

Question Skills Unit 3

English	**German**
What is there in your neighbourhood?	**Was gibt es in deiner Gegend?**
Where is your house?	**Wo befindet sich dein Haus?**
What is there near your house?	**Was gibt es in der Nähe von deinem Haus?**
Do you like your neighbourhood? Why? Why not?	**Gefällt dir deine Nachbarschaft? Warum? Warum nicht?**
What shops are there in your neighbourhood?	**Welche Geschäfte gibt es in deiner Nachbarschaft?**
Which is your favourite shop? Where is it?	**Was ist dein Lieblingsgeschäft? Wo ist es?**
What is the best thing about your area? What is the worst thing about your area?	**Was ist das Beste an deiner Gegend? Was ist das Schlechteste an deiner Gegend?**
What places do you NOT have near where you live?	**Was befindet sich NICHT in der Nähe von deinem Haus?**
What did you do recently in your area?	**Was hast du in letzter Zeit in deiner Gegend unternommen?**
What did you do last weekend?	**Was hast du letztes Wochenende gemacht?**
Where did you go?	**Wo warst du?**
How did it go?	**Wie war es?**
Did you have a good time?	**Hattest du Spaß?**

1. Match questions and answers

Gefällt dir deine Nachbarschaft?	In der Nähe vom Stadtzentrum.
Was hast du kürzlich in deiner Gegend gemacht?	Es gibt zum Beispiel einen Jugendklub.
Warum gefällt dir deine Nachbarschaft nicht?	In der Goethe Straße.
Welche Geschäfte gibt es?	Ich bin mit Lisa in den Park gegangen.
Wo befindet sich deine Nachbarschaft?	Nein, ich hasse es hier zu wohnen.
Was ist neben deinem Haus?	Es gibt alles: Kleidergeschäfte, ein Musikgeschäft, etc.
Was gibt es für junge Leute?	Weil es sehr laut und unsicher ist.
Ist deine Schule weit von dir entfernt?	Ein gutes chinesisches Restaurant.
In welcher Straße befindet sich dein Haus?	Nein, sie ist ganz in der Nähe.

2. Complete with the missing words

a. Wie h__________ deine Straße?	*What is your street's name?*
b. Wo b__________ sich deine Straße?	*Where is your street?*
c. G____________ dir deine Gegend?	*Do you like your neighbourhood?*
d. W_______ gefällt sie dir nicht?	*Why don't you like it?*
e. Was gibt es für J______________?	*What is there for young people?*
f. Welche G____________ gibt es in deiner Nachbarschaft?	*What shops are there in your neighbourhood?*
g. G______ es Sporteinrichtungen?	*Are there any sports facilities?*
h. Was befindet sich g_____________ deinem Haus?	*What is there opposite your house?*

3. Split questions

Wie	gefällt dir deine Gegend nicht?
Wo	wohnst du hier?
Gibt es	heißt deine Gegend?
Warum	befindet sich deine Wohnung?
Seit wann	für junge Leute?
Was gibt es	Sporteinrichtungen?
Welche	das Beste an deiner Gegend?
Mit	Sehenswürdigkeiten gibt es in deiner Gegend?
Wo	wem bist du ausgegangen?
Was ist	warst du gestern?

4. Translate into English

a. Wie heißt deine Straße?

b. In welchem Stadtteil ist das?

c. Erzähl mir von deiner Gegend. Gefällt sie dir?

d. Gibt es Sporteinrichtungen?

e. Was gibt es für junge Leute?

f. Was ist das Schlechteste an deiner Gegend? Und was das Beste?

g. Was ist gegenüber deinem Haus?

h. Was ist neben deinem Haus?

i. Was hast du letztes Wochenende gemacht?

5. Guided translation

a. W _ _ h_ _ _ _ d_ _ _ _ G_ _ _ _ _?	*What is your neighbourhood called?*
b. W_ b_ _ _ _ _ _ _ _ s_ _ s_ _ _?	*Where is it located?*
c. W _ _ g _ _ _ e_ i_ d_ _ _ _ _ _ G_ _ _ _ _ _?	*What is there in your neighbourhood?*
d. W_ _ i_ _ d_ _ B_ _ _ _?	*What's the best thing?*
e. W_ _ l_ _ _ _?	*For how long/since when?*
f. W_ w_ _ _ _ d_?	*Where did you go?*
g. S_ _ _ w_ _ _ w_ _ _ _ _ _ d_ h_ _ _?	*Since when do you live here?*
h. M_ _ w_ _ b_ _ _ d_ a_ _ _ _ _ _ _ _ _ _ _ _?	*Who did you go out with?*

Unit 4

Describing my home & furniture

In this unit you will learn:

- To say where your house is located
- To say what your house is like
- To describe what items are in each room

Key sentence patterns:

- *Ich wohne in/Ich lebe in* + location
- *In meinem Haus/in meiner Wohnung*
- *Mir gefällt + mein Haus/meine Wohnung (nicht), weil es/sie* + adjective + *ist*
- *In meiner Küche/Im Wohnzimmer/in meinem Zimmer + gibt es/steht/liegt/hängt* + piece of furniture

Grammar:

- Preposition *in* + Dativ (especially in combination with possessive adjective: *in meiner, in meinem*)
- Causal clause with *weil*

UNIT 4: Describing my home and furniture

Ich wohne *[I live]* **Ich lebe** *[I live]*	**in einem Haus** *[in a house]* **in einer Wohnung** *[in a flat]* **in einem Gebäude** *[in a building]*	**auf dem Land** *[in the countryside]* **im Stadtzentrum** **an der Küste** *[at the coast]* **in einem Vorort** *[in a suburb]* **in den Bergen** *[in the mountains]*

In meinem Haus *[In my house]* **In meiner Wohnung** *[In my flat]*	**gibt es** *[there are]*	**fünf** **sechs** **sieben**	**Zimmer,** *[rooms]*	**zum Beispiel** *[for example]*	**ein Elternschlafzimmer** *[a master bedroom]* **ein Badezimmer** *[a bathroom]* **ein Esszimmer** *[a dining room]* **ein Kinderzimmer** *[a child's bedroom]* **ein Spielzimmer** *[a playroom]* **ein Wohnzimmer** *[a living room]* **eine Küche** *[a kitchen]* **eine Speisekammer** *[a pantry]*

außerdem gibt es *[there is also]*	**einen Dachboden** *[an attic]* **einen Keller** *[a basement]*	**und**	**eine Garage** *[a garage]* **einen Garten** *[a garden]*

Mir gefällt mein Haus, weil *[I like my house because]* **Mir gefällt mein Haus nicht, weil** *[I don't like my house because]*	**es** *[it...]*	**abgewohnt** *[worn]* **alt** *[old]* **gut ausgestattet** *[well furnished]* **gemütlich** *[cosy]* **geräumig** *[spacious]* **hässlich** *[ugly]* **hell** *[well-lit]* **sauber** *[clean]* **schmutzig** *[dirty]* **schlecht gelegen** *[in a bad location]*	**ist** *[...is]*
Mir gefällt meine Wohnung, weil *[I like my flat because]* **Mir gefällt meine Wohnung nicht, weil** *[I don't like my flat because]*	**sie** *[it...]*		

In meiner Küche *[In my kitchen]*	**gibt es** *[there is]*	**eine Speisekammer** *[a pantry]* **ein Spülbecken** *[a sink]*
	steht *[stands]*	**ein Geschirrspüler** *[a dishwasher]* **ein Kühlschrank** *[a fridge]* **ein Ofen** *[an oven]* **ein Stuhl** *[a chair]* **ein Tisch** *[a table]*
Im Wohnzimmer *[In my living room]*	**gibt es** *[there is]*	**einen Kamin** *[a fireplace]*
	steht *[stands]*	**ein Bücherregal** *[a bookshelf]* **ein Couchtisch** *[a coffee table]* **ein Fernseher** *[a TV]* **ein Sessel** *[an armchair]* **ein Sofa**
	liegt *[lies]*	**ein Teppich** *[a rug]*
In meinem Zimmer *[In my room]*	**steht** *[stands]*	**ein Bett** *[a bed]* **ein Nachttisch** *[a bedside table]* **ein Schrank** *[a wardrobe]* **ein Schreibtisch** *[a desk]*
	hängt *[hangs]*	**ein Bild** *[a picture]* **ein Spiegel** *[a mirror]*

1. Translate into English

a. auf dem Land

b. am Stadtrand

c. in der Küche

d. im Wohnzimmer

e. im Spielzimmer

f. am Dachboden

g. im Garten

h. in der Garage

i. in meinem Zimmer

j. im Elternschlafzimmer

k. im Zimmer meines Bruders

l. im Keller

2. Match

eine Speisekammer	an armchair
ein Bett	a pantry
ein Bücherregal	a mirror
ein Stuhl	a television
ein Sessel	a desk
ein Schreibtisch	a fridge
ein Teppich	a bed
ein Fernseher	an oven
ein Kühlschrank	a bookshelf
ein Ofen	a rug
ein Spiegel	a chair

3. Write, in German, in which rooms the following objects are most likely to be found

a. der Stuhl	im Wohnzimmer, in der Küche	i. das Bücherregal	
b. der Schreibtisch		j. das Spielzeug	
c. der Teppich		k. das Bett	
d. der Sessel		l. der Fernseher	
e. die Dusche		m. das Auto	
f. das Spülbecken		n. der Baum	
g. der Ofen		o. die Vorhänge	
h. der Schrank		p. der Spiegel	

4. Complete with the missing letters

a. die D_ _ _ _ _ *the shower*

b. der T_ _ _ _ *the table*

c. das B_ _ _ *the bed*

d. der S_ _ _ _ _ _ _ _ _ _ _ *the desk*

e. der S_ _ _ _ *the chair*

f. das S_ _ _ _ _ _ _ _ _ *the toy*

5. Write "likely" or "unlikely" next to the statements

e.g. In der Küche steht ein Kühlschrank. *L*

a. Im Schlafzimmer steht ein Baum. ___

b. Im Wohnzimmer steht ein Sofa. ___

c. Im Elternschlafzimmer steht ein Ofen. ___

d. Im Kinderzimmer steht eine Lampe. ___

e. Im Garten liegt ein Hund. ___

f. Im Schlafzimmer steht ein Bett. ___

6. Multiple choice: choose the correct translation

	1	2	3
a. cupboard	der Schrank	die Tür	die Schachtel
b. armchair	der Stuhl	der Sessel	der Schrank
c. toys	die Bücher	die Spielsachen	die Sachen
d. oven	der Ofen	der Kamin	das Feuer
e. tree	der Tisch	der Kasten	der Baum
f. rug	der Boden	der Teppich	die Lampe
g. table	das Buch	der Tisch	das Haus
h. curtains	das Fenster	der Garten	die Vorhänge
i. desk	der Schreibtisch	der Baum	der Tisch
j. chair	der Stuhl	der Rasen	das Fenster
k. bookshelf	das Buch	das Bücherregal	der Teppich

7. Faulty translation: correct the mistakes in the translations below
Please note: not all translations are incorrect

a. In der Küche stehen ein Tisch und drei Stühle. — *In the kitchen there is a table and four chairs.*

b. In meinem Kinderzimmer liegt ein roter Teppich. — *In my bedroom there are red curtains.*

c. Im Elternschlafzimmer steht ein Bett. — *In the master bedroom there is a bed.*

d. In unserem Garten steht ein großer Baum. — *In our garden there aren't any trees.*

e. In unserem Wohnzimmer steht ein Bücherregal. — *In our living room there are two armchairs.*

f. Neben meinem Bett hängt ein Spiegel. — *Beside my bed there is a mirror.*

g. Auf meinem Schreibtisch steht eine Lampe. — *There is a book on my desk.*

8. Spot the hidden phrases, fill in the gaps and translate into English
HINT: the words are names of rooms + the furniture in it

a. I_ m_ _ _ _ _S_ _ _ _ _ _ _ _ _ _ _ s_ _ _ _e_ _B_ _ _.

b. I_ d_ _K_ _ _ _ g_ _ _e_ e_ _S_ _ _ _ _ _ _ _ _.

c. I_ G_ _ _ _ _s_ _ _ _e_ _B_ _ _.

d. I_ W_ _ _ _ _ _ _ _ _ _g_ _ _ e_e_ _ _ _F_ _ _ _ _ _ _ _.

e. I_ E_ _ _ _ _ _ _ _ _ _ _ _ _ _ _ _ s_ _ _ _e_ _B_ _ _.

f. I_ K_ _ _ _ _ _ _ _ _ _ _g_ _ _e_e_ _ _ _S_ _ _ _ _ _.

g. I_ W_ _ _ _ _ _ _ _ _ _s_ _ _ _e_ _ _ L_ _ _ _.

9. Write Richtig (true) or Falsch (false) next to each statement below

a. Neben dem Bett steht ein Nachttisch. ____________

b. Der Fernseher steht hinter dem Bett. ____________

c. Rechts von der Tür hängt ein Spiegel. ____________

d. Der Schreibtisch steht neben dem Fernseher. ____________

e. Der Schrank steht neben dem Bett. ____________

f. Der Fernseher steht zwischen dem Spiegel und dem Schreibtisch. ____________

g. Eine Lampe steht auf dem Schreibtisch. ____________

h. Die Katze liegt auf dem Bett. ____________

i. Die Tür ist zwischen dem Bett und dem Schrank. ____________

j. Das Nachkästchen ist zwischen dem Schrank und dem Bett. ____________

k. Der Stuhl steht in der Nähe vom Schreibtisch. ____________

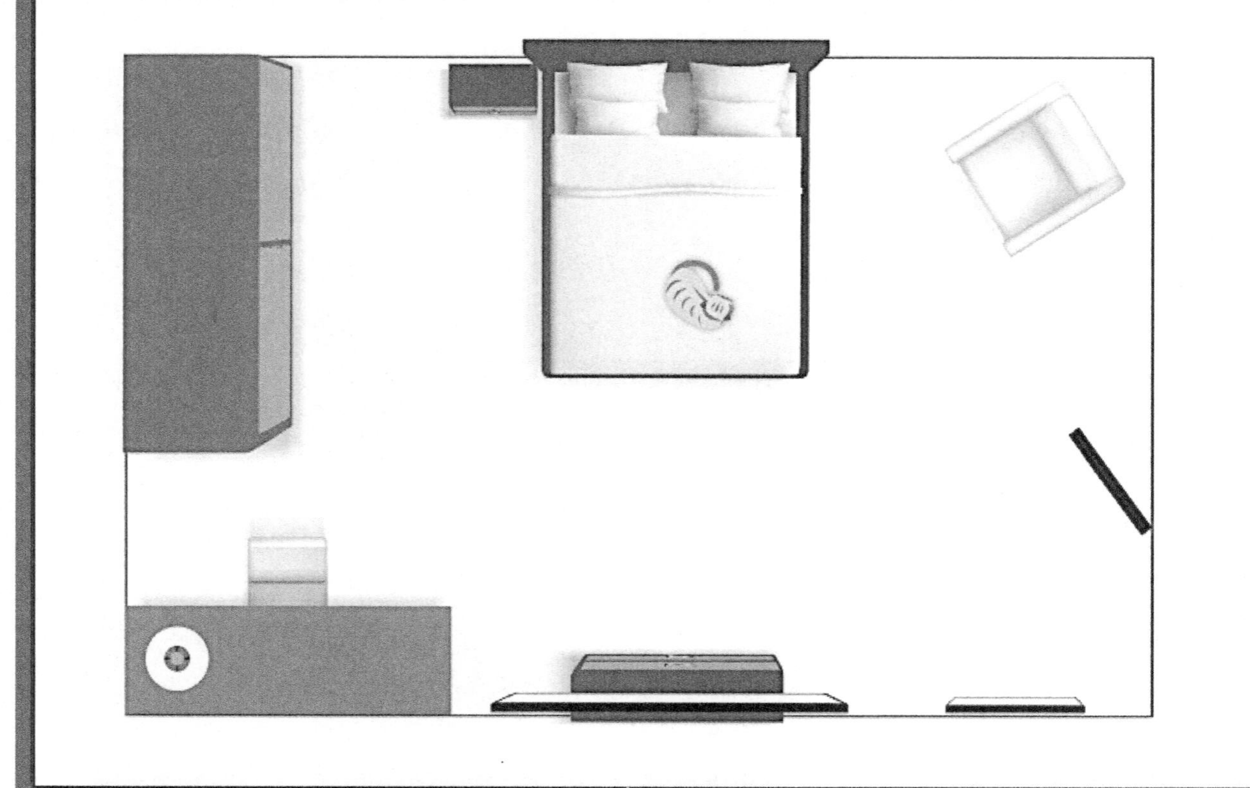

Ich heiße Martin und lebe in Innsbruck. Ich wohne mit meiner Familie in einer modernen Wohnung in einer schönen Gegend am Stadtrand.
Mir gefällt meine Gegend, weil es viele Angebote für junge Leute gibt. Es gibt einen tollen Park in der Nähe von meinem Haus, wo es eine Kletterwand, einen Eislaufplatz, eine Rutsche und viele andere Spielmöglichkeiten und Platz zum Spielen gibt.
Mit meinen Freunden treffe ich mich täglich im Park um Frisbee zu spielen, joggen oder Rad fahren zu gehen. Es gibt auch Sporteinrichtungen, zum Beispiel zehn Minuten von meinem Haus entfernt gibt es ein super Fitnessstudio und ein Schwimmbad. In meiner Gegend gibt es auch ein großes Einkaufszentrum, in dem es viele tolle Geschäfte gibt.
Ich wohne im siebten Stock eines modernen Gebäudes. In unserer Wohnung gibt es eine Küche, ein Wohnzimmer, zwei Badezimmer, ein Spielzimmer und drei Schlafzimmer: meines, das meiner großen Schwester und das meiner Mutter.
Mir gefällt mein Zimmer am besten, weil es gemütlich und hübsch dekoriert ist. Ich habe ein großes, bequemes Bett. Links davon steht ein geräumiger Schrank, rechts davon ein Nachttisch. Auf der anderen Seite meines Zimmers steht in der Ecke ein Schreibtisch. Neben dem Schreibtisch vor dem Bett steht ein alter Fernseher, der noch gut funktioniert.
Hinter dem Fernseher ist ein großes Fenster. Links davon hängt ein Spiegel. Ich verbringe viel Zeit in meinem Zimmer mit Musikhören, Bücherlesen und Hausaufgaben machen.
(Martin, 14 Jahre. Innsbruck)

10. Answer the questions below in English

a. In which part of Salzburg does Martin live?

b. Name three things one can find in the park near his home.

c. How often does he go there with his friends?

d. What three activities does he like to do with his friends?

e. What sports facilities are there in his area?

f. On which floor does he live?

g. What rooms does Martin list?

h. Why is his bedroom his favourite room in the house?

i. What is there to the right of his bed?

j. What is there to the left of his bed?

k. What is there in the corner, on the opposite side to the bed?

11. Find the German equivalent

a. near my house

b. a climbing wall

c. to ride a bike

d. ten minutes away from my house

e. on the seventh floor

f. a playroom

g. is very cosy

h. my older sister's bedroom

i. on the other side

j. in the corner

k. behind the TV

l. to the left of it (the window)

12. Spot the SIX words on the list below which are not contained in Martin's text

a. Motorrad	g. Wetter	m. weit
b. dekoriert	h. gemütlich	n. Ecke
c. Bett	i. Fernseher	o. Fenster
d. Schreibtisch	j. Tennisplatz	p. bequem
e. Ski	k. laut	q. Nachbarn
f. Zimmer	l. Bücher	r. Schrank

Ich heiße Martina und komme aus Dresden, lebe aber in Wien. Ich lebe in einer Altbauwohnung im ersten Bezirk in der Nähe der Hofburg.

Mir gefällt meine Gegend, weil sie sehr schön ist und es viel zu sehen gibt. In der Nähe von meinem Haus gibt es zwei große Parks, wo es viel Platz zum Spielen gibt. Dort treffe ich mich oft mit Freunden. In meiner Gegend gibt es viele Sehenswürdigkeiten, Theater, Kinos, Restaurants, Lokale im Freien und viele tolle Geschäfte. Außerdem gibt es in Wien einen berühmten Zoo mit Giraffen und Eisbären.

Ich wohne in einem sehr alten Gebäude im ersten Stock mit Blick auf die Innenstadt. In unserer Wohnung gibt es eine Küche, ein Wohnzimmer, ein Esszimmer, zwei Badezimmer, ein Spielzimmer und zwei Schlafzimmer: meines und das meiner Eltern.

Mein Lieblingszimmer ist mein eigenes Zimmer, weil es gemütlich ist und schön möbliert und dekoriert ist. Es gibt ein großes Bett, das sehr bequem ist. Links von meinem Bett steht ein großer Schreibtisch. Rechts von meinem Bett stehen ein Nachttisch und ein Spiegel. Auf der anderen Seite meines Zimmers steht in der Ecke ein großer Kleiderschrank. Daneben vor dem Bett stehen mein Computer und ein kleiner Fernseher, der neu ist. Hinter dem Fernseher befindet sich ein großes Fenster. Rechts vom Fenster steht ein großer Sessel. Ich verbringe sehr viel Zeit mit Lesen, Musikhören, Computer- oder Gitarrespielen in meinem Zimmer. Meine Hausaufgaben mache ich an meinem Schreibtisch.

(Martina, 13, Dresden)

15. List as many words from Martina's text as possible, under the following headings

1. Adjectives

2. Furniture

3. Verbs

4. Locative adverbs/prepositions *(e.g. next to, behind, to the right, etc.)*

13. Complete the sentences based on Martina's text, providing as many details as possible

a. She lives with her family in a…

b. In the two parks there is…

c. In her neighbourhood… (6 details)

d. Her building is….

e. In her flat there are… (6 details)

f. Her favourite room is… because…

g. The bed is…

h. To the right of the bed there is…

i. There is a big wardrobe in…

j. The TV is… but…

k. Behind the TV there is a…

14. Faulty translation: find the mistakes in the translation of the last paragraph of Martina's text

My favourite room is my parents' bedroom because it is very spacious and is very well furnished and decorated. There is a very big and soft bed. To the left of the bed there is a very spacious wardrobe. To the right there is a coffee table and a TV. On the other side of the room, in the corner, there is a big mirror. Next to the wardrobe, behind the bed, there is my computer and a TV. The TV is very small, but good. Next to the TV there is a large window. To the right of the window there is a plant. I spend a lot of time in my bedroom listening to music, playing the piano, writing and doing my homework on my bed.

16. Arrange the words in each sentence in the correct order, based on the translation

a. einen Computer gibt es weder In meinem Zimmer einen Fernseher noch.
In my room there is neither a TV or a computer.

b. ein Tisch, ein Kühlschrank, ein Ofen und zwei Stühle, ein Schrank In der Küche stehen.
In the kitchen there are a table, two chairs, a fridge, an oven and a cupboard.

c. stehen zwei Sessel, ein Sofa und Im Wohnzimmer ein Fernseher.
In the living room there are two armchairs, a sofa and a TV.

d. Stühle in Es gibt keine meinem sehr bequemen einen Zimmer, aber Sessel.
There are no chairs in my bedroom but there is a very comfortable armchair.

e. dem Schreibtisch neben der Tür hängt und das Fenster ist hinter Der Spiegel.
The mirror is next to the door and the window is behind the desk.

17. Translate into German

a. a beautiful chair e___ s_________ S_____________

b. a bright kitchen e____ h_________ K____________

c. a red rug e___ r_____________T_________

d. blue curtains b____________ V_____________

e. a spacious flat e___ g________W_____________

f. an old wardrobe e__ a___________ S____________

g. a comfortable bed e___ b___________B___________

h. a building e___ G_________________________

i. a new television e___ n________F______________

18. Complete with a suitable word

a. In meiner Gegend gibt es viele ___________ ______________.

b. Mein Lieblingszimmer ist das ______________, weil es ________________ ist.

c. Neben dem Schrank steht ein _______________.

d. Der Spiegel ____________ neben ________________.

e. In meinem Haus ___________ sieben Zimmer.

19. Insert *von der/vom/dem* as appropriate

a. Das Esszimmer liegt rechts _________Küche.

b. Der Spiegel hängt links_______ Bild.

c. Mein Haus liegt zehn Minuten _______ Kirche entfernt.

d. Das Bett steht gegenüber _______ Fenster.

e. Meine Gegend ist in der Nähe _______ Zentrum.

f. Meine Wohnung hinter _______ Museum.

g. Das Kino ist neben _______ Einkaufszentrum.

20. Spot and add the missing words

a. Die Küche neben dem Wohnzimmer.

b. In meinem Haus gibt drei Badezimmer.

c. Im Wohnzimmer ein grüner Teppich.

d. Ich lebe in kleinen Wohnung.

e. Der Spiegel hängt an Wand.

f. Mir gefällt Küche.

g. Der Fernseher steht gegenüber Bett.

h. Mein Zimmer ist neben Küche.

21. Translate into German

a. *In my flat there are six rooms.* I_ m_ _ _ _ _ W_ _ _ _ _ _ _ g_ _ _ e_ s_ _ _ _ Z_ _ _ _ _.

b. *My favourite room is...* M_ _ _ L_ _ _ _ _ _ _ _ _ _ _ _ _ _ _ i_ _ ...

c. *I also love my room.* I_ _ l_ _ _ _ a_ _ _ m_ _ _ Z_ _ _ _ _ .

d. *My room is very cosy.* M_ _ _ Z_ _ _ _ _ i_ _ s_ _ _ g_ _ _ _ _ _ _ _ _.

e. *There is also a big desk.* E_ g_ _ _ a_ _ _ e_ _ _ _ g_ _ _ _ _ S_ _ _ _ _ _ _ _ _ _ _ _.

f. *There is a big and comfortable bed.* E_ g_ _ _ e_ _ g_ _ _ _ _ u_ _ b_ _ _ _ _ _ _ _ B_ _ _.

g. *I live in a modern building.* I_ _ w_ _ _ _ i_ e_ _ _ _ m_ _ _ _ _ _ _ _ G_ _ _ _ _ _.

h. *I don't like my living room.* M_ _ g_ _ _ _ _ _ _ m_ _ _ W_ _ _ _ _ _ _ _ _ _ n_ _ _ _.

22. Spot and correct the errors

a. In meinem Zimmer gibt haben eine Lampe.

b. In meinem Haus gibt es zwei Bett.

c. In meiner Nachbarschaft haben wir viel Geschäfte.

d. Mein Lieblingsgeschäft sind das Schuhgeschäft.

e. Mein Zimmer bin groß und gemütlich.

f. Ich wohne in einer alten Gebäude.

g. Der Wohnzimmer sind gut möbliert. (2 errors)

h. Neben der Tisch sind eine Lampe. (2 errors)

24. Translate into German

I live in a beautiful neighbourhood on the outskirts of Berlin, a city in the East of Germany. I like my neighbourhood a lot because there are lot of things to do for people of my age. There are many great shops, two beautiful parks, three big shopping centres and many sports facilities. There are also a lot of bars and restaurants.

I live in a big flat in a modern building. In my flat there are seven rooms. My favourite room is my bedroom because it is spacious and well-furnished. Also, the bed is big and comfortable and there is a big desk with a new computer.

23. Complete each sentence with an appropriate verb

a. Meine Stadt ___________ Berlin.

b. Berlin ______ die Hauptstadt Deutschlands.

c. Meine Nachbarschaft ___________ am Stadtrand von Berlin.

d. In meiner Gegend __________ es viele Angebote für junge Leute.

e. Zum Beispiel kann man in den Park __________, im Stadtzentrum __________ _______ und in der Altstadt Sightseeing ___________.

f. Mir ___________ mein Zimmer, weil es gemütlich ist.

g. Das Wohnzimmer ________ gut ausgestattet.

h. Ich ____________ viel Zeit in meinem Zimmer mit Computerspielen.

i. Meistens _________ ich meine Hausaufgaben im Esszimmer.

j. Ich __________ mit meinem Hund spazieren.

k. Ich gehe Rad _________ im Park in der Nähe von meinem Haus.

25. Write two 80-100 word paragraphs in the first person in which you say:

▪ You live in Frankfurt. ▪ Your neigbourhood is situated in the centre of the city. ▪ You like your neighbourhood because there are many good shops and excellent sports facilities. ▪ There are many bars and restaurants. ▪ There is a beautiful park near your house. ▪ You live in a flat with six rooms. ▪ Your favourite room is your bedroom because it is spacious, bright and is well-furnished. ▪ You hate the living room because it is badly furnished. ▪ It is small and the sofa is old and ugly.	▪ Your house is big and modern. ▪ You love your living room because it is well-furnished and bright. ▪ In the living room there is a big sofa. Next to the sofa there is a little table. ▪ Opposite the sofa there is a TV. ▪ You also love your bedroom because it is cosy. ▪ In your bedroom there is a big and comfortable bed. ▪ Next to the bed there is a bedside table and next to the bedside table there is a big wardrobe. ▪ Opposite the wardrobe there is a big desk with a computer.

26. Write a paragraph in German in the first person in which you say:

a. You live in Bern, the capital of Switzerland.

b. You live on the outskirts, in a residential neighbourhood.

c. You like your neighbourhood because one can do a lot of sports.

d. There are many sports facilities, such as gyms, a sports centre, two football pitches, some tennis and golf clubs, some swimming pools and a stadium.

e. Also, there is a big shopping centre, a beautiful park and a river.

f. Last weekend you did a lot of sports. You went cycling in the park, you lifted weights in the gym, played football with your school friends and went to your favourite shopping centre with your boyfriend/girlfriend. You had a great time.

g. In your street there are many good shops and restaurants. For instance, there is a good Italian restaurant next to your house.

h. In your flat there are 7 rooms: a kitchen, two bathrooms, three bedrooms and a living room.

i. Your favourite room is the living room because it is big, well-furnished and bright. There is also a very comfortable sofa and a new television.

j. The sofa is opposite the television. To the left of the sofa there is an armchair and to its right there is a big plant. In front of the sofa there is a small black table. Between the sofa and the television there is an old rug.

Question Skills Unit 4

English	German
Do you live in a house or in a flat?	**Wohnst du in einem Haus oder einer Wohnung?**
How many rooms are there in your house?	**Wie viele Zimmer gibt es in deinem Haus?**
How many bathrooms are there?	**Wie viele Badezimmer gibt es in deinem Haus?**
What is your favourite room? Why?	**Was ist dein Lieblingszimmer? Warum?**
Where do you spend most of your time?	**Wo verbringst du die meiste Zeit?**
Where do you do your homework?	**Wo machst du deine Hausaufgabe(n)?**
Describe your bedroom.	**Beschreib dein Zimmer.**
Do you share your bedroom with anyone?	**Teilst du dein Zimmer mit jemandem?**
What do you like most about your bedroom?	**Was gefällt dir am besten an deinem Zimmer?**
What posters are there on the walls?	**Welche Poster hängen an deinen Wänden?**

1. Faulty translation: spot and fix the incorrect translations
Please note: not all the translations are wrong

a. Wohnst du in einer Wohnung? — *Do you live in a house?*
b. Beschreib deine Straße. — *Describe your street.*
c. Seit wann wohnst du in Wien? — *Since when have you been living there?*
d. Teilst du dein Zimmer mit jemandem? — *Do you share your room with a sibling?*
e. Was gefällt dir am besten an deinem Haus? — *What do you like best about your living room?*
f. Wie viele Schlafzimmer gibt es? — *How many bathrooms are there?*
g. Wie viele Zimmer gibt es in deinem Haus? — *How many floors are there in your house?*
h. Warum gefällt dir dein Wohnzimmer nicht? — *Why don't you like the dining room?*
i. Wo verbringst du die meiste Zeit? — *Where do you spend most of your time?*
j. Gibt es einen Dachboden in deinem Haus? — *Is there an attic in your house?*

2. Complete with the missing words

a. ______ befindet sich in deinem Zimmer?	*What is there in your room?*
b. ______ _____ Zimmer gibt es in deiner Wohnung?	*How many rooms are there in your flat?*
c. Was _____ dein Lieblingszimmer?	*Which is your favourite room?*
d. In ________ Zimmer machst du deine Hausaufgaben?	*In which room do you do your homework?*
e. Warum ________ dir dein Zimmer nicht?	*Why don't you like your room?*
f. Seit _______ lebst du da?	*Since when have you been living there?*
g. _____ _____ wohnst du zusammen?	*Who do you live with?*

3. Match questions and answers

Wohnst du in einer Wohnung oder einem Haus?	Ich bevorzuge das Wohnzimmer, weil es schön eingerichtet ist.
Wie viele Zimmer gibt es in deinem Haus?	Es ist klein, gemütlich und sehr hell.
Seit wann wohnst du da?	Die meiste Zeit verbringe ich in meinem Zimmer.
Was ist dein Lieblingszimmer? Warum?	Das Beste an meinem Zimmer ist mein gemütliches Bett.
In welchem Zimmer verbringst du die meiste Zeit?	Insgesamt gibt es sieben Zimmer.
Wo machst du deine Hausaufgaben?	Ja, ich teile es mit meiner kleinen Schwester.
Beschreib dein Zimmer.	Seit fünf Jahren.
Teilst du dein Zimmer mit jemandem?	Sie ist sehr alt und der Kühlschrank ist hässlich.
Was gefällt dir am besten an deinem Zimmer?	Meine Hausaufgaben mache ich in der Küche.
Wie ist deine Küche?	Ich wohne in einem Haus.

4. Guided translation

a. B_ _ _ _ _ _ _ _ d_ _ _ Z_ _ _ _ _ .	*Describe your bedroom*
b. W_ _ _ _ _ d_ i_ e_ _ _ _ H_ _ _ o_ _ _ e_ _ _ _ W_ _ _ _ _ _?	*Do you live in a house or a flat?*
c. W_ m_ _ _ _ _ d_ d_ _ _ _ H_ _ _ _ _ _ _ _ _ _ _ _?	*Where do you do your homework?*
d. M_ _ w_ _ w_ _ _ _ _ d_ z_ _ _ _ _ _ _?	*Who do you live with?*
e. T_ _ _ _ _ d_ d_ _ _ Z_ _ _ _ _ m_ _ j_ _ _ _ _ _ _?	*Do you share your bedroom?*
f. G_ _ _ _ _ _ d_ _ d_ _ _ H_ _ _?	*Do you like your house?*
g. W_ _ l_ _ _ _ l_ _ _ _ d_ s_ _ _ _ d_?	*How long have you lived there?*
h. W_ _ i_ _ d_ _ _ L_ _ _ _ _ _ _ _ _ _ _ _ _ _ _?	*Which is your favourite room?*

Vocab Revision Workout 2

1. Match

am Ende der Straße	far from
neben	a ten minute walk
hinter	opposite
weit entfernt von	near
zehn Minuten zu Fuß entfernt	to the left of
gegenüber	at the end of the street
in der Nähe von	behind
rechts von	to the right of
links von	in front of
an der Ecke	on the corner
vor	next to

2. Missing letters

a. Es gibt eine B_ _ _ _ _ _ _ _ _ _.

b. Es gibt einen F_ _ _ _ _ _ _ _ _ _ _ _ _.

c. Es gibt eine B_ _ _ _ _ _ _ _ .

d. Es gibt einen S_ _ _ _ _ _ _ _ _ _ _ .

e. Es gibt ein K_ _ _ _ _ _ _ _ _ _ _ _ _ _ _ _ _ _.

f. Es gibt keine K_ _ _ _ _ _ .

g. Es gibt kein S_ _ _ _ _ _ _ _ _ _ _.

h. Ich mag mein G_ _ _ _ _ _ _.

i. Ich gehe ins T_ _ _ _ _ _ _ .

j. Meine Schule liegt zwischen dem P_ _ _ und der K_ _ _ _ _ _ .

3. Break the flow

a. InderNähevonmeinemHausgibteseinenkleinen Park.

b. InmeinemHausgibtesfünfZimmer.

c. InmeinerStraßegibtesvieleGeschäfte.

d. IchwohneimSüdenvonDeutschland,inderNähevon München.

e. MirgefälltmeineGegend,weilesvieleAngebotegibt.

f. IchwohneineinertouristischenStadtinderSchweiz.

g. MeineStadtistlangweiligundhässlich.

4. Correct the nouns and add capital letters as required.

a. gemütlich	j. alt
b. hübsch	k. palast
c. fernseher	l. schloss
d. klein	m. haus
e. langweilig	n. hässlich
f. sportzentrum	o. land
g. geschäft	p. zimmer
h. grünfläche	q. stadt
i. geräumig	r. hell

5. Spot the incorrect translations and fix them. Note: not all the translations are wrong

a. Ich wohne in einem gemütlichen Haus.	*I live in a cosy house.*
b. Ich lebe in einer industriellen Gegend.	*I live in an industrial town.*
c. In meinem Zimmer hängen gelbe Vorhänge.	*In my kitchen there are red curtains.*
d. Mein Haus ist gegenüber dem Fleischer.	*My house is opposite the butcher's.*
e. In meiner Küche steht ein sehr großer Ofen.	*In my kitchen there is a very big fridge.*
f. Ich wohne in einem Haus am Stadtrand.	*I live in a house on the outskirts of the city.*
g. Meine Wohnung ist in einem modernen Gebäude.	*My flat is an old building.*
h. In der Nähe von meinem Haus gibt es eine Kirche.	*Near my house there is a big park.*
i. In meiner Straße gibt es einen Supermarkt.	*Near my street there is a supermarket.*
j. In meinem Gebäude gibt es sieben Stockwerke.	*In my building there are six floors.*

6. Complete

a. In der N______ von meinem Haus *Near my house*

b. In meiner N____________ *In my neighbourhood*

c. Es gibt viel V__________. *There is a lot of traffic*

d. Gestern war ich j______. *Yesterday I did jogging*

e. Am Ende der S_________ *At the end of the street*

f. Ich wohne in einer W__________. *I live in a flat*

g. In meinem D_________ *In my village*

h. Mein Haus ist s_________. *My house is beautiful*

i. Mir gefällt meine S_______. *I like my town*

7 Complete with gemacht, *gegangen, gesehen, gespielt*

a. Ich habe einen Film im Kino ____________.

b. Ich bin mit meinem Hund spazieren ________________.

c. Ich habe Tennis im Sportzentrum ________________.

d. Ich habe gestern nichts ____________.

e. Ich habe letzte Woche Fußball ________.

f. Ich habe mir letzten Montag ein Match im Fernsehen ______________.

8. Slalom writing

Mir gefällt	bin ich	steht	dem Geschäft.	***e.g.* I like my flat because it is cosy.**
Gestern	zwei Tagen	alleine	ein Schreibtisch.	a. Yesterday I went to the pool alone.
In meiner	Zimmer	gibt es	**gemütlich ist.**	b. In my town there is a lot on offer.
In meinem	**meine Wohnung, weil**	habe ich	geräumig.	c. In my bedroom there is a desk.
Vor	ist	ziemlich	ins Schwimmbad gegangen.	d. Two days ago, I didn't do anything.
Die Bibliothek	ist	**sie**	zu Fuß entfernt.	e. The library is opposite the shop.
Mein Wohnzimmer	Stadt	Minuten	viele Angebote.	f. My living room is quite spacious.
Es ist	fünf	gegenüber	nichts gemacht.	g. It is five minutes away on foot.

9. Translate into German

a. I live in the north-east of Germany, on the coast.

b. I live in a neighbourhood on the outskirts.

c. I live with my parents and my two brothers.

d. My neighbourhood is boring and dangerous.

e. There is nothing on offer for young people.

f. There is only a sports centre and a few shops.

g. Last weekend I played tennis and basketball.

h. I also went to the city centre. I watched a film.

Unit 5

Saying what I did & am going to do at the weekend

In this unit you will learn:

- To say what plans I am making for the future and how it will be
- To say what I and others did in the recent past

Key sentence patterns:

- Time marker + *werde* + prepositional phrase + infinitive
- *Das wird* + intensifier + adjective
- Time marker + perfect tense + prepositional phrase

Grammar:

- Future (1st person singular & plural)
- perfect tense (1st person singular & plural) of *machen, gehen, spielen, (an)sehen*

UNIT 5: Saying what I did & am going to do at the weekend

<table>
<tr><td rowspan="4">Nächstes Wochenende
[Next weekend]

Nächsten Samstag
[Next Saturday]

Nächsten Sonntag
[Next Sunday]</td><td rowspan="3">werde ich
[I am going...]

wird meine Schwester
[my sister is going...]

werden mein Bruder und ich
[my brother and I are going...]

werden meine Eltern
[my parents are going...]</td><td>Hausaufgaben [homework]
Sport [sports]</td><td>machen
[...to do]</td></tr>
<tr><td>auf ein Konzert [to a concert]
auf eine Party [to a party]
einkaufen [shopping]
ins Einkaufszentrum
[to the shopping centre]
Rad fahren [bike riding]
reiten [horse riding]</td><td>gehen
[...to go]</td></tr>
<tr><td>am Computer
[on the computer]
Basketball [basketball]</td><td>spielen
[...to play]</td></tr>
<tr><td>werde ich mir [I am going...]
werden wir uns
[we are going...]</td><td>ein Fußballspiel
[a football match]
einen Film [a film]</td><td>ansehen
[...to watch]</td></tr>
<tr><td colspan="4">Author's notes: 1) Instead of "werden + [infinitive]" one can also use the present tense to express the future, e.g. "Ich gehe morgen ins Einkaufszentrum" [Tomorrow I am going to the shopping centre].
2) Without a time expression, the subject moves to the first position, e.g. "Ich werde reiten gehen."</td></tr>
</table>

<table>
<tr><td>Das/Es wird
[It will be]</td><td>ziemlich [quite]
ein bisschen [a bit]
sehr [very]
überhaupt nicht [not at all]</td><td>langweilig [boring]
lustig [fun]
interessant [interesting]</td></tr>
</table>

<table>
<tr><td rowspan="4">Letztes Wochenende
[Last weekend]

Letzten Freitag
[Last Friday]

Letzten Sonntag
[Last Sunday]</td><td>bin ich [I...]
sind wir [we...]</td><td>zu meinem Freund
[to my friend's place]
ins Stadion [to the stadium]</td><td>gegangen [...went]</td></tr>
<tr><td>habe ich [I...]
haben wir [we...]</td><td>Sport [sports]
meine Hausaufgaben
[my homework]</td><td>gemacht [...did]</td></tr>
<tr><td>habe ich [I...]
haben wir [we...]</td><td>Videospiele [video games]
am Computer
[on the computer]</td><td>gespielt [...played]</td></tr>
<tr><td>habe ich mir [I...]
haben wir uns
[we...]</td><td>ein Fußballspiel
[a football match]
einen Film [a film]</td><td>angesehen [...saw]</td></tr>
</table>

<table>
<tr><td>Das/Es war
[It was]</td><td>ziemlich [quite]
ein bisschen [a bit]
sehr [very]</td><td rowspan="2">anstrengend [exhausting]
aufregend [exciting]
cool</td></tr>
<tr><td colspan="2">Das/Es war überhaupt nicht... [It was not ... at all]</td></tr>
</table>

1. Match: near future recap

Wir werden einkaufen gehen.	We are going to go bike riding.
Wir werden Basketball spielen.	We are going to do homework.
Wir werden uns einen Film ansehen.	We are going to go to the stadium.
Wir werden ein Buch lesen.	We are going to go to a concert.
Wir werden Sport machen.	We are going to go swimming.
Wir werden schwimmen gehen.	We are going to do sports.
Wir werden ins Stadion gehen.	We are going to play videogames.
Wir werden Hausaufgaben machen.	We are going to read a book.
Wir werden Videospiele spielen.	We are going to watch a film.
Wir werden auf ein Konzert gehen.	We are going to go shopping.
Wir werden Rad fahren gehen.	We are going to play basketball.

2. Complete with *gehen*, *machen*, *spielen* or *ansehen*

a. Ich werde einkaufen _________.

b. Ich werde auf ein Konzert _________.

c. Wir werden Tennis _________.

d. Wir werden ins Einkaufszentrum _________.

e. Ich werde Sport _________.

f. Ich werde mir einen Film im Kino _________.

g. Ich werde ins Stadion _________.

h. Ich werde auf dem Land reiten __________.

3. Complete with the missing letters

a. Ich w____ m__ e____ F__m i_ Ki__ an_______.

b. Ich w____e i___ S_____on ge______ .

c. W__ w_____ Sp___ m______n .

d. Wir w_____ Bas__________ sp______.

e. Ich w____ in d____ P___k g_______ .

f. D__ w____ lus_____.

g. Wir w______ rei_____ g_______.

h. Wir w____ i__ Einka_________ g____.

i. Wir w_______ schw_________ g____n.

4. Faulty translation: correct the mistakes in the translations below (not all are wrong!)

a. Nächsten Samstag werde ich mir einen Film ansehen. *Next Friday I am going to watch a film.*

b. Nächstes Wochenende werde ich Rad fahren gehen. *Next weekend I am going to go horse riding.*

c. Mein Freund und ich werden wandern gehen. *My friend and I are going to go hiking.*

d. Am Sonntagmorgen werde ich in die Kirche gehen. *Sunday night I am going to go to church.*

e. Nächsten Samstag wird meine Tante ins Schwimmbad gehen. *Next Saturday my aunt is going to go to the beach.*

f. Morgen werde ich meine Hausaufgaben machen. *Tomorrow I will do my homework.*

5. Sentence puzzle: rewrite the sentences in the correct order

a. Nächsten wir Stadion Samstag werden ins gehen.

b. ins werde Wochenende ich Nächstes Einkaufszentrum gehen.

c. Nächstes gehen werden wir Wochenende einkaufen.

d. werde Sonntagmorgen Kirche Am ich gehen in die.

e. Eltern Meine im sich werden Film Kino einen ansehen.

f. Schwester Meine ins wird gehen Schwimmbad Freundinnen mit ihren.

g. mit Bruder wird Freitag Mein seinen feiern Freunden nächsten gehen.

6. Multiple choice: choose the correct translation

	1	2	3
a. Sport machen	to ride a bike	to do sports	to go hiking
b. einkaufen gehen	to go out	to go shopping	to do nothing
c. sich einen Film ansehen	to watch a game	to go running	to watch a film
d. in die Kirche gehen	to go to church	to go hunting	to go shopping
e. auf ein Konzert gehen	to play guitar	to go to a concert	to watch a film
f. Rad fahren	to ride a bike	to ride a horse	to play games
g. ein Buch lesen	to read an article	to read a magazine	to read a book
h. spazieren gehen	to go for a walk	to go running	to stay at home
i. nichts tun	to do homework	to go to a concert	to do nothing

7. Find in the wordsearch the German translations of the phrases below and write them as shown in the example

```
R N C K B P V Y K W S A J X D Y N G U C
E L E S S S R Q P N G V G L I I Y Q E F
T Z E H V M H T I Y Q S Q W A U Q N P F
S A I T C R J C V X N E Y Y Y T J P F I
E J C E D A H V N X I B I M O P J I I S
W N B U M T M C S N J A L Q I T D J Y Z
H W D W S L U T B D N E G N E R T S N A
C I A T W F I U R K C R Q O K R M Y A D
S D U Q J D C C G O E A C A D P V Q N J
E N I T R H H O H D P C N H X Q P E K I
N H F N L L M C P S G S A P H S G R V A
I W R E N E F U A K N I E S S E I R G L
E O S R K R O O D S S W J D R T W O L M
M E N G U I V Z W M G W X F R M I K C V
N E G L E G N A T L P U U U D I E G U D
U L Q S D H T T A H M A Q Q A X Y S T A
N Ä C H S T E S W O C H E N E N D E S Y
M D R Y V J H H J C R R G O T L S R E Q
Y C Q L R Q T Y M I V R R L L Y G M H M
E Y Q J Z K H J B H T C I M N L R U R D
```

e.g. next weekend — ***nächstes Wochenende***

a. to read a book

b. exhausting

c. exciting

d. very

e. quite

f. to do nothing

g. shopping

h. to do sports

i. my sister

8. Translate into English

a. Nächsten Samstag werden meine Freundin und ich uns einen Film ansehen.

b. Am Wochenende werden mein Bruder und ich Badminton spielen.

c. Nächsten Freitag werden meine Eltern auf ein Konzert gehen.

d. Nächsten Sonntagnachmittag werde ich mit meiner Mutter einkaufen gehen.

e. Nächstes Wochenende wird meine Schwester mit ihrem Freund ins Schwimmbad gehen.

f. Nächstes Wochenende werde ich meine Mathematikhausaufgaben machen.

g. Nächsten Samstagmorgen werde ich mit meinem kleinen Bruder in den Park gehen.

9. Match

Ich bin einkaufen gegangen.	I went to the library.
Ich habe ein Buch gelesen.	I went bike riding.
Ich habe mir einen Film angesehen.	We did sports.
Ich bin Rad gefahren.	I watched a film.
Ich habe nichts gemacht.	We went jogging.
Ich bin in die Bibliothek gegangen.	I played basketball.
Wir haben Sport gemacht.	I read a book.
Ich habe Basketball gespielt.	I didn't do anything.
	I went shopping.

10. Complete with the missing letters

a. Ich b ___ einkaufen g_________.

b. Wir si___ Rad fah____ g_________.

c. Wir ha____ Sport ge_______.

d. Ich ha__ mir einen Film ang_______.

e. Ich b___ ins Stadion g_________.

f. Ich habe ein Buch gel______.

g. Wir ha____ Basketball ge___________.

h. Wir haben viele Denkmäler. ges__________.

11. Choose the correct verb and cross out the wrong ones

a. Wir haben Basketball gemacht / gekauft / gespielt.

b. Ich habe mir nichts gemacht / angesehen / gespielt.

c. Ich bin Rad fahren gegangen / gelaufen / gemacht.

d. Ich habe Musik gegangen / gesungen / gehört.

e. Ich habe Sport gemacht / getanzt / gegessen.

f. Ich bin auf ein Konzert gesessen / gegangen / gelaufen.

g. Ich bin in die Kirche gegangen / gekauft / gelesen.

h. Ich habe einen Freund gelesen / getroffen / gespielt.

i. Ich habe ein Buch gegessen / gemalt / gelesen.

12. Anagrams: rewrite the jumbled-up words correctly

a. chI nib fakeennui genengga

b. hcI beha rim niene mFli nseagehen

c. chI ehab tihncs gahmcte

d. hcI abeh keBabstall gipsetle

e. riW ndis nsi Staniod ngagenge

f. irW hanbe poStr etchgam

g. chI beha emnie uaHsufabagne thcin echtmag

h. Ihc ibn Rda egefhrna

13. Slalom writing

e.g. Yesterday I rode my bike in the park.

a. Last Saturday I went shopping with my girlfriend.

b. Last Friday I did my homework after school.

c. Last Sunday I didn't do anything. I only watched a film.

d. Three days ago I went to the gym with my older brother.

e. The day before yesterday I played basketball with my friends.

Gestern	habe ich	mit meinem älteren Bruder	einkaufen	gemacht.
Letzen Samstag	**bin ich**	nichts gemacht.	Ich habe mir nur einen Film	**gegangen.**
Letzten Freitag	bin ich	mit meinen Freunden	ins Fitnessstudio	gegangen.
Letzten Sonntag	habe ich	**im Park**	**Rad fahren**	gegangen.
Vor drei Tagen	habe ich	mit meiner Freundin	nach der Schule	gespielt.
Vorgestern	bin ich	meine Hausaufgaben	Basketball	angesehen.

14. Translate into English

a. Ich bin ins Schwimmbad gegangen.

b. Ich werde einkaufen gehen.

c. Wir haben Bowling gespielt.

d. Mein Freund und ich haben Sport gemacht.

e. Wir werden Rad fahren gehen.

f. Ich bin schwimmen gegangen.

g. Ich werde ins Stadion gehen.

h. Wir haben Basketball gepielt.

i. Wir haben Sightseeing gemacht.

j. Wir haben Pizza gegessen.

k. Ich habe ein Buch gelesen.

l. Wir haben uns Zeichentrickfilme angesehen.

m. Wir sind ins Stadion gegangen.

15. Complete the hidden sentences
HINT: they are all in the perfect tense

a. I _ _ b_ _ R _ _ g _ _ _ _ _ _ _ _ .

b. I _ _ b_ _ e _ _ _ _ _ _ _ _ _ g _ _ _ _ _ _ _ _.

c. I _ _ h_ _ _ B_ _ _ _ _ _ _ _ _ _ g _ _ _ _ _ _ _ _.

d. W _ _ h_ _ _ _ B _ _ _ _ _ _ _ g _ _ _ _ _ _ _ _.

e. I _ _ b_ _ i _ _ S _ _ _ _ _ _ _ g _ _ _ _ _ _ _ _.

f. I _ _ h_ _ _ n _ _ _ _ _ _ g _ _ _ _ _ _ _.

g. I _ _ h_ _ _ m _ _ _ _ _ H _ _ _ _ _ _ _ _ _ _ _ _ _ g _ _ _ _ _ _ _.

16. Complete the table using the words listed below. Note: four of the words are distractors HINT: all the sentences are in the perfect tense

Auto	Schule	Strand	Rad
Schwimmbad	angesehen	Letzte	Pinguin
Zentrum	Haus	Einkauf	Gestern
Kino	Freitag	Vor	Park
Letzten	gespielt	Film	Letzten
Fernsehen	gegangen	gegangen	Tagen

Wann?	Was?	Wo? / Wohin?	Was?
a. _________ Samstag	bin ich	im ______________	______ fahren gegangen.
b. Letzten __________	haben wir uns	im ______________	ein Fußballspiel ____________.
c. _________ Sonntag	sind wir	im ___________szentrum	einkaufen ____________.
d. _____________	sind wir	ins städtische _________________	schwimmen ____________.
e. ____ drei ________	habe ich mir	im _______ in der Nähe von meinem _______	einen ________ angesehen.
f. _________ Woche	haben wir	in meiner _____________	Basketball ____________.

17. Complete the table below with the missing verb forms, as shown in the example

PERFECT TENSE (Perfekt)	PRESENT TENSE (Präsens)	FUTURE TENSE (Futur I)
*Ich **bin** ins Kino **gegangen**.*	*Ich **gehe** ins Kino.*	*Ich **werde** ins Kino **gehen**.*
	Wir gehen einkaufen.	Wir werden einkaufen gehen.
		Ich werde meine Hausaufgaben machen.
Ich bin skateboarden gegangen.	Ich gehe skateboarden.	
	Ich gehe ins Stadion.	
	Ich gehe reiten.	
Ich bin auf eine Party gegangen.	Ich gehe auf eine Party.	
	Ich gehe Rad fahren.	Ich werde Rad fahren gehen.
	Ich sehe mir einen Film an.	

Letztes Wochenende habe ich nicht viel gemacht. Am Freitag nach der Schule bin ich gegen vier Uhr nach Hause gekommen. Ich habe ein Sandwich gegessen und mich für eine Weile beim Musikhören entspannt *[relaxed]*. Danach habe ich wie immer meine Hausaufgaben gemacht und bin mit meinem älteren Bruder ins Fitnessstudio gegangen. Es war anstrengend, aber lustig. Am Nachmittag habe ich mir einen Actionfilm im Fernsehen angesehen. Er war überhaupt nicht spannend.

Am Samstagmorgen bin ich mit meiner Mutter einkaufen gegangen. Ich habe ein T-Shirt und eine Jeans gekauft. Am Nachmittag bin ich mit meiner besten Freundin im Park Rad gefahren und dann gegen sieben Uhr mit meiner Freundin Anna ins Kino gegangen. Ich hatte eine tolle Zeit mit ihr. Sie ist sehr klug und lustig!

Am Sonntag habe ich wenig gemacht. Ich bin sehr spät aufgewacht, dann mit meinen Eltern in die Kirche gegangen und habe mich dann beim Computerspielen entspannt. Es war nichts Besonderes. **(Roman, 14 Jahre. Bern)**

18. Find in the text the German equivalent for the phrases below.

a. I didn't do a lot

b. I came home

c. I ate a sandwich

d. as always, I did my homework

e. then I went to the gym

f. it was tiring

g. I watched a film on TV

h. it wasn't exciting at all

i. I went shopping

j. in the afternoon

k. I went bike riding

l. with my girlfriend

m. a good time

n. very clever and funny

o. then my parents and I went to church

p. afterwards I relaxed

q. nothing special

19. Answer the questions below in the first person, as if you were Roman

a. Um wie viel Uhr bist du letzten Freitag nach Hause gekommen?

b. Was hast du gegessen?

c. Was hast du am Freitag getan, um dich zu entspannen?

d. Mit wem bist du ins Fitnessstudio gegangen?

e. Wie war das Training?

f. Was für einen Film hast du dir im Fernsehen angesehen?

g. Wo warst du am Samstagmorgen?

h. Mit wem?

i. Was hast du gekauft?

j. Um wie viel Uhr bist du mit deiner Freundin ins Kino gegangen?

20. Spot and correct the mistakes in these sentences from Roman's text

a. Ich habe nicht fiel gemacht. (1 mistake)

b. An Freitag nach die Schule bin ich gegen vier Uhr nach Hause gekomen. (3)

c. Ich habe ein Sändwich gegeßen. (2)

d. Ich habe mein Hausaufgaben gemacht und bin in Fitnessstudio gegangen. (2)

e. Ich habe mir ein Film angesehen. (1)

f. Am Samstagmörgens. (2)

g. Ich bin einkäufen gegangen. (1)

h. Ich habe eine Hemd gekauft. (1)

i. Am Sontag habe ich nicht gemacht. (2)

j. Ich bin spat aufgestanden. (1)

Letzten Samstagmorgen bin ich mit meiner älteren Schwester in der Innenstadt spazieren gegangen. Ich bin in mein Lieblings-kleidergeschäft gegangen und habe ein cooles rosa Kleid gekauft. Am Nachmittag bin ich mit meinem Freund ausgegangen. Wir sind in den Park in der Nähe von meinem Haus gegangen und dann gegen sieben Uhr bin ich mit meiner Familie in ein italienisches Restaurant gegangen. Es ist hundert Meter von meinem Haus entfernt, also sind wir zu Fuß dorthin gegangen. Wir haben sehr gut gegessen!

Am Sonntag habe ich nichts Besonderes gemacht. Ich bin ziemlich spät aufgewacht und dann mit meiner älteren Schwester ins Schwimmbad gegangen. Es war ein sehr erholsames Wochenende. **(Monika, 13 Jahre).**

Letzten Samstagmorgen bin ich mit meiner jüngeren Schwester in der Innenstadt spazieren gegangen. Ich bin in mein Lieblings-kleidergeschäft gegangen und habe einen coolen rosa Rock gekauft. Am Nachmittag bin ich mit meiner besten Freundin ausgegangen. Wir haben Eis gegessen, sind ins Einkaufszentrum gegangen und haben uns Schaufenster angesehen. Dann bin ich mit meiner Familie in ein japanisches Restaurant gegangen.

Am Sonntag habe ich nichts gemacht. Ich bin früh aufgestanden, um mit meiner Mutter joggen zu gehen. Ich versuche in Form zu kommen! Dann habe ich mich beim Musikhören und Online-Videospielen bis fünf Uhr nachmittags entspannt. Dann habe ich mir einen Film im Fernsehen angesehen und meine Hausaufgaben gemacht. **(Anna, 13 Jahre. Kassel)**

24. Translate the words underlined below. HINT: the phrases are from Anna's text

a. Ich bin mit meiner Tante ausgegangen.

b. ein sehr cooler rosa Rock

c. Ich bin früh aufgewacht.

d. Wir haben uns Schaufenster angesehen.

e. Ich versuche in Form zu kommen.

21. Richtig oder Falsch? Write R or F next to each statement about Monika's text

a. Ich bin laufen gegangen. _____

b. Ich habe ein Kleid gekauft. _____

c. Wir sind in den Park gegangen. _____

d. Wir sind in ein chinesisches Restaurant gegangen. _____

e. Am Sonntag habe ich etwas ganz Besonderes gemacht. _____

f. Es war ein anstrengendes Wochenende. _____

22. *Monika*, *Anna* or *Neither* of them?

a. went to the park with her boyfriend

b. relaxed reading a book

c. had an ice cream with her best friend

d. went to the restaurant by car

e. went for a walk with her younger sister

f. went window shopping

g. relaxed playing guitar

h. lives close to a restaurant

i. went to the pool on Sunday morning

j. woke up early to go jogging

23. Find the German equivalent of the items below in Anna's text. HINT: they are not listed in the same order as in the text

a. Saturday morning

b. until 5 pm in the afternoon

c. to go jogging with my mum

d. early

e. trying to get fit

f. with my best friend

g. my homework

h. my favourite clothes shop

i. we ate ice cream

j. then

h. Japanese restaurant

Silvia: Letzten Sonntag habe ich nichts Besonderes gemacht. Morgens bin ich in die Bibliothek gegangen und dann nachmittags in das Einkaufszentrum in der Nähe von meinem Haus. Dann habe ich meine Mathe-Hausaufgaben gemacht. Als ich mit meinen Hausaufgaben fertig war, habe ich mir einen romantischen Film im Fernsehen angesehen.

Martina: Der letzte Sonntag hat überhaupt keinen Spaß gemacht. Ich habe meine Hausaufgaben gemacht, mit meinem Hund im Garten gespielt und meiner Mutter bei der Hausarbeit geholfen. Gegen sieben Uhr nachmittags ging ich mit meiner Mutter zu meinen Großeltern und wir haben dort zu Abend gegessen.

Paul: Der letzte Sonntag war sehr aufregend, weil ich mit meinen besten Freunden viel Sport gemacht habe. Morgens bin ich mit meiner Freundin Anna Mountainbike gefahren, das war sehr anstrengend, aber auch sehr lustig. Es war aufregend. Dann habe ich mit meinem Freund Jonas Gewichte gehoben. Es war phänomenal! Meine Arme tun immer noch weh.

Susanne: Letzten Sonntag habe ich gar nichts gemacht. Ich habe nur geschlafen, gegessen und ferngesehen.

Julian: Letzten Sonntag hatte ich eine tolle Zeit. Ich habe den ganzen Tag mit meiner Freundin verbracht. Am Morgen sind wir in die Innenstadt einkaufen gegangen. Dann haben wir etwas in einer Cafeteria getrunken und sind durch die Altstadt spaziert. Wir haben Sightseeing gemacht und viele Fotos gemacht. Es hat Spaß gemacht! Wir hatten eine schöne Zeit!

25. Find someone who...

a. ...didn't do anything special

b. ...had a nice day with his girlfriend

c. ...went mountain biking

d. ...still has sore arms from their work-out

e. ...spent the evening with their grandparents

f. ...watched a romantic film on TV

g. ...spent the whole Sunday eating, sleeping and watching television

26. Find the German equivalent

a. last Sunday

b. to the library

c. when I was finished with my homework

d. and I helped my mother with chores

e. and we had dinner there

f. because I did a lot of sports

g. with my best friends

27. Tick or cross? Tick the phrases below that are contained in the text above and cross out the ones that are not.

a. Ich hatte eine tolle Zeit.	f. Wir hatten eine schöne Zeit!	k. Ich habe Gewichte gehoben.
b. Ich habe eine Kerze gemacht.	g. Es war interessant.	l. Am Morgen sind wir einkaufen gegangen.
c. Ich habe viele Fotos gemacht.	h. Wir haben etwas getrunken.	m. Ich bin im Internet gesurft
d. Ich bin Rad gefahren.	i. Wir sind durch die Altstadt spaziert.	n. Ich habe gar nichts gemacht
e.Wir haben dort zu Abend gegessen.	j. Ich bin ins Schwimmbad gegangen.	o. Wir haben Sightseeing gemacht.

28. Sentence puzzle: rewrite the sentences in the correct order

a. früh Ich aufgestanden bin.	*I got up early.*
b. gemacht Ich viele habe Fotos.	*I took many pictures.*
c. nichts Ich habe gemacht Besonderes.	*I didn't do anything special.*
d. Ich gegangen allein ins bin Kino.	*I went to the cinema alone.*
e. Musikhören Ich beim mich entspannt habe.	*I relaxed listening to music.*
f. Stadtzentrum Wir Sightseeing haben im gemacht.	*We did some sightseeing in the centre.*
g. fahren sind Wir auf Land Rad dem gegangen.	*We did some biking in the countryside.*
h. gegangen sind wandern Wir.	*We went hiking.*
i. Samstag sind einkaufen Letzten wir gegangen.	*Last Saturday we went shopping.*

29. Complete the translation

a. *I had a great time.*	I_ _ h_ _ _ _ e_ _ _ s_ _ _ _ _ _ Z_ _ _.
b. *I went to the old part of town.*	I_ _ b_ _ i_ d_ _ A_ _ _ _ _ _ _ _ _ g_ _ _ _ _ _ _ _ _.
c. *Last Saturday.*	L_ _ _ _ _ _ _ S_ _ _ _ _ _ _.
d. *I went bike riding.*	I_ _ b_ _ R_ _ f_ _ _ _ _ _ g_ _ _ _ _ _ _ _.
e. *We did some sightseeing.*	W_ _ h_ _ _ _ S_ _ _ _ _ _ _ _ _ _ _ _ g_ _ _ _ _ _ _.
f. *I went to the stadium with my dad.*	I_ _ b_ _ m_ _ m_ _ _ _ _ _ V_ _ _ _ _ i_ _ S_ _ _ _ _ _ _ g_ _ _ _ _ _ _ _.
g. *I relaxed listening to music.*	I_ _ h_ _ _ m_ _ _ b_ _ _ M_ _ _ _ _ _ _ _ _ _ e_ _ _ _ _ _ _ _ _.
h. *I did not do anything special.*	I_ _ h_ _ _ n_ _ _ _ _ _ B_ _ _ _ _ _ _ _ _ _ _ g_ _ _ _ _ _ _.
i. *I got up late.*	I_ _ b_ _ s_ _ _ a_ _ _ _ _ _ _ _ _ _ _ _ _ _.

30. Rewrite the sentences on the left in the perfect tense and the right in the future

Indikativ Perfekt	Indikativ Präsens	Futur I
Ich bin Rad fahren gegangen.	Ich gehe Rad fahren.	Ich werde Rad fahren gehen.
	Ich gehe ins Stadion.	
	Ich mache meine Hausaufgaben.	
	Ich reite.	
	Ich spiele Basketball.	
	Ich entspanne mich.	
	Ich esse ein Sandwich.	
	Ich höre Musik.	

31. Split sentences

Ich habe	ein Fußballspiel	gegessen.
Ich habe	im Fernsehen	gemacht.
mich	ins Schwimmbad	aufgestanden.
Ich habe	früh	gekauft.
Ich habe	Steak mit Salat	gespielt.
Ich habe	Rad	gefahren.
Ich bin	ein rosa Kleid	entspannt.
Ich bin	beim Lesen	schwimmen
Ich bin	Basketball	gegangen.
Ich bin	ins	angesehen.
Ich habe	Einkaufszentrum	gegangen.
mir	nichts	

32. Translate into German

a. I had a great time.

b. I went to the cinema.

c. We went sightseeing.

d. I am going to play basketball.

e. I didn't do anything.

f. We went shopping.

g. We are going to go to a party.

33. Complete with the missing verbs. Please note: use the first person singular of the perfect tense (e.g. bin gegangen, habe gemacht, etc.)

a. Ich ________ mit meinem Hund in den Park ________________.

b. Ich ________ mir ein Hemd __________.

c. Gestern _________ ich mir im Fernsehen eine Serie ______________.

d. Ich ______ im Park Rad _____________.

e. Ich _________ mit meinem Opa Karten ______________.

f. Ich _____________ mich beim Musikhören _____________.

g. Am Samstag ____________ ich früh _______________.

34. Write a paragraph in which you include as much of the information below as possible

Things to see in your neighbourhood	shops a medieval castle a big museum
Things one can do in your neighbourhood	eat well go shopping go to concerts go to the cinema
Sports facilities	a big sports centre gyms a swimming pool a climbing wall *(Kletterwand)*
Things you did last weekend	went shopping watched a football match went to a party at a friend's
Things you are going to do next weekend	go to a concert play basketball with friends go sightseeing in the old town

35. Write a 200 word description of your neighbourhood including the following information

- Where it is located.
- What one can see and do in your neighbourhood (***Man kann*** **+ verb**).
- A brief description of your street.
- What sports facilities can be found.
- What you usually do at the weekend (**present tense**).
- What you are planning to do next weekend (**near future tense**).
- What you did last weekend (**perfect tense**).

Question Skills Unit 5

English	German
What are you going to do next weekend?	**Was wirst du nächstes Wochenende machen?**
At what time are you going to get up?	**Um wie viel Uhr wirst du aufstehen?**
Where are you going to go?	**Wo wirst du hingehen?**
Who are you going to go with?	**Mit wem wirst du hingehen?**
What do you think it will be like?	**Wie glaubst du wird es werden?**
What did you do last weekend?	**Was hast du letztes Wochenende gemacht?**
Where did you go? With whom?	**Wo warst du? Mit wem warst du dort?**
How did it go? What was the best thing?	**Wie ist es gelaufen? Was war das Beste?**
What was the weather like?	**Wie war das Wetter?**
When did you get up?	**Wann bist du aufgestanden?**
When did you go to bed?	**Wann bist du ins Bett gegangen?**
Author's note: like in English, "Um wie viel Uhr?" *[At what time?]* **and "Wann"** *[When?]* **are often interchangeable. However, the former needs to be answered with a specific time, while the latter can be answered more vaguely, e.g. "morgen"** *[tomorrow]* **or "sehr früh"** *[very early]*.	

1. Sentence puzzle: rewrite the sentences in the correct order

a. wem hin Mit du gehst?

b. wirst Wochenende du nächstes Was machen?

c. spät es Wie war?

d. gemacht Welchen hast Sport du?

e. letztes hast Was du gemacht Wochenende?

f. viel Bett du ins Um bist gegangen wie Uhr?

g. war Beste Was das?

h. dort wem warst Mit du?

2. Gapped questions: complete with a suitable word

a. Was wirst du _______________ Wochenende _______________?

b. Um wie viel Uhr bist du _______________ Sonntag _______________?

c. Wo bist du _______________? Mit ___________ warst du dort?

d. Wie ist es ___________? Wie war das _____________?

e. Wann bist du _______________ Samstag ins Bett _______________?

f. Um wie viel Uhr bist du _______________ Samstagmorgen _______________?

g. Was wirst du _______________ Sonntag _______________?

3. Write the questions to the answers below

a.	*Ich werde ins Einkaufszentrum gehen.*
b.	*Mit meinem besten Freund.*
c.	*Ich werde mir ein Paar Jeans kaufen.*
d.	*Es wird lustig werden.*
e.	*Ich bin mit meinem Papa und meiner Schwester ins Schwimmbad gegangen.*
f.	*Es war fantastisch.*
g.	*Dann sind wir in den Park gegangen und haben einen Spaziergang gemacht.*

4. Break the flow

a. WannwirstduinsBettgehen?

b. WashastduletztesWochenendegemacht?

c. Mitwemwirstduhingehen?

d. Wowarstdu?

e. UmwievielUhrbistduaufgestanden?

f. WaswardasBeste?

g. WiewardasWetter?

h. Wieistesgelaufen?

i. WaswirstdunächstesWochenendemachen?

5. Spot and add in the one word missing

a. Was hast letztes Wochenende gemacht?

b. Um wie viel Uhr du aufgestanden?

c. Wie ist gelaufen?

d. Wie war Wetter?

e. Mit hast du Sport gemacht?

f. Wo warst du Wochenende?

g. Wo du nächsten Samstag hingehen?

h. Wo wirst nächsten Sonntag hingehen?

i. Wann bist du Bett gegangen?

6. Complete the answers to the questions

a. Um wie viel Uhr bist du letzten Sonntag aufgestanden?	Ich bin…
b. Was hast du am Morgen gemacht?	Am Morgen…
c. Was hast du am Nachmittag gemacht?	Am Nachmittag…
d. Wie war das Wetter?	Es…
e. Wie ist es gelaufen?	Es war…
f. Was wirst du nächstes Wochenende machen?	Ich werde…
g. Wo wirst du hingehen?	Ich werde…
h. Mit wem wirst du hingehen?	Mit…
i. Wie glaubst du wird es werden?	Es wird …
j. Wo wirst du zu Abend essen?	Ich werde...
k. Was wirst du zu Abend essen?	Ich werde…

Unit 6

Talking about my daily routine & activities

In this unit you will learn:

- To say what daily activities you do
- To say what time you do things at
- To describe what you "can", "have to" and "want" to do

Key sentence patterns:

- Time adverbial + verb phrase + *um* + time + noun phrase + adversative clause
- Time adverbial + verb phrase + *um* + time + prepositional phrase + adversative clause
- *Aber/jedoch* + time adverbial + modal verb + infinitive

Grammar:

- Reflexive constructions with reflexive pronoun in dative (*mir*) or accusative (*mich*)
- Present of modal verbs

UNIT 6: Talking about my daily routine & activities

<table>
<tr><td rowspan="13">Unter der Woche [During the week]

Vor der Schule [Before school]

Am Morgen/ Morgens [In the morning]

Am Nachmittag/ Nachmittags [In the afternoon]

Am Abend/ Abends [In the evening]

In der Nacht/ Nachts [At night]</td><td>dusche ich mich [I shower]
frühstücke ich [I have breakfast]
wasche ich mich [I wash]</td><td colspan="2">um *[ZEIT]
[at TIME o‘clock]</td></tr>
<tr><td>gehe ich [I go/leave]</td><td rowspan="12">um *[ZEIT]</td><td>aus dem Haus [the house]
ins Bett [to bed]
nach Hause [home]</td></tr>
<tr><td>putze ich mir [I brush]</td><td>die Zähne [my teeth]</td></tr>
<tr><td>stehe ich [I get up]</td><td>auf</td></tr>
<tr><td>wasche ich mir [I wash]</td><td>das Gesicht [my face]</td></tr>
<tr><td>ziehe ich mich [I get dressed]
ziehe ich mir meine Uniform</td><td>an</td></tr>
<tr><td>esse ich [I eat]</td><td>Frühstück [breakfast]
einen Snack [a snack]
zu Mittag/Abend [lunch/dinner]</td></tr>
<tr><td>komme ich [I arrive at]</td><td>in der Schule an [at school]</td></tr>
<tr><td>lese ich [I read]</td><td>ein Buch [a book]</td></tr>
<tr><td>mache ich [I do]</td><td>Hausaufgaben [homework]</td></tr>
<tr><td>ruhe ich mich [I rest]</td><td>aus</td></tr>
<tr><td>sehe/schaue ich [I watch TV]</td><td>fern</td></tr>
<tr><td>spiele ich [I play]</td><td>Videospiele [video games]</td></tr>
</table>

<table>
<tr><td colspan="2">*[ZEIT] [TIME]</td></tr>
<tr><td>eins zwei drei vier fünf sechs sieben acht neun zehn elf zwölf</td><td>Uhr</td></tr>
<tr><td>Viertel nach [quarter past] **halb [half past] Viertel vor [quarter to]</td><td>eins zwei drei vier fünf sechs
sieben acht neun zehn elf zwölf</td></tr>
</table>

<table>
<tr><td rowspan="2">, aber [but]

, jedoch [however]</td><td rowspan="2">heute [today]</td><td colspan="2">***kann ich (nicht) [I can –not-]
muss ich (nicht) [I -don’t- have to]
werde ich (nicht) [I am -not- going to]</td><td>in die Schule gehen [go to school]
früh aufstehen [get up early]
mit meinen Freunden ausgehen [go out with my friends]
im Haushalt helfen [help at home]</td></tr>
<tr><td>will ich
[I don’t want to]</td><td colspan="2">meine Hausaufgaben nicht machen [do my homework]
mein Bett nicht machen [make my bed]</td></tr>
<tr><td colspan="5">Author’s notes: 1) **half an hour to the next hour, e.g. “halb acht” = 7:30. 2) ***The verbs “ich kann/ich will/ich muss” are “modal verbs”. They are used to say what you can, want to or have to do. Without a time expression, the subject moves to the first position of the sentence, e.g. “Ich wache auf.”</td></tr>
</table>

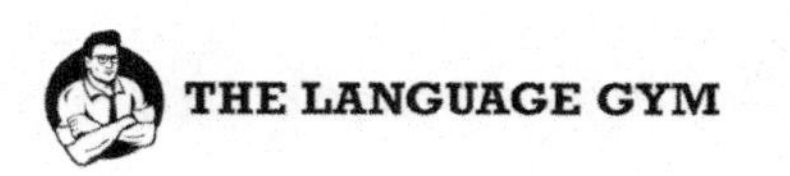

1. Match

Ich frühstücke.	I go to bed.
Ich mache Hausaufgaben.	I wash my face.
Ich gehe aus dem Haus.	I read a book.
Ich stehe auf.	I do my homework.
Ich komme in der Schule an.	I have breakfast.
Ich gehe ins Bett.	I rest.
Ich lese ein Buch.	I leave the house.
Ich wasche mir das Gesicht.	I arrive at school.
Ich ziehe mich an.	I get dressed.
Ich dusche mich.	I shower.
Ich ruhe mich aus.	I get up.

2. Missing letters

a. Ich frü_stücke.
b. Ich ru_e mich aus.
c. Ich wa_che mich.
d. Ich le_e ein Bu_h.
e. Ich ma_he Hausaufgaben.
f. Ich ste_e auf.
g. Ich ge_e aus dem Haus.
h. Ich es_e z_ A_end.
i. D_nn ge_e ich in die Schu_e.
j. Ich zi_he mich a_.
k. Ich d_sche mic_.
l. Heute k_nn i_h ni_ht.

3. Multiple choice: choose the correct translation

	1	2	3
a. I get dressed	ich wasche mich	ich ziehe mich an	ich mache Yoga
b. I have lunch	ich frühstücke	ich esse zu Mittag	ich esse zu Abend
c. I have dinner	ich esse zu Abend	ich arbeite	ich esse einen Snack
d. I wash	ich dusche mich	ich ziehe mich an	ich wasche mich
e. I want	ich will	ich muss	ich kann
f. I read a book	ich lese eine Zeitung	ich lese in Magazin	ich lese ein Buch
g. I watch a film	ich sehe mir einen Film an	ich gehe spazieren	ich gehe ins Bett
h. I have to	ich muss	ich kann	ich werde

4. Complete with the missing verb phrase

a. _ _ _ _ _ _ _ _ _ _ _ _ _ _ _ *I get dressed*
b. _ _ _ _ _ _ _ _ _ _ _ _ _ _ *I wash*
c. _ _ _ _ _ _ _ _ _ _ _ _ _ _ _ _ _ *I have lunch*
d. _ _ _ _ _ _ _ _ _ _ _ _ _ _ _ _ *I read a book*
e. _ _ _ _ _ _ _ *I want*
f. _ _ _ _ _ _ _ _ _ *I play*
g. _ _ _ _ _ _ _ *I have to*
h. _ _ _ _ _ _ _ _ _ _ _ _ _ _ _ _ *I go to bed*
i. _ _ _ _ _ _ _ *I can*

5. Match action and place

Ich wasche mich	im	Garten.
Ich esse		Park joggen.
Ich ziehe mich		Schlafzimmer an.
Ich gehe		Kino an.
Ich hebe		Badezimmer.
Ich sehe mir einen Film		Restaurant zu Mittag.
Ich spiele mit dem Hund		Fitnessstudio Gewichte.

6. Arrange the actions below in the correct chronological order

Ich stehe auf.	1
Ich esse zu Mittag.	
Ich esse zu Abend.	
Ich gehe ins Bett.	
Ich frühstücke.	
Ich verlasse die Schule.	
Ich gehe in die Schule.	
Ich komme in der Schule an.	
Nach dem Abendessen sehe ich fern.	

7. Faulty translation: correct the English

a. Ich stehe um sechs Uhr auf. *I get up at 6:15.*

b. Ich dusche mich gleich. *I shower much later.*

c. Ich ziehe mich an. *I have breakfast.*

d. Ich ziehe meine Uniform an. *I take off my uniform.*

e. Ich komme in der Schule an. *I go to school.*

f. Ich gehe joggen. *I have feet.*

g. Ich frühstücke. *I have dinner.*

h. Ich verlasse die Schule. *I go to school.*

i. Ich ruhe mich aus. *I read.*

j. Ich gehe schlafen. *I shower.*

8. Complete with the options below

a. Normalerweise stehe ich um ___________ sieben auf. *I usually get up at 6:30.*

b. Ich frühstücke gegen _________ vor sieben. *I have breakfast around 6:40.*

c. Ich verlasse das Haus um circa ________ nach sieben. *I leave my home around 7:10.*

d. Ich nehme den Bus um ____________ sieben. *I catch the bus at 7:15.*

e. Ich komme um ________ acht in der Schule an. *I arrive at school at 7:45.*

f. Der Unterricht beginnt um ________ vor acht. *Lessons start at 7:55.*

g. Um _________ eins esse ich zu Mittag. *I have lunch at 12.30.*

h. Um zwanzig nach ______ nehme ich den Bus nach Hause. *I get back home on the 4:20 bus.*

i. Um _____________ sechs essen wir zu Abend. *Shortly after 6 we have dinner.*

j. Um halb _____ gehe ich ins Bett. *I go to bed at 10.30.*

Viertel vor	zwanzig	halb	kurz nach	Viertel nach
halb	zehn	fünf	vier	elf

9. Match

um Viertel nach acht	um zehn nach acht	um halb neun	um fünf nach acht	um fünf vor neun	um zehn vor neun	um Viertel vor neun
8:05	8:10	8:15	8:30	8:50	8:45	8:55

10. Sentence puzzle: rewrite the sentences in the correct order

a. machen Heute muss meine Hausaufgaben ich nicht. *Today I don't have to do my homework.*

b. früh aufstehen Morgen muss ich nicht. *Tomorrow I don't have to get up early.*

c. kann Heute ich mit Abend meinen Freunden ausgehen. *This evening I can go out with my friends.*

d. Schule Morgen nicht in muss ich die gehen. *Tomorrow I don't have to go to school.*

e. Stadion Dieses gehe ich ins Wochenende. *This weekend I am going to go to the stadium.*

f. Nächsten Hausarbeit Freitag die muss machen ich. *Next Friday I have to do chores.*

g. ins Samstag Bett kann ich spät Nächsten gehen. *Next Saturday I can go to bed late.*

h. Sonntag Am nächsten kann ich zu gehen Party Pauls. *Next Sunday I can go to Paul's party.*

Peter: Morgen kann ich nicht mit meiner Freundin ausgehen, weil ich Hausaufgaben machen muss.

Paula: Nächstes Wochenende gehe ich auf die Party von Karin.

Hans: Nächsten Sonntag gehe ich an den Strand.

Elke: Heute Nachmittag gehe ich mit meiner Mutter einkaufen.

Thomas: Heute will ich keine Hausaufgaben machen, weil ich total müde bin.

Richard: Jeden Tag nach dem Aufstehen muss ich mein Bett machen.

Susanne: Normalerweise helfe ich meiner Mutter im Haushalt, aber heute kann ich leider nicht, weil ich für eine Prüfung lernen muss.

Lotte: Dieses Wochenende will ich mit meiner Familie verbringen. Wir werden in einen Freizeitpark gehen und danach im Zentrum in ein italienischen Restaurant gehen.

Christian: Heute kann ich nicht mit dem Mountainbike fahren gehen, weil schlechtes Wetter ist.

Pia: Nächsten Samstag werde ich absolut nichts machen, außer mich zu entspannen.

11. Find someone who…

a. …has to revise for an exam.

b. …can't go mountain biking today.

c. …has a lot of homework so can't go out with his girlfriend.

d. …wants to spend the weekend with their family.

e. …has to go shopping with their mother.

f. …is going to an amusement park with their mother.

g. …mentions bad weather.

h. …who has to make their bed after getting up.

i. …will go to the beach at the weekend.

j. …is going to a party at the weekend.

k. …won't do anything other than relax at the weekend.

12. Gapped translation

a. Morgen kann ich nicht mit meiner Freundin ausgehen, weil ich viele Hausaufgaben habe.

Tomorrow I ___________ *go out with my girlfriend because I have* ________________________.

b. Nächstes Wochenende gehe ich zur Party von Karin.

Next ________________ *I am going to go to Karin's* __________________.

c. Nächsten Sonntag will ich an den Strand fahren.

Next _______________ *I* ___________ *to go to the beach.*

d. Heute Nachmittag gehe ich mit meiner Mutter einkaufen.

This ________________ *I am going to go* _______________ *with my mother.*

e. Heute will ich keine Hausarbeit machen, weil ich total müde bin.

_____________ *I don't want to do chores. I am very* _______________.

f. Jeden Tag nach dem Aufstehen muss ich mein Bett machen.

Every day after __________________ *I* __________ ______ *make my bed.*

g. Heute kann ich nicht Mountainbike fahren gehen, weil schlechtes Wetter ist.

Today I ______________ *go mountain biking because* _______________________________.

h. Nächsten Samstag werde ich gar nichts machen, außer mich zu entspannen.

Next _________________ *I am not going to do anything. I am only going to* _______________.

13. Sort the activities below in the appropriate box

a. Rad fahren gehen
b. Hausaufgaben machen
c. für eine Prüfung lernen
d. das Bett machen
e. bummeln gehen
f. einkaufen gehen
g. Kleidung kaufen
h. Basketball spielen
i. Geschirr spülen
j. in den Deutschunterricht gehen
k. Gewichte heben
l. kochen
m. Auto waschen

Sport *(sports)*	**Einkaufen** *(shopping)*
Schule/Ausbildung *(studies)*	**Hausarbeit** *(chores)*

14. Complete with a suitable word

a. Heute muss ich meine Hausaufgabe ___________.

b. Morgen will ich mich _____________.

c. Heute Nachmittag werde ich meiner Mutter _____________.

d. Heute Morgen werde ich nicht in die Schule _________________

e. Heute will ich _______________.

f. Ich muss für eine Prüfung ____________.

g. Ich will Rad fahren _______________.

h. Ich komme um 8 in der _____________ an.

i. Ich frühstücke in der _____________.

j. Heute mache ich gar ______________.

Unter der Woche stehe ich normalerweise sehr früh auf, also so gegen sechs Uhr, damit ich den Bus zur Schule um Viertel vor sieben nehmen kann. Nach dem Aufstehen dusche ich mich gleich und esse einen Toast mit einem Glas Orangensaft.

Nach dem Frühstück ziehe ich meine Schuluniform an und verlasse das Haus, um den Bus zu nehmen. Normalerweise komme ich ungefähr um halb acht in der Schule an. Der Unterricht beginnt um Viertel vor acht und endet um Viertel nach drei.

Circa um vier Uhr nachmittags komme ich nach Hause. Dann entspanne ich mich ein wenig *[a bit]*, bevor ich meine Hausaufgaben mache. Heute muss ich für meine Prüfungen lernen, weshalb ich nicht mit meinen Freunden ausgehen kann.

Normalerweise kann ich mit meinen Freunden zwischen fünf und halb sieben im Einkaufszentrum bummeln gehen. Heute allerdings muss ich zu Hause bleiben, um zu lernen. Das wird langweilig werden.

(Florian, 14 Jahre, St Wolfgang)

16. Complete the sentences

a. During the week I get up ______________.

b. At 6.45 I have to ______________________ to go to school.

c. For breakfast I have ___________________ with __________________.

d. After breakfast I put on my school uniform and _________________ to take the bus.

e. Lessons start at___________________ and end at _____________________.

f. At four I ____________________.

g. Before doing my homework I ______________________________.

h. Today I have to revise for my exams, so I ______________________________.

15. Find the German equivalent

e.g. during the week: ***unter der Woche***

a. early

b. so that I can take

c. I shower right away

d. toast with a glass of orange juice

e. after breakfast

f. I arrive at

g. lessons start

h. I relax a bit

i. I cannot go out

j. to go window shopping

k. in order to study

17. Find in the text and write below

a. Two reflexive verbs:

b. Two modal verbs:

c. Two types of food:

d. One verb associated with school:

e. Two verbs usually associated with free-time activities:

f. A time adverb starting with "h":

g. A time phrase starting with "u":

h. A time preposition with "b":

18. Answer the questions in German in full sentences, as if you were Florian.

a. Wann stehst du auf, Florian?

b. Um wie viel Uhr nimmst du den Bus?

c. Was isst du zum Frühstück?

d. Wann ziehst du deine Schuluniform an?

e. Um wie viel Uhr beginnt dein Unterricht?

f. Warum kannst du heute nicht mit deinen Freunden ausgehen?

g. Was machst du normalerweise mit deinen Freunden?

h. Was machst du heute Abend?

Unter der Woche stehe ich normalerweise sehr früh auf. Ich muss ungefähr um halb sieben aufstehen, weil ich den Bus um Viertel nach sieben nehmen muss, um in die Schule zu kommen. Ich dusche mich gleich nach dem Aufstehen und dann frühstücke ich einen Toast mit Butter und Marmelade und trinke einen Apfelsaft. Nach dem Frühstück putze ich mir die Zähne und bevor ich das Haus verlasse, ziehe ich mir meine Schuluniform an. Danach verlasse ich das Haus, um den Bus zu nehmen.

Normalerweise komme ich circa um halb acht in der Schule an. Der Unterricht beginnt um Viertel vor acht und endet um drei oder vier Uhr. Bevor ich nach Hause gehe, verbringe ich eine Stunde in der Bibliothek, um zu lernen. Oft ist das sehr schwierig und langweilig, aber zum Glück bin ich nicht alleine. Meine beste Freundin Eva hilft mir beim lernen und so helfen wir uns gegenseitig, wenn wir etwas nicht verstehen.

Ich komme circa um fünf von der Schule nach Hause. Dann ruhe ich mich ein wenig aus, bevor ich meine Aufgaben mache. Weil ich bald Prüfungen habe, kann ich weder mit meinen Freundinnen ausgehen noch mit ihnen online chatten. Wenn ich mit ihnen chatte, habe ich immer sehr viel Spaß. Wir erzählen uns Witze *[we tell each other jokes]*, den neuesten Tratsch *[gossip]* und unterhalten uns über die Jungen und Mädchen in unserer Klasse. In meiner Gegend gibt es schöne Geschäfte und nette Cafés, wo wir manchmal einen Tee trinken gehen. Mein Freund heißt Klemens. Er sieht super aus und ist sehr witzig. Normalerweise treffe ich mich mit ihm am Wochenende.

(Kerstin, 14 Jahre. Stuttgart)

19. Find the German equivalent

a. during the week

b. I have to get up

c. right away

d. I brush my teeth

e. I leave the house

f. I arrive at school

g. lessons start

h. before leaving school

i. we help each other

j. I spend one hour

k. since I have exams soon

20. Translate into English the following extracts from the text above

a. ich stehe normalerweise sehr früh auf

b. ich muss ungefähr um halb sieben aufstehen

c. bevor ich das Haus verlasse

d. wir helfen uns gegenseitig

e. ich komme nach Hause

f. ich ruhe mich ein wenig aus

g. ich kann weder mit meinen Freundinnen ausgehen noch mit ihnen online chatten

21. Tick the phrases below that you can find in Kerstin's text

a. wir gehen spazieren	e. den neuesten Tratsch	i. meine Freundin
b. mein Freund heißt	f. online chatten	j. nach dem Abendessen
c. wir gehen in den Zoo	g. helfen wir uns gegenseitig	k. einen Toast mit Butter
d. bevor ich das Haus verlasse	h. ich jogge	l. wir erzählen uns Witze

22. Complete the text with one of the options below

Unter der Woche __________ normalerweise sehr früh auf. ____________ ungefähr um halb sieben aufstehen, weil ich den Bus um Viertel nach sieben nehmen muss, um in die Schule zu kommen. Ich dusche mich gleich nach dem ____________ und dann _____________ ich einen Toast _____________ und Marmelade und trinke einen Apfelsaft. Nach dem Frühstück putze ich mir die Zähne und bevor ich das Haus verlasse, ziehe ich mir meine _________________ an. Danach verlasse ich das Haus, um den Bus zu nehmen.

_____________ komme ich circa um halb acht in der Schule an. Der ____________ beginnt um Viertel vor acht und endet um drei oder vier Uhr. Bevor ich nach Hause gehe, verbringe ich eine Stunde in der Bibliothek, um zu ______________. Ich komme circa ___________ von der _________ nach Hause. Dann ruhe ich mich ein wenig aus bevor ich meine Aufgaben mache. Wegen meinen Prüfungen _____________ weder mit meinen Freundinnen _____________ noch mit ihnen online chatten. Wenn ich mit ihnen chatte, habe ich immer sehr viel Spaß. Wir erzählen uns Witze, den neuesten Tratsch und _______________ uns über die Jungen und Mädchen unserer Klasse.

normalerweise	Schuluniform	stehe ich	frühstücke	kann ich	Unterricht	ausgehen
circa fünf	Aufstehen	Schule	lernen	mit Butter	ich muss	unterhalten

23. Jigsaw reading: arrange the text in the correct order

Normalerweise stehe ich um halb sieben auf	
und dusche mich anschließend.	
Hallo, ich heiße Emma und ich	1
Dann ziehe ich meine Schuluniform an	
und mache mich auf den Weg	
Um halb vier ist die Schule aus.	
will dir ein wenig über meine Tagesroutine erzählen.	
in die Schule.	
Dann frühstücke ich Cornflakes und trinke einen Tee.	
Ich nehme meistens den Bus, mit dem ich	
pünktlich um halb acht in die Schule komme.	

24a. Translate the sentences below into German using *Ich muss* + infinitive

a. I have to get up early.

b. I have to do my homework.

c. I have to help my friend.

d. I have to go to school.

e. I have to make my bed.

f. I have to go to bed early.

g. I have to revise for the exams.

24b. Translate the sentences below into German using *Ich kann (nicht)* + infinitive

a. I can go out with my friends.

b. I cannot play on my computer.

c. I can go bike riding in the park.

d. I can go to bed late.

e. I cannot have breakfast.

f. I can go to school by bike.

g. I can get up early.

24c. Translate the sentences below into German using *ich will / ich muss / ich kann* + infinitive

a. I have to work.

b. I don't want to shower.

c. I can't go to the party.

d. I have to tidy up my room.

e. I want to watch TV.

f. I don't want to go fishing.

g. I can't get up early.

h. I want to eat pizza.

i. I don't want to play.

j. I have to go home.

k. I don't want to study.

l. I have to do my homework.

25. Guided translation

a. M_ _ _ _ _ m_ _ _ i_ _ m_ _ m_ _ _ _ _ M_ _ _ _ _ e_ _ _ _ _ _ _ _ g_ _ _ _.
Tomorrow I have to go shopping with my mother.

b. H_ _ _ _ A_ _ _ _ k_ _ _ i_ _ n_ _ _ _ m_ _ m_ _ _ _ _ F_ _ _ _ _ _ _ a_ _ _ _ _ _ _.
This evening I can't go out with my friends.

c. H_ _ _ _ k_ _ _ i_ _ n_ _ _ _ V_ _ _ _ _ _ _ _ _ _ s_ _ _ _ _ _.
Today I can't play videogames.

d. H_ _ _ _ w_ _ _ i_ _ n_ _ _ _ m_ _ _ _ H_ _ _ _ _ _ _ _ _ _ _ m_ _ _ _ _.
Today I don't want to do my homework.

e. D_ _ _ _ _ W_ _ _ _ _ _ _ _ _ _ w_ _ _ i_ _ Z_ _ _ m_ _ m_ _ _ _ _ F_ _ _ _ _ _ v_ _ _ _ _ _ _ _ _.
This weekend I want to spend time with my family.

f. U_ _ _ _ d_ _ W_ _ _ _ m_ _ _ i_ _ f_ _ _ a_ _ _ _ _ _ _ _.
During the week I have to get up early.

g. H_ _ _ _ M_ _ _ _ _ k_ _ _ i_ _ n_ _ _ _ i_ d_ _ S_ _ _ _ _ g_ _ _ _.
This morning I can't go to school.

h. M_ _ _ _ _ w_ _ _ i_ _ n_ _ _ _ a_ _ d_ _ P_ _ _ _ g_ _ _ _.
Tomorrow I don't want to go to the party.

26. Translate the following text into German

Hi. My name is Maria. I am going to tell you about my daily routine.

During the week I have to get up early because I have to catch the bus to go to school at six thirty. I get up at six and shower right away. I then have breakfast. Generally, I eat two eggs, a piece of toast and a banana. After breakfast I leave home and catch the bus to go to school.

I usually arrive at school at seven thirty. Lessons start at 7:40 am and end at 2:20 pm. My favourite subject is German because the teacher is very good, cool and funny.

I come back home at three o'clock. After coming back I rest a bit, I shower and then I have to do my homework or else I'm not allowed to go out. Around 6 I go out with my friends. We usually go to the shopping centre near my house. We go window shopping, buy clothes and gossip about the boys in our school.

I have to come home at eight for dinner. After dinner I watch TV and then go to bed.

27. Write a 150 to 250 words paragraph in which you:

- Briefly describe yourself and your family.
- Say where you live and where your town is located.
- Describe your neighbourhood and what one can do there.
- Say what you do on a typical weekday.
- Say what you normally do at the weekend and your plans for next weekend.
- Say what you did yesterday (3 things minimum).
- List three things you want to do today (feel free to make them up).
- List three things you have to do today (feel free to make them up).

Question Skills Unit 6

English	German
Tell me about your daily routine.	**Erzähl mir etwas über deine tägliche Routine.**
What do you do in the morning?	**Was machst du am Morgen?**
When do you wake up?	**Wann wachst du auf?**
At what time do you get up?	**Um wie viel Uhr stehst du auf?**
What do you normally have for breakfast?	**Was isst du normalerweise zum Frühstück?**
Who do you have breakfast with?	**Mit wem frühstückst du?**
When do you leave the house?	**Wann verlässt du das Haus?**
How do you get to school?	**Wie kommst du zur Schule?**
What do you do when you come back from school?	**Was machst du, wenn du von der Schule nach Hause kommst?**
What do you have to do after school?	**Was musst du nach der Schule machen?**
What do you like to do when you get home from school?	**Was machst du gerne, wenn du von der Schule nach Hause kommst?**
What are you going to do next weekend?	**Was wirst du nächstes Wochenende machen?**
What chores do you have to do?	**Welche Aufgaben übernimmst du im Haushalt?**

1. Split questions

Um wie viel Uhr	den Bus?
Mit wem	stehst du auf?
Wo gehst du	kommst du zur Schule?
Wie	Lieblingsbeschäftigung?
Was machst	du nach der Schule?
Was wirst du	nach der Schule hin?
Gefällt dir	nächsten Samstag machen?
Was ist deine	frühstückst du normalerweise?
Nimmst du	deine Schule?

2. Find and write in the missing words

a. Erzähl mir etwas deine tägliche Routine.

b. Um wie viel Uhr du auf?

c. Was frühstückst?

d. Wann gehst in die Schule?

e. Was du nach der Schule?

f. Um wie Uhr machst du deine Hausaufgaben?

g. Wann du das Haus?

3. Match questions and answers

Wann wachst du auf?	Normalerweise esse ich einen Toast mit Honig.
Um wie viel Uhr stehst du auf?	Meistens frühstücke ich in der Küche.
Was frühstückst du normalerweise?	Ich verlasse das Haus um Viertel vor acht.
Mit wem frühstückst du?	Am liebsten schaue ich fern.
Wo frühstückst du?	Meistens fahre ich mit dem Bus in die Schule.
Um wie viel Uhr verlässt du das Haus?	Ich wache jeden Tag um sechs Uhr auf.
Wie kommst du in die Schule?	Ich mache meine Hausaufgaben.
Was machst du gleich nach der Schule?	Ich frühstücke mit meinen Eltern.
Was musst du nach der Schule machen?	Ich werde mit meinem Freund ins Theater gehen.
Was machst du gerne nach der Schule?	Ich muss mein Zimmer aufräumen. Wie langweilig.
Was machst du nächstes Wochenende?	Ich stehe um sieben Uhr auf.

4. Guided translation

a. Mit w_ _ f_ _ _ _ _ _ _ _ _ _ du?	*Who do you have breakfast with?*
b. U_ w_ _ v_ _ _ U_ _ s_ _ _ _ _ d_ a_ _?	*What time do you get up?*
c. W_ _ k_ _ _ _ _ d_ i_ d_ _ S_ _ _ _ _?	*How do you get to school?*
d. G_ _ _ _ _ _ d_ _ d_ _ _ _ S_ _ _ _ _?	*Do you like your school?*
e. W_ f_ _ _ _ _ _ _ _ _ _ d_?	*Where do you have breakfast?*
f. U_ w_ _ v_ _ _ U_ _ w_ _ _ _ _ d_ a_ _?	*At what time do you wake up?*
g. N_ _ _ _ _ d_ d_ _ B_ _?	*Do you take the bus?*
h. W_ _ i_ _ d_ _ _ L_ _ _ _ _ _ _ _ _ _ _ _ _?	*What is your favourite hobby?*
i. W_ _ m_ _ _ _ _ d_ n_ _ _ d_ _ S_ _ _ _ _?	*What do you do after school?*

5. Translate into German

a. At what time do you wake up?

b. At what time do you get up?

c. Who do you have breakfast with?

d. How do you get to school?

e. Do you like school?

f. At what time do you get back home?

g. What chores do you have to do?

h. What is your favourite hobby?

i. What are you going to do next weekend?

6. Answer the following questions in your own words, using full sentences

Um wie viel Uhr wachst du auf?

Um wie viel Uhr stehst du auf?

Was frühstückst du? Mit wem?

Wann verlässt du das Haus?

Wie kommst du in die Schule?

Was machst du nach der Schule?

Welche Aufgaben machst du im Haushalt?

Was machst du am Wochenende?

Vocab Revision Workout 3

1. Translate into English

a. Wir werden Basketball spielen.
b. Meine Mama wird ins Büro fahren.
c. Ich gehe heute nicht in die Schule.
d. Und was machst du morgen?
e. Was werdet ihr morgen machen?
f. Morgen werde ich nicht lernen.
g. Mein Bruder und ich werden Fußball spielen.
h. Meine Geschwister werden ins Fitnessstudio gehen.
i. Meine Schwester wird nichts machen.
j. Ich bleibe morgen zuhause.

2. Complete with the correct form of "*werden*"

a. Nächstes Wochenende _ _ _ _ _ ich an den Strand gehen.
b. Am Nachmittag _ _ _ _ sie ein Konzert besuchen.
c. Heute Morgen _ _ _ _ _ _ _ meine Brüder nicht in die Schule gehen.
d. Morgen _ _ _ _ _ _ _ meine Eltern nicht ins Büro gehen.
e. Mein Bruder und ich _ _ _ _ _ _ _ Tennis spielen.
f. Und du, was _ _ _ _ _ _ du am Samstag machen?
g. Was _ _ _ _ _ _ _ ihr heute Abend machen?
h. Meine Brüder _ _ _ _ _ _ _ reiten gehen.

3. Gapped translation

a. D_ _ S_ _ _ _ _ _ _ _ _ _ _ _ _ i_ _ n_ _ _ _ d_ _ K_ _ _. *The sports shop is next to the cinema.*
b. D_ _ S_ _ _ _ _ _ _ _ _ _ _ i_ _ g_ _ _ _ _ _ _ _ _ _ d_ _ S_ _ _ _ _. *The pool is opposite the school.*
c. D_ _ E_ _ _ _ _ _ _ _ _ _ _ _ _ _ _ _ i_ _ a_ E_ _ _ d_ _ S_ _ _ _ _. *The shopping centre is at the end of the street.*
d. D_ _ B_ _ _ i_ _ h_ _ _ _ _ diesem Gebäude. *The bank is behind this building.*
e. D_ _ S_ _ _ _ _ _ _ _ _ _ _ i_ _ i_ d_ _ N_ _ _ v_ _ m_ _ _ _ _ H_ _ _. *The supermarket is near my house.*

4. Guided translation

a. *a beautiful chair* e___ s___________ S___________
b. *a bright kitchen* e___ h___________ K___________
c. *a red rug* e___ r___________ T___________
d. *blue curtains* b___________ V___________
e. *a spacious room* e___ g___________ Z___________
f. *an old wardrobe* e__ a___________ S___________
g. *a comfortable bed* e___ b___________ B___________
h. *a modern building* e__ m___________ G___________
i. *a new TV* e___ n___________ F___________

5. Complete with a suitable word

a. In meiner Stadt gibt es viele _________ ______________.
b. Mein Lieblingszimmer ist das_______________, weil es _______________ ist.
c. Neben dem Schrank steht ein _________________________.
d. Der Spiegel _______ an der Wand.
e. In meiner Wohnung gibt es fünf _____________.

6. Faulty translation: correct the mistakes in the translations below
Please note: not all translations are incorrect.

a. In der Küche stehen vier alte Sessel.	*In the kitchen there are 4 old armchairs.*
b. In meinem Zimmer hängen rote Vorhänge.	*In my living-room there are red curtains.*
c. In meiner Küche steht ein alter Fernseher.	*In the kitchen there is a small television.*
d. In unserem Garten gibt es keine Bäume.	*In our garden there are many trees.*
e. In unserem Wohnzimmer gibt es zwei Sessel.	*In our playroom there are two armchairs.*
f. Neben meinem Bett steht ein Nachttisch.	*Opposite my bed there is a bedside table.*
g. In meiner Küche steht ein Kühlschrank.	*In my kitchen there is a lamp.*
h. In meinem Haus gibt es einen Fernseher.	*In my house there is no TV.*

7. Translate the sentences below into German using *Ich will / Ich muss / Ich kann (nicht)* + infinitive

a. I have to study.	g. I can't get up early.
b. I don't want to go out.	h. I want to eat pasta.
c. I can't go to the party.	i. I don't want to go jogging.
d. I have to tidy up the kitchen.	j. I have to go to the gym.
e. I want to watch a film.	k. I don't want to work.
f. I want to go to school.	l. I have to do my homework.

9. Translate into German

a. In my neighbourhood there is a lot on offer for young people.

b. Last week I went to the shopping centre with my mother.

c. Three days ago I went bike riding and played with my friends in the park.

d. I don't want to go to the party this evening.

e. We relaxed listening to music.

f. We went to the old town and took many photos.

g. Next week we will go to Berlin. It will be fun.

h. Every day I help my mother with the chores.

i. I usually get up very early in the morning because I have to leave the house at seven to go to school.

8. Complete with the missing verbs. NOTE: use the first person singular of the perfect tense (e.g. *bin gelaufen*, etc.)

a. Ich _____ mit meinem Vater ins Geschäft ________________.

b. Ich _____ letztes Wochenende nichts _______________.

c. Gestern Nachmittag ______ ich mir einen Film im Kino _________.

d. Ich _____ mit dem Fahrrad ins Zentrum _______________.

e. Ich ______ mit meinem Vater Tennis ________________.

f. Ich ______ Musik _____________.

g. Ich ______ früh ______________, um mit meinem Vater Fußball zu spielen.

h. Ich ______ auf die Party von meiner besten Freundin Bettina ________________.

i. Ich ______ viele Fotos in der Galerie ________________.

j. Vorgestern ______ ich im Park Basketball ________________.

k. Ich ______ mir einen neuen Pullover ___________________.

Unit 7

Saying what I do to help at home – present & past

In this unit you will learn:

- To say what chores I and other family members have to do
- To say what chores I did in the recent past
- To say why I didn't help at home in the recent past

Key sentence patterns:

- *Ich muss* + time + infinitive + adversative clause + causal clause
- *Aber/jedoch* + time marker + perfect tense with *nicht*
- *weil* + imperfect tense

Grammar:

- Use of *müssen:* first and third person
- Perfect tense: first person
- Imperfect tense of *haben*

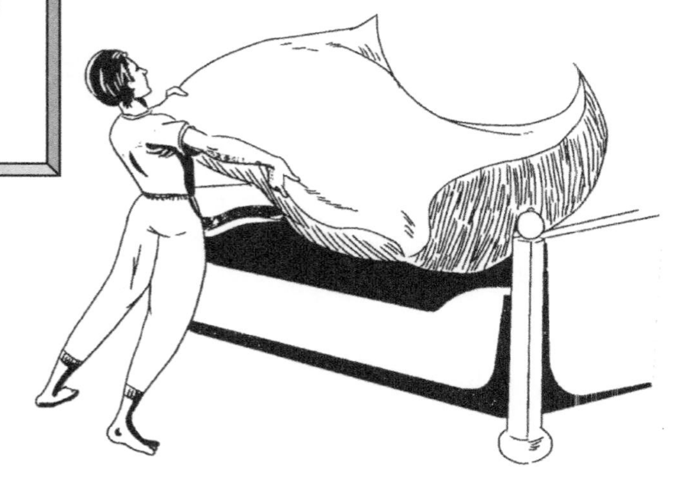

UNIT 7: Saying what I do to help at home – present & past

Ich *[I]* **Mein Bruder** *[My brother]* **Meine Schwester** *[My sister]*	**muss** *[have to/has to...]*	**einmal pro Woche** *[once a week]* **zweimal pro Woche** *[twice a week]* **normalerweise** *[usually]* **heute** *[today]* **jeden Tag** *[every day]*	**das Bett machen** *[...make the bed]* **das Geschirr spülen** *[...wash the dishes]* **den Boden wischen** *[...mop the floor]* **den Müll hinausbringen** *[...take the rubbish out]* **den Rasen mähen** *[...mow the lawn]* **den Tisch decken** *[...lay the table]* **die Blumen gießen** *[...water the plants]* **einkaufen gehen** *[...go shopping]* **im Haushalt/bei der Hausarbeit helfen** *[...help at home/do chores]* **kochen** *[...cook]* **meinen Eltern helfen** *[...help my parents]* **mit dem Hund spazieren gehen** *[...walk the dog]* **Staub saugen** *[...vacuum]* **Wäsche waschen** *[...do the laundry]*
Ich muss *[I have to]*			**mein Zimmer aufräumen** *[tidy my room]* **meinem Bruder helfen** *[help my brother]* **meiner Oma helfen** *[help my grandmother]*

Mein Bruder **Meine Schwester**	**muss** *[has to]*	**mir mit den Hausaufgaben helfen** *[help me with my homework]*	
Mein Bruder		**sein**	**Zimmer aufräumen** *[tidy his/her room]*
Meine Schwester		**ihr**	

, aber *[but]*	**gestern** *[yesterday]*	**bin ich nicht** *[I did not...]*	**mit dem Hund spazieren** *[walk the dog]* **einkaufen** *[shopping]*	**gegangen** *[...go]*
		habe ich *[I did not...]*	**meinen Eltern nicht geholfen** *[help my parents]* **mein Zimmer nicht aufgeräumt** *[tidy my room]* **den Boden nicht gewischt** *[mop the floor]* **das Bett nicht gemacht** *[make the bed]*	
			nicht **gekocht** *[...cook]* **Staub gesaugt** *[...vacuum]*	

, weil *[because]*	**ich** *[I ...]*	**müde** *[tired]* **krank** *[sick]*	**beschäftigt** *[busy]*	**war** *[...was]*
	mir *[my]*	**der Arm** *[arm]* **der Fuß** *[foot]*	**der Kopf** *[head]* **der Rücken** *[back]*	**weh getan** **hat** *[hurt]*
	ich keine Lust hatte *[I didn't feel like it]* **ich viele Hausaufgaben hatte** *[I had a lot of homework to do]*			

1. Match

Ich muss einkaufen gehen.	I have to wash the dishes.
Ich muss das Geschirr spülen.	I have to go shopping.
Ich muss die Betten machen.	I have to lay the table.
Ich muss den Boden wischen.	I have to mow the lawn.
Ich muss den Tisch decken.	I have to walk the dog.
Ich muss mit dem Hund spazieren gehen.	I have to tidy my room.
Ich muss mein Zimmer aufräumen.	I have to mop the floor.
Ich muss den Rasen mähen.	I have to make the beds.

2. Missing letters

a. Ich muss d_n T_sch deck_n.

b. Ich mus_ S_aub s_ugen.

c. Ich muss d_n Ra_en m_hen.

d. Ich mu_s d_e B_umen gi_ßen.

e Ic_ mu_s m_i_ Zi_mer au_r_umen.

f. Ich mu_s _ochen.

g. Ic_ m_ss meine_ B_uder he_fen.

3. Complete

a. Ich muss mein Z_______________aufräumen.

b. Ich muss meinem B________ regelmäßig bei seinen Hausaufgaben helfen.

c. Ich muss k______________.

d. Ich muss mit dem H________ spazieren gehen.

e. Ich muss den Boden w____________.

f. Ich muss das G___________ spülen.

g. Ich muss meiner Oma h_________.

4. Give your opinion about the activities listed, using the following expressions

– Das macht mir Spaß. *[I enjoy it]*
– Das finde ich ok. *[I don't mind it]*
– Das gefällt mir nicht *[I don't like it]*

a. mein Zimmer aufräumen

____

b. die Blumen gießen

____

c. das Auto waschen

____

d. den Tisch decken

____

e. mit dem Hund spazieren gehen

____

f. meinem Bruder helfen

____

g. mich mit meinen Freunden treffen

____

5. Write P for probable and I for improbable for the sentences below

a. Ich muss meine Schwester gießen.

b. Ich muss mit meiner Katze spazieren gehen.

c. Ich muss meinem Papa helfen das Auto zu waschen.

d. Ich koche regelmäßig den Tisch.

e. Ich gehe regelmäßig mit meiner Mama einkaufen.

f. Ich muss den Papa wischen.

6. Complete the table with the missing present forms of the verbs *können*, *wollen* and *müssen*

	können	wollen	müssen
ich	kann		muss
du		willst	musst
er/sie/es	kann		
wir		wollen	
ihr	könnt		ihr müsst
sie		wollen	

Hallo,

ich heiße Lukas. In meiner Familie gibt es fünf Personen: meine Eltern, meinen großen Bruder, meinen kleinen Bruder und mich.

Wir alle müssen im Haushalt helfen. Mein Papa kocht normalerweise und wäscht die Wäsche. Meine Mama kocht ebenfalls, kümmert sich außerdem um den Garten und deckt den Tisch.

Mein Bruder muss sein Bett machen, den Tisch abräumen und nach dem Frühstück das Geschirr spülen. Am Wochenende muss er das Auto meiner Mama waschen.

Mein kleiner Bruder muss ebenfalls sein Bett machen. Er muss auch den Tisch abräumen und nach dem Frühstück das Geschirr spülen. Samstags muss er auch das Auto meines Papas waschen.

Ich muss selbstverständlich mein Bett machen. Ich muss außerdem den Tisch abräumen und nach dem Abendessen das Geschirr spülen. Zusätzlich muss ich meinem Papa im Garten helfen und meinem Bruder bei seiner Mathematikaufgabe.

(Lukas, 17 Jahre. Klagenfurt)

7. Find in the text

a. there are five people

b. we all have to share the chores

c. my little brother has to also make his bed

d. I have to clear the table

e. he has to wash the car

f. help my father in the garden

g. my dad usually cooks

h. she looks after the garden

i. I have to make my bed

j. of course

k. moreover

l. after breakfast

m. to wash the dishes

n. after dinner

o. on Saturdays

p. additionally

8. Translate into English

a. In meiner Familie gibt es fünf Personen.

b. Mein großer Bruder ist faul.

c. Mein kleiner Bruder ist fleißig.

d. Meine Mama kocht ebenfalls.

e. Mein Papa muss im Garten arbeiten.

f. Ich muss normalerweise das Auto waschen.

g. Mein Bruder muss sein Bett machen.

h. Normalerweise decke ich den Tisch.

i. Meine Schwester spült das Geschirr.

j. Außerdem muss mein Bruder mit meiner Mutter einkaufen gehen.

9. Sentence puzzle: rewrite the sentences in the correct order

a. die muss ich das waschen Woche Auto meines Zweimal Papas.

Twice a week I have to wash my father's car.

b. Garten die Einmal muss ich Woche Papa im meinem helfen.

Once a week I have to help my father in the garden.

c. mein Ich muss jeden Tag Bett und gehen mit dem machen spazieren Hund.

Every day I have to make my bed and walk the dog.

d. Samstag den Rasen letzten habe muss nicht ich mähen Samstag es gemacht ich Jeden, aber .

Every Saturday I have to mow the lawn, but last Saturday I didn't do it.

e. Nach ich normalerweise Tisch dem räume , aber heute ab den konnte ich das nicht, weil ich viele Hausaufgaben Mittagessen hatte.

After lunch I usually clear the table, but today I couldn't because I had a lot of homework.

10. Rock climbing translation: translate the sentences by selecting each tile in the wall below and numbering them off, as shown in the example

e.g. I usually help my brother with his homework. Ich helfe meinem Bruder normalerweise mit seinen Hausaufgaben.

a. *Today I have to water the plants after lunch.*

b. *This afternoon I have to walk the dog.*

c. *After getting up I always have to make my bed.*

d. *Every day I have to lay and clear the table.*

e. *On Saturdays I usually wash my father's car.*

machen	Vaters	**Hausaufgaben**	und abräumen	gießen	gehen
spazieren	**seinen**	Blumen	meines	Bett	decken
den Tisch	die	dem Hund	Auto	**mit**	mein
dem Mittagessen	ich	immer	**normalerweise**	mit	das
muss ich	muss	**meinem Bruder**	ich normalerweise	muss ich	nach
muss ich	Nachmittag	Tag	**helfe**	dem Aufstehen	wasche
Heute	Heute	**Ich**	Nach	Jeden	Samstags

HELP BOX	
Ich habe mein Zimmer nicht aufgeräumt.	I didn't tidy up my room.
Ich habe meinen Eltern nicht geholfen.	I didn't help my parents.
Ich habe nicht das Geschirr gespült.	I didn't wash the dishes.
Ich habe nicht mein Bett gemacht.	I didn't make my bed.
Ich war nicht mit dem Hund spazieren.	I didn't walk the dog.
Ich habe nichts gemacht.	I didn't do anything.
Ich habe nicht gekocht.	I didn't cook.
Ich habe nicht Staub gesaugt.	I didn't vacuum.
Ich konnte nicht.	I wasn't able to.

11. Complete with the missing letters

a. Ich habe n_chts gem_cht .

b. Ic_ war n_cht m_t dem Hun_ spazieren.

c. Ich _abe _ein Bett nich_ gemacht.

d. Ich ha_e nicht Stau_ gesa_gt.

e. Ich kon_te _icht.

f. Ich _abe mein Zimm_r nicht aufgeräu_t.

g. Ich w_llte _icht helfen.

h. Ich _abe nic_t das G_schirr gespült

i. Ic_ ha_e nicht _ekoch_

12. Faulty translation

a. Ich habe Staub gesaugt.	*I mopped the floor.*
b. Ich habe nichts gemacht.	*I didn't want anything*
c. Ich habe nicht den Tisch gedeckt.	*I didn't lay the table.*
d. Ich konnte nicht.	*I didn't want to.*
e. Ich wollte nicht helfen.	*I couldn't help.*
f. Ich habe meinen Eltern nicht geholfen.	*I helped my parents.*

13. Spot and correct the errors. HINT: not all sentences contain mistakes

a. Ich habe nicht Staub gesaugt.	*I didn't vacuum.*
b. Ich hab nichts gemacht.	*I didn't lay the table.*
c. Ich war mit dem Hund spazieren.	*I walked the dog.*
d. Ich konnte nicht.	*I didn't want to.*
e. Ich habe mein Bett gemacht.	*I made my bed.*

14. Tangled translation: rewrite in German

a. Jeden **day** gehe ich normalerweise mit dem **dog** spazieren, aber gestern **could I not**.

b. Jeden **Saturday** muss ich **the car wash, but** letzten Samstag **I didn't want to**.

c. Nach dem Frühstück räume **I usually** den **table** ab, aber gestern **I didn't do it**.

d. Vorgestern habe ich **my room tidied** und **dishes** gespült, aber gestern habe ich **nothing** gemacht.

e. Jeden **day** muss ich mein **bed** machen, aber heute **morning I didn't want to**.

f. Montags **make** ich immer **my bed** und **water** die Blumen.

HELP BOX

IMPERFECT TENSE		
Ich hatte keine Lust *[I didn't feel like it]*		
Ich musste viele Hausaufgaben machen *[I had to do a lot of homework]*		
Ich konnte nicht	*I wasn't able to*	
Ich wollte nicht	*I didn't want to*	
Ich war *[I was]*	**beschäftigt** *[busy]* **krank** *[ill]* **müde** *[tired]* **sauer** *[angry]*	
PERFECT TENSE		
Mir hat der *[My]*	**Arm** *[arm]* **Kopf** *[head]* **Rücken***[back]*	**wehgetan** *[hurt]*
PAST PERFECT TENSE		
Ich hatte vergessen es zu machen *[I had forgotten to do it]*		

15. Complete with a suitable word based on the HELP BOX. Please ensure no word is repeated twice

a. Gestern hatte ich ____________ Lust.

b. Ich wollte ____________.

c. Ich ___________ beschäftigt.

d. ______ konnte ________.

e. ______ hat der Arm wegetan.

f. ___________ viele Hausaufgaben machen.

g. ______ war müde.

h. Mir hat der Rücken __________.

i. Ich ___________ vergessen es zu machen.

16. Multiple choice: choose the correct translation

	1	2	3
a. Ich war müde.	I was lazy.	I was tired.	I was ill.
b. Ich musste meine Hausaufgaben machen.	I had no homework.	I was too busy.	I had lots of homework.
c. Ich wollte nicht.	I could not.	I didn't want to.	I didn't do it.
d. Ich war krank.	I was in shape.	I was ill.	I was happy.
e. Ich hatte vergessen.	I didn't want to.	I didn't like it.	I had forgotten.
f. Mein Kopf tat weh.	My head hurt.	My arm hurt.	My back hurt.
g. Ich konnte nicht.	I didn't remember.	I didn't want to.	I wasn't able to.
h. Ich hatte keine Lust.	I had no game.	I didn't feel like it.	I had no time.

17. Translate into English

a. Gestern konnte ich nicht mit dem Hund spazieren gehen, weil ich krank war.

b. Vorgestern habe ich das Geschirr nicht gespült, weil ich müde war.

c. Diese Woche bin ich nicht in die Schule gegagen, weil mir der Kopfweh wehgetan hat.

d. Heute Nachmittag habe ich den Müll nicht hinausgebracht, weil mir der Arm wehgetan hat.

e. Letztes Wochenende habe ich nicht das Auto gewaschen, weil mir der Rücken wehgetan hat.

f. Letzen Sonntag habe ich nichts für die Schule gemacht, weil ich sehr beschäftigt war.

18. Wordsearch: find the German translation of the sentences below and write them as shown in the example

T	I	V	Q	N	H	U	D	S	Q	Y	B	F	I	V	U	X	Z	H	A
S	C	M	C	O	H	Y	D	O	C	H	L	C	P	D	V	L	Z	L	U
U	H	A	D	I	V	D	Y	H	Q	A	H	I	T	I	X	K	B	G	K
L	W	L	U	E	K	Z	D	I	E	W	D	O	I	H	X	U	X	E	N
E	A	R	I	R	Q	Y	T	R	A	L	N	E	L	V	T	P	J	E	L
N	R	E	S	E	E	E	R	R	L	X	U	F	I	D	I	Q	A	M	Z
I	B	B	K	S	W	D	M	N	Y	L	S	I	P	R	W	L	K	J	M
E	E	R	J	L	K	Ü	E	S	I	E	W	R	E	L	A	M	R	O	N
K	S	F	R	F	D	T	H	C	I	N	E	T	N	N	O	K	H	C	I
E	C	D	B	E	Z	C	B	C	C	I	L	M	F	Z	N	O	H	T	S
T	H	H	A	N	R	C	V	I	I	C	B	N	H	U	H	A	W	A	T
T	Ä	T	S	Z	Q	C	V	O	R	H	E	A	S	P	E	M	U	V	E
A	F	W	I	Y	J	K	M	N	I	W	Y	D	B	T	A	E	M	W	L
H	T	S	B	P	B	D	T	A	W	A	V	S	H	H	R	A	Z	F	H
H	I	T	G	Y	F	P	G	C	Z	R	M	U	N	J	N	I	V	A	E
C	G	J	I	X	R	G	C	A	C	K	M	U	N	U	U	G	U	R	R
I	T	P	S	Q	N	A	H	S	A	R	Q	D	J	U	Y	N	H	F	S
N	F	D	E	B	Q	M	D	C	A	A	N	A	U	S	Z	U	O	V	U
T	H	O	Q	R	U	P	P	E	Z	N	D	T	U	V	V	S	M	L	U
M	D	H	Y	R	B	I	H	M	H	K	J	R	Y	A	I	I	W	Y	R

e.g. I was sick — ***ich war krank***

a. I was tired

b. I wasn't able to

c. I didn't feel like it

d. I was busy

e. angry

f. normally

g. because

19. Match

Ich konnte nicht.	I have to lay the table.
Ich habe meinen Papa nicht geholfen.	I didn't wash the dishes.
Ich hatte keine Lust.	I was busy.
Ich war beschäftigt.	I was angry.
Ich habe nichts gemacht.	I usually wash the car.
Mir hat der Arm wehgetan.	My arm hurt.
Ich wasche normalerweise das Auto.	I didn't do anything.
Ich habe das Geschirr nicht gespült.	I didn't want to.
Ich muss den Tisch decken.	I didn't feel like it.
Ich war sauer.	I didn't help my father.
Ich wollte nicht.	I wasn't able to.

20. Missing letters

a. Ich habe de_ Tisch nic_t ged_ckt, weil ich keine Lust hatte.

b. Ich bi_ nicht _it dem Hun_ s_azieren gegan_en, weil ic_ keine Lust hat_e.

c. Ich habe _ichts g_macht, _eil ich mü_e wa_.

d. Ich hab_ mei_em _apa nich_ geholfen, wei_ ich ni_ht w_llte.

e. G_stern h_be ich _ein_r Mam_ nicht beim Einkaufen geho_fen, weil ich sau_r w_r.

f. Ic_ habe _en Tisch n_cht gedeckt, weil ich keine Zeit h_tte.

g. Ich hab_ gestern ni_ht mit _einem Bruder ges_ielt, weil ich ni_ht kon_te.

h. Ich ha_e gest_rn nicht ge_ocht, weil ich Kopf_eh h_tte.

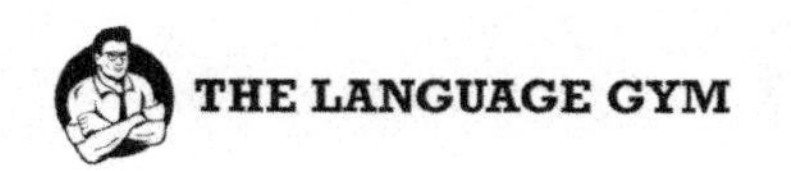

Ich heiße Paul und bin fünfzehn Jahren alt. Ich komme aus Köln in Deutschland. In meiner Stadt gibt es viele Angebote für junge Leute. Mir gefällt meine Stadt, weil es viele Sporteinrichtungen gibt und ich sehr sportlich bin. In meiner Freizeit gehe ich schwimmen, klettern und Rad fahren. Mir gefallen diese Sportarten. Außerdem gibt es in meiner Stadt viele tolle Geschäfte, und gute Bars.

In meiner Familie teilen wir die Aufgaben im Haushalt auf. Meine Mama kocht normalerweise und kümmert sich um den Garten. Mein Papa muss das Auto waschen und mit dem Hund spazieren gehen. Mein Bruder und ich müssen die Betten machen, unsere Zimmer aufräumen, den Müll hinausbringen und den Tisch abräumen.

Unsere Eltern freuen sich, wenn wir ihnen helfen. Gestern konnte ich das allerdings nicht, weil ich krank war. **(Paul, 15 Jahre. Köln)**

21. Find the German equivalent in Paul's text

a. a lot on offer for young people

b. because I am very sporty

c. in my free time

d. rock climbing

e. these sports

f. we share the chores

g. usually cooks

h. looks after the garden

i. to walk the dog

j. make the bed

k. tidy up our bedroom

22. Gapped translation

My name is Paul. I am _________ years old and I am from Köln in Germany. In my city there is a lot to do _____________________________. There are many _____________ __________________, which is very important _________ _________ because I am very ________________. In my __________ _________ I go swimming, _________ _______________ and cycling. I love these sports. In my city there are also lots of _____________ that I ________ and many good bars.

In my family we always _____________ the ________________. My mother usually __________________ and looks after ________ ________________. My father has to ____________ _______ __________ and ___________ the _________. My brother and I have to _____________ the _____________, tidy up _________ ______________, take ________ _____________ out and _____________ the ______________. Our parents are glad when we __________ ________. However, yesterday I couldn't because I was __________.

23. Answer the following questions in German, as if you were Paul

a. Woher kommst du, Paul?

b. Was machst du in deiner Freizeit?

c. Was gibt es in deiner Stadt zu tun?

d. Welche Aufgaben macht dein Papa im Haushalt?

e. Welche Aufgaben macht deine Mama?

f. Was machst du im Haushalt?

24. Tick the items below which are contained in Paul's text and cross out the ones which aren't. Can you do it under two minutes?

a. mein Bruder	h. tanzen
b. Aufgaben	i. dennoch
c. gestern	j. helfen
d. Sporteinrichtungen	k. sportlich
e. Eltern	l. aufräumen
f. Kindergarten	m. sehr gut
g. allerdings	n. Bett machen

Hallo, ich heiße Nele und wohne in Eisenstadt, das in der Nähe von Ungarn liegt. Ich wohne am Stadtrand, wo es wenige Angebote für junge Leute gibt. Es gibt wenige Sporteinrichtungen und keine guten Geschäfte.
Ich lebe mit meiner Familie in einem ziemlich großen Haus. Mir gefällt mein Haus, weil es sehr geräumig und hell ist. Es gibt einen schönen, großen Garten. Mein Zimmer ist sehr gemütlich. Es steht ein Schreibtisch neben einem gemütlichen Bett.
In meiner Familie sind die Aufgaben im Haushalt aufgeteilt. Meine Mama muss den Müll hinausbringen und sich um den Garten kümmern. Mein Papa muss kochen und die Wäsche waschen. Mein großer Bruder, meine Schwester und ich müssen unsere Betten machen und unsere Zimmer aufräumen.
Außerdem muss mein älterer Bruder meiner Mama im Garten helfen und das Auto meiner Eltern waschen. Zusätzlich muss mein Bruder auch meiner Schwester zwei Mal pro Woche bei ihren Französischhausaufgaben helfen. Gestern allerdings konnte er das nicht, weil er krank war.
Meine Schwester muss jeden Tag den Tisch decken, mit dem Hund spazieren gehen und meinem Bruder bei seinen Mathematikhausaufgaben helfen.
Was mich betrifft, räume ich immer den Tisch ab, bügle die Wäsche und helfe meiner Schwester bei ihren Englischhausaufgaben. Gestern allerdings habe ich das nicht getan, weil ich keine Lust hatte.

(Nele, 15 Jahre. Eisenstadt)

25. True, False or Not mentioned?

a. Eisenstadt is near Hungary.

b. Nele's neighbourhood has many good shops.

c. Her house is small.

d. Her bedroom is big.

e. Apart from her father, every member of her family shares the chores.

f. Nele and her siblings have to all tidy-up their respective rooms.

g. Yesterday her older brother was so busy that he couldn't help her sister with her homework.

h. Her sister does the ironing.

i. Nele helps her sister with her homework.

26. Who does what?

a. Who has to wash their parents' cars?

b. Who has to help with French homework?

c. Who has to take the rubbish out?

d. Who has to make their beds?

e. Who has to look after the garden?

f. Who didn't feel like helping her sister?

g. Who does the laundry?

h. Who has to walk the dog?

i. Who was sick yesterday?

j. Who always clears the table?

27. Find the German equivalent for the following items in Nele's text

a. outskirts	f. desk	k. to help	p. I clear the table
b. there aren't	g. we share	l. to wash	q. lay the table
c. bright	h. chores	m. he wasn't able to	r. I help my sister
d. cosy	i. however	n. I iron the clothes	s. always
e. beautiful	j. our	o. unwell	t. because I didn't feel like it

28. Complete

a. I___ g______ n____________ m___ d___ H_____ s__________. *I usually walk the dog.*

b. I___ m_______ d____ T_______ d____________. *I have to lay the table.*

c. I___ h_______ n__________ g____________. *I didn't do anything.*

d. M______ B_________ m______ k___________. *My brother has to cook.*

e. I___ m_______ W________ w__________. *I have to do the laundry.*

f. M_____ ä__________ S____________ h_______ m_________ B________ j_______ T_____. *My older sister helps my brother every day.*

g. G__________ w________ i___ m__________ E_________ n_________ h_________. *Yesterday I didn't want to help my parents.*

h. N_________________ h_______ i___ m__________ B_________, a_________ g_________ k__________ i___ n___________. *I normally help my brother but yesterday I wasn't able to.*

i. I___ m___________ F__________ s______ d____ A___________ i___ H____________ a_______________. *In my family we all share the chores.*

29. Write two paragraphs for Franz in the first person singular (*ich*) and for Tina in the third person singular (*sie*)

Name and age	Franz, 13 years old	Tina, 17 years old
Description of neighbourhood	on the outskirts ugly many factories	in the city centre historic beautiful
What one can do in their neighbourhood	not much there is a stadium not many sports facilities	a lot for young people many green areas many sports facilities
What they do at the weekend	rides bike in the park goes to friend's house goes to cinema with his family	goes window shopping goes out with her friends goes partying
What they did last weekend	went to Jürgen's party did a lot of sports relaxed listening to music and watching TV	went sightseeing took many pictures went shopping visited her cousins
What they usually do to help at home	lays and clears the table makes his bed tidies up his room helps his father in the garden	prepares the food washes her mother's car makes her bed looks after her younger brother
What they didn't do yesterday and why	he didn't help his father in the garden because he was ill	she didn't wash her mother's car because she was busy

Question Skills Unit 7

English	German
Do you help your parents at home?	**Hilfst du deinen Eltern bei der Hausarbeit?**
How often do you help your parents?	**Wie oft hilfst du deinen Eltern?**
When do you help at home?	**Wann hilfst du deinen Eltern?**
What do you do to help your parents at home?	**Wie hilfst du deinen Eltern im Haushalt?**
What chores do you not like to do? Why?	**Welche Aufgaben gefallen dir? Warum?**
What does your brother/sister do to help at home?	**Was macht dein Bruder/deine Schwester im Haushalt?**
Who normally cooks in your family?	**Wer kocht normalerweise in deiner Familie?**
Who mows the lawn?	**Wer mäht den Rasen?**
Who washes your mum/dad's car?	**Wer wäscht das Auto deiner Mama/deines Papas?**
What did you do yesterday to help at home?	**Was hast du gestern im Haushalt gemacht?**
Why did you not help at home yesterday?	**Warum hast du gestern nicht im Haushalt geholfen?**

1. Sentence puzzle: rewrite the German

a. hast du im Was Haushalt gemacht gestern?

b. Wer Rasen den mäht?

c. deinen geholfen Wer hat gestern Eltern?

d. kocht Wer in deiner normalerweise Familie?

e. Haushalt oft hilfst Wie du Eltern im deinen?

f. hilfst du Wann Eltern deinen?

g. Familie das Auto wäscht in deiner Wer?

h. hast du gestern Warum nicht im geholfen Haushalt?

2. Match the sentences below with the questions in Exercise 1

a. Ich habe nichts gemacht, um ihnen zu helfen.

b. Mein Papa, weil er gerne kocht.

c. Mein Bruder, weil er den Garten liebt.

d. Ein- bis zweimal die Woche.

e. Ich habe das Geschirr gespült.

f. Weil ich krank war.

g. Das mache ich.

h. Wenn ich nicht viele Hausaufgaben habe.

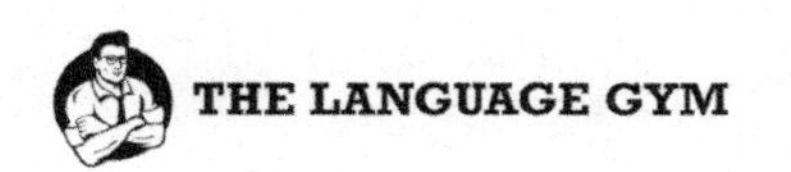

Ich heiße David. In meiner Familie ist die Hausarbeit aufgeteilt, was ich normal finde. Mein Papa bringt den Müll hinaus und kümmert sich um den Garten. Meine Mama kocht und wäscht die Wäsche. Mein großer Bruder, meine Schwester und ich müssen jeden Tag unsere Betten machen.
Zusätzlich muss mein Bruder Mark meinem Papa einmal pro Woche im Garten helfen. Gestern allerdings wollte er das nicht, weil er sauer war.
Meine Schwester Lisa muss meinem kleinen Bruder bei seinen Mathe- und Physikhausaufgaben helfen. Sie ist sehr intelligent und fleißig und hilft ihm täglich. Sie will Biologin werden wie meine Tante Renate. Gestern allerdings konnte Lisa ihm nicht helfen, weil sie krank war.
(David, 14 Jahre. Bern)

3. Answer the questions below as if you were David

a. Wer macht die Hausarbeit in eurer Familie?

b. Was musst du und deine Geschwister im Haushalt machen? Wie oft?

c. Was macht dein Papa im Haushalt?

d. Wem hilft dein Bruder Mark im Garten?

e. Warum hat dein Bruder gestern nicht geholfen?

f. Womit hilft deine Schwester deinem kleinen Bruder?

g. Wie ist Lisa?

h. Wer ist bereits Biologin in deiner Familie?

i. Warum konnte deine Schwester eurem Bruder gestern nicht helfen?

4. Translate into English

a. Wer war gestern krank?

b. Was machst du im Haushalt?

c. Wie oft hilfst du im Haushalt?

d. Wer kocht bei euch zu Hause?

e. Wer räumt dein Zimmer auf?

f. Was hast du letztes Wochenende im Haushalt gemacht?

g. Welche Art von Hausarbeit hasst du?

h. Erzähl mir von deiner täglichen Routine.

i. Um wie viel Uhr hast du gestern das Geschirr gespült.

j. Warum hast du gestern deinen Eltern nicht im Haushalt geholfen?

5. Complete with the missing words

a. _______ heißt du?

b. Wie ________ bist du?

c. _______ wohnst du?

d. Mit wem _________ du zusammen?

e. In welchem Teil der __________ wohnst du?

f. Was _________ du im Haushalt?

g. Gibt es ____________Geschäfte?

h. Welche ______________ gibt es in deiner Gegend?

i. Was hast du gestern in deiner Gegend _________?

j. Was hat dir am besten ___________?

k. Was __________ du nächstes Wochenende in deiner Nachbarschaft machen?

l. Sie liebt Mathe und ist sehr _____________.

tolle	wie	Restaurants	gemacht	gefallen	machst
wohnst	wo	alt	Stadt	wirst	intelligent

Unit 8
Describing a typical day at school

In this unit you will learn:
- To say what you have to do at school
- To say what you can and cannot do
- To say where certain actions are allowed and where they are not

Key sentence patterns:
- Verb phrase + time of the day
- Place (prepositional phrase) + modal verb + verb phrase (infinitive)

Grammar:
- Use of present tense modal verbs in their positive and negative forms

UNIT 8: Describing a typical day at school

<table>
<tr><td colspan="2">Die Pause ist [Breaktime is at]
Ich mache außerschulische Aktivitäten
[I do extra-curricular activities]
Der Unterricht beginnt [Lessons start]
Der Unterricht endet [Lessons finish]
Das Mittagessen ist [Lunchtime is at]</td><td rowspan="2">um</td><td>sieben Uhr
acht Uhr
neun Uhr
zehn Uhr
elf Uhr</td><td>morgens
[in the morning]</td></tr>
<tr><td>Die erste / zweite / letzte Stunde
[The first / second / last lesson]
Mathematik [maths]</td><td>ist [is]
habe ich
[I have]</td><td>zwei Uhr
drei Uhr
vier Uhr</td><td>nachmittags
[in the afternoon]</td></tr>
<tr><td colspan="2">Ich gehe [I go]</td><td rowspan="3">mittags
[at noon]</td><td colspan="2">in den Schachklub [to the chess club]
in die Schule [to school]
nach Hause [home]</td></tr>
<tr><td colspan="2">Ich komme [I arrive]</td><td colspan="2">in der Schule an [at school]</td></tr>
<tr><td colspan="2">Ich mache meine Hausaufgaben
[I do my homework]</td><td colspan="2">in der Bibliothek [in the library]</td></tr>
</table>

<table>
<tr><td rowspan="2">In meiner Schule
[In my school]</td><td rowspan="2">muss man
[one has to...]
darf man
[one is allowed to...]
darf man nicht
[one must not...]
kann man [one can...]
kann man nicht
[one cannot...]
muss ich [I have to...]
darf ich
[I'm allowed to...]
kann ich (nicht)
[I can -not-...]</td><td colspan="2">dem Lehrer/der Lehrerin zuhören [listen to the teacher]
im Klassenzimmer essen [eat in the classroom]
rauchen [smoke]
sich in der Kantine anstellen [queue up in the canteen]
während des Unterrichts auf die Toilette gehen
[go to the toilet during lessons]
aufzeigen, bevor man spricht
[raise one's hand before speaking]
Kaugummi kauen [chew chewing gum]
das Handy benutzen [use one's mobile phone]</td></tr>
<tr><td>eine Schuluniform [school uniform]
kurze Röcke [short skirts]
Make-up [make-up]
Ohrringe [earrings]
Sportschuhe [trainers]</td><td>tragen [...wear]</td></tr>
<tr><td colspan="4">Author's note: The word order in German is relatively flexible due to the various case endings. If some information is very important, you may move it to the front of the sentence. Usually, this information is also emphasized vocally. The conjugated verb in a sentence however is always in second position, no matter how we begin the sentence.</td></tr>
</table>

1. Match

Ich gehe nach Hause.	I eat in the canteen.
Ich mache meine Hausaufgaben.	I go home.
Ich gehe in die Kantine.	I go to the canteen.
Ich esse in der Kantine.	Break is at noon.
Die Pause ist mittags.	I do my homework.
Die letzte Stunde ist...	The last lesson is…
Ich habe Englisch.	I go to the library.
Ich höre dem Lehrer/der Lehrerin zu.	I arrive at school.
Ich gehe in die Bibliothek.	I have English.
Ich komme in der Schule an.	I listen to the teacher.

2. Missing letters

a. Die e_ste Stunde ist u_ neun Uhr.

b. Ich _omme in der Schule an.

c. Ich ge_e nach Hause.

d. Ich mache Hausauf_aben.

e. Ich höre der Lehrer_n zu.

f. Ich unterhal_e mich mit meinen Sc_ulkollegen und -kolleginnen.

g. Ich stehe Schlange in der Ka_tine.

3. Complete with the missing words

a. Normalerweise k_ _ _ _ ich um acht Uhr dreißig in der Schule an.

b. Montags habe ich M_ _ _ _ _ _ _ _ _ _ in der ersten Stunde.

c. Danach haben wir eine P_ _ _ _.

d. In der Pause u_ _ _ _ _ _ _ _ _ _ ich mich mit meinen Schulkollegen.

e. Dann habe ich G_ _ _ _ _ _ _ _ _ _.

f. Geschichte gefällt mir nicht, w_ _ _ es langweilig ist.

g. Normalerweise esse ich Hühnchen mit Reis in der K_ _ _ _ _ _.

h. Die letzte S_ _ _ _ _ endet um drei Uhr.

4. Put the actions below in chronological order

Ich komme um 8 in der Schule an	
Der Unterricht beginnt	
Der Unterricht endet	
Ich stehe auf	1
Ich habe eine Pause	
Ich dusche mich	
Ich gehe nach Hause	
Ich ziehe die Uniform an	
Ich esse in der Kantine	
Ich esse mit meinen Eltern zu Abend	

5. Spot and correct the grammar/spelling mistakes

a. Ich gehe in Schachklub.

b. Ich komme um acht in Schule an.

c. In der ersten Stunden habe ich Deutsch.

d. In das Pause.

e. Ich gehe nach die Schule in die Bibliothek.

f. Ich gebe nach Hause.

g. Ich darf ich nicht kurze Röcke trägen.

h. Ich darf kein Ohrringe tragen.

i. Ich muss eine Uniform trage.

j. Die letzter Stunde ist um drei.

k. In der zweiten Stunden habe ich Biologie.

l. Die Unterricht endet um vier.

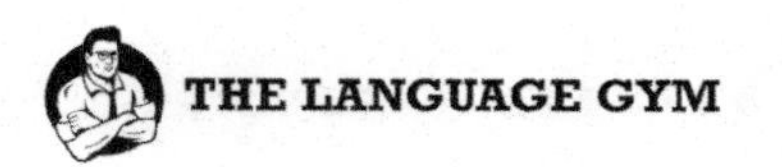

6. Gapped translation

a. In der ersten Stunde habe ich Englisch.	*My ________________ lesson is English.*
b. Freitags habe ich Informatik in der letzen Stunde.	*On Fridays my last lesson is ___________.*
c. Die Pause ist um halb zehn.	*Break is at ________________________.*
e. Während der Pause spiele ich Basketball.	*During break I play _________________.*
f. In meiner Schule darf man keine Ohrringe tragen.	*In my school one cannot wear __________.*
g. Ich mache meine Hausaufgaben normalerweise in der Bibliothek.	*I usually do my homework in the ________.*
h. In der Kantine muss man sich anstellen.	*You have to______________ in the canteen.*
i. Ich muss eine Schuluniform tragen.	*I have to wear a _________ __________.*

7. Which of the following are unlikely to be REAL school rules? Write I for *improbable* or P for *probable* next to the rule below

a. Man darf nicht rauchen.

b. Man darf in der Klasse essen.

c. Man darf keine Ohrringe tragen.

d. Man darf in der Stunde Kaugummi kauen.

e. Man muss die Lehrer und Lehrerinnen respektieren.

f. Man darf Haustiere in die Schule mitnehmen.

g. Man darf nicht lernen in der Schule.

h. Man kann die Lehrer und Lehrerinnen beleidigen.

i. Man muss die Mitschüler und Mitschülerinnen ärgern.

8. Sentence puzzle: rewrite the sentences in the correct order

a. nicht Man darf rauchen.

b. Man muss eine Schuluniform tragen.

c. muss Kantine Man sich der anstellen in.

d. verwenden Man das darf nicht Handy.

e. Hausaufgaben Du machen deine musst.

f. um Der beginnt Uhr Unterricht acht.

g. Kaugummi Man keinen darf kauen.

h. Ohrringe Man keine darf tragen.

i. Lehrer Man muss die und respektieren Lehrerinnen.

9. Complete with a suitable word

a. Man darf __________ rauchen.

b. Der Unterricht __________ um acht.

c. Ich nehme den ________ nach Hause.

d. Zu Mittag ________ ich in der Kantine.

e. Man muss sich in der _______ anstellen.

f. Ich mache meine Hausaufgaben in der ________________.

g. Man muss die Lehrer und Lehrerinnen _________.

h. Man muss seine ________________ machen.

i. Man darf keinen __________________ kauen.

j. Der Unterricht __________________ um acht.

k. Ich __________ in den Schachklub.

l. Um zwei Uhr _______ ich Geografie und danach ________________.

DIE SCHULFÄCHER
(SCHOOL SUBJECTS)

Chemie	**gefällt mir (nicht)** *[I -don't- like]*
Deutsch *[German]*	
Englisch	
Französisch	
Geografie	
Informatik *[IT]*	
Kunst *[art]*	
Mathematik	
Musik	
Physik	
Religion	
Spanisch	
Sport	

10. Translate into English

a. In der ersten Stunde habe ich Englisch.

b. Mein Lieblingsfach ist Physik.

c. Ich hasse *[I hate]* Chemie.

d. Informatik ist ein spannendes Fach.

e. Französisch ist langweilig.

f. Ich liebe den Deutschunterricht.

g. Montags habe ich Sport in der letzten Stunde.

h. Meine Mathematiklehrerin ist sehr streng.

i. In Musik müssen wir hart arbeiten.

j. Religion habe ich einmal pro Woche.

k. Mein Geografielehrer ist sehr sympathisch.

11. Faulty translation

a. Man darf im Unterricht nicht essen.	*One must eat during lessons.*
b. Man darf keine Ohrringe tragen.	*One must not wear trainers.*
c. Bevor man spricht, muss man aufzeigen.	*One must raise their hand before moving around.*
d. Man darf nicht Kaugummi kauen.	*One must not use the mobile phone.*
e. Man darf nicht in der Klasse rauchen.	*One must not run in the corridors.*
f. Man darf keine Turnschuhe tragen.	*One must not wear smart shoes.*
g. Man darf kein Make-up tragen.	*One must not wear glasses.*
h. Man muss den Lehrern zuhören.	*One must ignore the teachers.*

12. Spot and correct the nonsense sentences

a. Man darf in der Schule rauchen.

b. Man muss aufzeigen, bevor man spricht.

c. Der Unterricht beginnt um 5 Uhr morgens.

d. In der Pause mache ich Sightseeing.

e. Man muss in der Schule schlafen.

f. Man darf keinen Kaugummi kauen.

g. Die letzte Stunde endet um halb vier.

h. Ich spiele gerne Basketball in der Pause mit meiner Oma.

13. Split sentences

Man darf keine	bevor man spricht.
Man darf das Handy	ist um halb vier.
Auf den Gängen	Ohrringe tragen.
Man muss aufzeigen,	um acht Uhr.
Ich muss meine	ist total nett.
Der Unterricht beginnt	nicht benutzen.
In der Pause spiele ich	darf man nicht laufen.
Die letzte Stunde	oft Basketball.
Meine Deutschlehrerin	Hausaufgaben machen.

14. Gapped translation

a. Man darf im Unterricht _____ __________.	*One must not eat during lessons.*
b. Man darf keine __________ tragen.	*One must not wear earrings.*
c. Man muss ____________, bevor man spricht.	*One has to raise one's hand before speaking.*
d. Man darf nicht ____________ kauen.	*One must not chew gum.*
e. Man darf auf den Gängen ______ _________.	*One must not run in the corridors.*
f. Man darf keine ___________ tragen.	*One must not wear trainers.*
g. Man darf kein Make-up ___________.	*One must not wear make-up.*
h. Man muss die _____________ beachten.	*One has to respect the rules.*
i. Man muss die Lehrer und Lehrerinnen ____________.	*One has to respect the teachers.*

Emma: In meiner Schule darf man keine Ohrringe tragen.

Tobias: In meiner Schule muss man viel lernen.

Karl: In meiner Schule darf man mittags nicht im Klassenzimmer essen.

Dietmar: In meiner Schule muss man aufzeigen bevor man spricht.

Johannes: In meiner Schule darf man nicht auf die Toilette gehen während des Unterrichts.

Franz: In meiner Schule darf man das Handy nicht benützen.

Peter: In meiner Schule darf man weder kurze Röcke noch Sportschuhe tragen.

Susanne: In meiner Schule darf man weder auf dem Gang essen noch Kaugummi kauen.

Ruth: In meiner Schule kann man nicht viel Sport machen. Schwimmen kann man auch nicht, weil es kein Schwimmbecken gibt.

Thomas: In meiner Schule muss man jeden Tag Hausaufgaben machen.

Lotte: In meiner Schule darf man kein Make-up tragen.

15. Read the box on the left and find someone who, in their school...

a. …cannot do a lot of sports

b. …must not eat in a classroom at lunchtime

c. …must not chew gum

d. …must not talk without raising their hand

e. …has to study a lot

f. …must not go to the toilet during lessons

g. …must not wear make-up

h. …must not wear short skirts

i. …must not use their mobile phone

j. …must do homework every day

k. …must not wear trainers

l. …must not wear earrrings

16. Wordsearch: find the German translation of the sentences below and write them as shown in the example

N E S I C H E N F W W D N W R D H N R J
R E D L B Q C N N J L J W E I C E E I G
G Y L B O Z F A A Y J G G E H G F L R A
G E R L V C J K R Y Q M P B A C O L T T
X J L I E P M N S V E A Q R B F U G E L
D I E S A T U A G X U M T K R A B A X U
A O G I S K S M N S G P V V E Q S N R H
P Y W C H L T N E D U T K Z N Q J Y U C
P V X E L J Q I A E A P W G S T B J J S
D Z N G U I S F K H T R D A E S D Q E N
I U K G D T D A O E C U F D Y A W T D V
J I U T U Z M V S Y Z I F N S G L H E O
E W C M D A Q Z L I L W S V I T D D N Z
K A U G U M M I K A U E N P L C N Y T T
Z X E G S P O J H J K S J V Z L H O A F
V J H Z M E O C I K Z A G G E B G T G B
F H Y C P G F O N J V O C R W Z G G E S
Y D N A H L K S V H T R K M F E P I Q P
G N P R B S R S O C C H N X J F F W E S
G R T I Y L Q P N P I H O D J R L Q U B

*e.g. chew chewing gum — **Kaugummi kauen***

a. one can

b. wear make-up

c. sich anstellen

d. one must not

e. every day

f. break is at

g. mobile phone

h. smoke

i. school day

17. Complete the two texts with the options below

a. Ich werde dir nun von einem _______________ Schultag erzählen. Ich gehe in London in __________ in die Schule. Der _____________ beginnt um Viertel nach acht. Montags habe ich Kunst in der ____________ Stunde. Mir gefällt das Fach Kunst sehr gut, ____ die _____________ nett ist. Danach haben wir eine __________ bis um zehn. In der Pause spiele ich _______________ mit meinen Freunden. Dann habe ich Deutsch. Ich liebe den Deutschunterricht, weil er Spaß macht und ich viel ___________. Die Mittagspause _____ um Viertel vor eins. Die __________ Stunde beginnt um zehn vor zwei. Normalerweise ________ ich so um halb vier nach dem ________________ von der Schule nach Hause. Ich liebe Tennis. Mir ________ meine Schule sehr.

gehe	Tennisklub	ist	gefällt	lerne	England	ersten
Schach	Pause	Unterricht	letzte	Lehrerin	typischen	weil

b. Ich werde dir nun von einem typischen Tag in meiner Schule _____________. Ich gehe in eine internationale ___________ in Wien. Der Unterricht beginnt um zwanzig vor acht. In der _________ Stunde habe ich Physik. Dann ________ wir Musik. Mir gefällt dieses _____ nicht, weil es langweilig ist. Außerdem ist mir der ____________ unsympathisch. Die Pause ___________ um Viertel nach zehn und ________ um halb elf. __________ haben wir Chemie. Mittags ________ ich mit meinen Freunden in der Kantine. Normalerweise esse ich __________ mit Reis. Die letzte ________ beginnt um halb zwei. Mir gefällt ______ Schule nicht. Ich hasse es zu __________, obwohl ich weiß, dass es sehr wichtig für meine Zukunft ist.

ersten	erzählen	Schule	haben	Fach	Danach	meine
Stunde	esse	Lehrer	beginnt	Hähnchen	endet	lernen

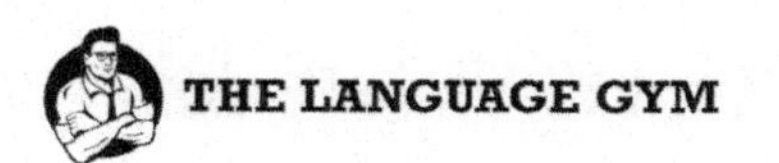

Hallo, ich heiße Jens. So sieht ein typischer Schultag bei mir aus: Normalerweise komme ich gegen acht in der Schule an, also circa eine viertel Stunde vor Unterrichtsbeginn.

Montags habe ich in der ersten Stunde Geografie. Ich kann Geografie nicht ausstehen, weil die Lehrerin langweilig ist und wir nie Gruppenarbeit machen. Dann haben wir eine Pause.

In der Pause spiele ich Basketball mit meinen Freunden. Danach haben wir Deutsch. Ich liebe das Fach Deutsch, weil der Lehrer witzig ist, wir spielerisch den Stoff durchmachen und ich viel lerne. Später habe ich Englisch. Dieses Fach macht mir keinen Spaß, weil der Lehrer streng ist und sehr viel schreit. Anschließend ist Mittagspause.

Ich verbringe die Mittagspause mit meinen Freunden in der Kantine. Wir essen und plaudern dabei. Letzten Montag habe ich ein Schnitzel mit Kartoffelsalat gegessen und eine Cola getrunken. Cola ist nicht sehr gesund, aber hin und wieder gönne ich mir eine. In der letzten Stunde haben wir Sport, was mein absolutes Lieblingsfach ist.

In meiner Schule gibt es strenge Regeln: man muss eine Schuluniform tragen, man darf das Handy nicht benutzen und man muss jeden Tag Hausaufgaben machen. Wenn man gegen diese Regeln verstößt, sind die Konsequenzen schwerwiegend. Gestern habe ich meine Hausaufgaben nicht gemacht und musste deshalb eine Stunde das Büro unserer Direktorin aufräumen. Das war irre langweilig.

(Jens, 13 Jahre. Bonn)

18. Find the German equivalent

a. normally I arrive at school
b. beginning of lessons
c. because we never do group work
d. during break
e. later I have English
f. it is lunch break
g. we eat and chat
h. I treat myself to one
i. which is by far my favourite subject
j. the consequences are severe

19. Correct the statements

a. Jens loves geography.
b. At lunchtime he plays basketball.
c. He learns little in the German lessons.
d. The English teacher never shouts.
e. Every Monday he has Schnitzel with potato salad.
f. He hates sports.
g. He never drinks Coke.
h. Every Friday he has to tidy up the headteacher's office.

20. Correct the mistakes in these sentences from Jens's text and then translate them

a. Normalerweise komme ich in der Schule an.
b. In der spiele ich Basketball.
c. Danach wir Deutsch.
d. Essen und plaudern dabei.
e. In der letzten haben wir Sport.
f. Man muss Schuluniform tragen.
g. Man muss Tag Hausaufgaben machen.
h. Wenn man diese Regeln verstößt...
i. ...sind die schwerwiegend.
j. Ich musste das unserer Direktorin aufräumen.

21. Answer the following questions

a. When does he get to school?
b. When do the lessons start?
c. What does he do during break?
d. What is his German teacher like?
e. How much does he learn in German?
f. What 2 things make him dislike English?
g. What 2 things did he eat last Monday?
h. Does he drink Cola very often?
i. Name 2 school rules he mentions.
j. What happens if one breaks the rules?
k. What did he do wrong yesterday?
l. What were the consequences?

Hallo, ich bin Pia. Ich werde dir nun von einem typischen Schultag erzählen. Normalerweise komme ich so gegen halb neun in der Schule an. Der Unterricht beginnt um zwanzig vor neun.

Freitags habe ich in der ersten Stunde Geschichte. Ich mag Geschichte nicht, weil mir die Lehrerin unsympathisch ist und wir nie etwas Lustiges im Unterricht machen. Ich lerne sehr wenig. Dann haben wir eine Pause. In der Pause spiele ich mit meinen Freunden am Schulhof und esse etwas in der Kantine. Nach der Pause habe ich Französisch. Ich liebe Französisch, weil mein Lehrer freundlich ist und uns immer Witze erzählt. Außerdem lerne ich etwas, indem ich mich mit meinen Freunden unterhalte. Ich lerne sehr viel. Dann habe ich das Fach Kunst, was mir gar nicht gefällt. Mein Lehrer erklärt nicht gut und hat oft schlechte Laune. Dann ist Mittagspause.

In der Mittagspause spiele ich mit meinen Freunden Fußball. Danach essen wir gemeinsam und erzählen uns Witze. Gestern hatte ich Fischstäbchen und dazu einen Orangensaft. In der letzten Stunde habe ich Biologie, was mein absolutes Lieblingsfach ist, weil die Lehrerin so einen tollen Unterricht macht.

Grundsätzlich sind die Regeln in meiner Schule sehr strikt: Man muss eine Schuluniform tragen, man muss pünktlich sein, man darf keine Handys benutzen, man darf nicht rauchen oder auf dem Gang laufen. Außerdem darf man den Lift nicht benutzen. Es ist auch wichtig im Unterricht aufzuzeigen, bevor man etwas sagt. Wenn man die Regeln bricht, sind die Konsequenzen schwerwiegend. Letzte Woche war ich fünf Minuten zu spät in der Schule und musste dann das Büro unserer Direktorin aufräumen. Das war mühsam. **(Pia, 12 Jahre. Vaduz)**

23. Find in the last paragraph of Pia's text the German equivalent of the following items

a. The rules in my school are strict.

b. One has to wear a school uniform.

c. One must not use a mobile phone.

d. One must not smoke.

e. One must not run.

f. It is important to raise one's hand before speaking.

g. The consequences are severe.

22. Complete the sentences below based on the text

a. My name is Pia. I am going to talk to you about a typical _________ _____.

b. I usually get to school at around ______

c. On Fridays my first lesson is _______________.

d. I don't like history because the teacher is very _________________ and we don't do anything ______________.

e. I have French after ______________.

f. The French teacher is friendly and tells us _______________.

g. I don't like art a lot because the teacher _____________ well and is often in a bad _____________.

h. I spend lunch break playing _________ with my friends.

i. We _________ and tell each other jokes.

j. Yesterday I ate _______________ and drank an ____________________.

k. My _____________ lesson is Biology. I love the teacher because her classes are __________.

24. Correct the false statements

a. Pia isst nichts in der Mittagspause.

b. Pia hasst Französisch.

c. Der Kunstlehrer hat immer guter Laune.

d. Pia isst keinen Fisch.

e. Pia hasst Biologie.

f. Es gibt keine Schulregeln.

g. Pia ist immer pünktlich.

25. Translate the last paragraph of Pia's text into English

26. Match questions and answers

Wie kommst du in die Schule?	Weil sie sehr hilfsbereit ist.
Um wie viel Uhr kommst du in der Schule an?	Ja, wir machen Leichtathletik.
Was hast du freitags in der ersten Stunde?	Ich fahre mit dem Rad.
Wer ist deine Lieblingslehrerin?	Ich esse und plaudere mit meinen Freunden.
Warum?	So ungefähr gegen halb neun am Morgen.
Was machst du in der Pause?	Man darf nicht rauchen oder auf dem Gang laufen.
Macht ihr Sport in deiner Schule?	Meine Deutschlehrerin.
Um wie viel Uhr kommst du nach Hause?	In der ersten Stunde habe ich Kunst.
Welche Regeln gibt es in deiner Schule?	Dass man kein Make-up tragen darf.
Welche Regel magst du am Wenigsten?	Um halb fünf nachmittags.

27. Translate into German

a. *I arrive at school at around 8.* I____ k_______ u___ c____ a__ U___ i_ d__ S_______ a_.

b. *Today my first lesson is English.* H____ h____ i__ E__________ i_ d___ e________ S______.

c. *Afterwards, I have German.* D_________ h_______ i____ D_____________.

d. *Lunch starts at 12 o'clock.* D____ M______________ b________ u_ z________ U____.

e. *My last lesson is ICT.* I_ d___ l_________ S_________ h_____ i____ I___________.

f. *I hate this subject.* I____ h______ d____________ F_________.

g. *In my school there are many rules.* I_ m_________ S________ g____ e__ v_____ R________.

h. *One must not wear make-up.* M_____ d_____ k_______ M______________ t_________.

28. a) Translate the two paragraphs into German

b) Write a 150-250 words text about a typical school day of yours, listing five key rules

1. I usually arrive at school at 8.15. On Mondays, my first lesson is history. I love history because the teacher is friendly. Then I have break until 9.30. During break I usually chat with my best friend Bernd or with my girlfriend. My second lesson is English. I don't like this subject. Lunch starts at 12. After lunch I have two more lessons: English and maths. I don't like these subjects because they are too hard. In my school, the rules are very strict. One must not run in the corridors; one must not wear make-up or earrings; one must not use the lift and one must not talk without putting their hand up.

2. The rules of my school are very strict. First of all, one has to arrive at 7.45 sharp *[pünktlich]*. Secondly, one has to wear a uniform. I hate it, because I must not wear my favourite baseball cap *[Baseballkappe]* and trainers. Also, I must not chew gum and use my mobile phone. I also must not play videogames during break and lunch break. In class, one must not talk without raising one's hand and must not go to the toilet. What I like about my school, however, is that the teachers are nice, I learn a lot and one can do a lot of sports.

Question Skills Unit 8

English	Deutsch
What is a typical school day like?	**Wie sieht ein typischer Schultag bei dir aus?**
At what time do classes start?	**Um wie viel Uhr beginnt der Unterricht?**
At what time do classes end?	**Um wieviel Uhr endet der Unterricht?**
How many lessons do you have per day?	**Wie viele Stunden hast du pro Tag?**
What is your first / last class?	**Was hast du in der ersten / letzten Stunde?**
What extra-curricular activities can one do in your school?	**Welche außerschulischen Aktivitäten werden in deiner Schule angeboten?**
At what time do you leave school?	**Um wie viel Uhr gehst du/fährst du von der Schule nach Hause?**
Which is your favourite subject?	**Was ist dein Lieblingsfach?**
Which subjects can't you stand? Why?	**Welches Fach kannst du nicht ausstehen? Warum?**
Who is your favourite teacher?	**Wer ist dein Lieblingslehrer (masc.)/-lehrerin? (fem.)**
What are you not allowed to do in your school?	**Was darfst du in deiner Schule nicht tun?**
What are the rules in your school?	**Welche Regeln gibt es in deiner Schule?**
Is one allowed to wear make-up?	**Darf man Make-up tragen?**
Are you allowed to use a mobile phone?	**Darfst du ein Handy benutzen?**
Do you have to queue up in the canteen?	**Musst du dich in der Kantine anstellen?**

1. Complete with the missing words

a. Um wie viel ____ stehst du normalerweise auf?

b. Um wie viel Uhr ___________ der Unterricht?

c. Wie viele Stunden ________ du pro Tag?

d. Wann kommst du _____ der Schule an?

e. Wie sieht ein typischer Schultag bei ___ aus?

f. Darf man ____________ tragen?

g. Wer ist ______ Lieblingslehrer?

h. Was ________ man nicht in deiner Schule?

i. Was ist dein _______________?

j. Welche außerschulischen Aktivitäten ______ es?

Make-up	gibt	Uhr	dein	darf
hast	in	beginnt	Lieblingsfach	dir

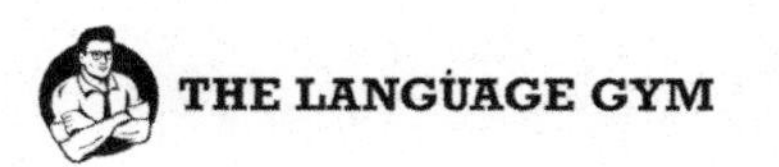

2. Write the questions to the answers below

a. ______________________________?	Der Unterricht beginnt um halb neun.
b. ______________________________?	Ich habe fünf Stunden.
c. ______________________________?	Deutsch ist mein Lieblingsfach, weil es Spass macht.
d. ______________________________?	Ich fahre um fünf mit dem Bus nach Hause.
e. ______________________________?	Ich kann das Fach Kunst nicht ausstehen, weil es langweilig ist.
f. ______________________________?	Mein Deutschlehrer, weil er sehr witzig ist.
g. ______________________________?	Man darf nicht rauchen oder das Handy benützen.

3. Guided translation

a. *At what time do lessons end?*	U___ w___ v___ U___ e_____ d___ U___________?
b. *What are the rules in your school?*	W_____ R_________ g_____ e_____ i_ d________ S_____?
c. *What is your favourite subject?*	W____ i______ d________ L__________________?
d. *Is one allowed to wear make-up?*	D______ m_____ M____________ t________?
e. *How many lessons do you have per day?*	W___ v____ S_________ h_______ d__ p____ T____?
f. *What is a typical school day like?*	W___ s________ e___ t__________ S___________ a__?
g. *Who is your favourite teacher (fem.)?*	W___ i___ d______ L___________________?
h. *Is one allowed to wear short skirts?*	D_______ m_____ k________ R_________ t_________?

4. Spot and correct the errors in the sentences below. HINT: sometimes words are missing

a. Was hast in der letzten Stunde?

b. Wie viele Stunden hast du Tag?

c. Wann beginnt Unterricht?

d. Darf man kurz Röcke tragen?

e. Darfst ein Handy?

f. Was dein Lieblingsfach?

g. Welche außerschulischen Aktivitäten werden?

h. Wer sind deiner Lieblingslehrerin?

i. Welches kannst du nicht ausstehen?

j. Um wie viel ist die Schule aus?

k. Warum magst du Mathematiks nicht?

5. Translate into German

a. How many lessons do you have?

b. What is your favourite subject?

c. Why can't you stand maths?

d. Who is your favourite teacher?

e. What subjects do you not like?

f. At what time do lessons start and end?

g. What is a typical school day like?

h. What is one not allowed to do in your school?

i. Is one allowed to smoke?

j. Is one allowed use the mobile phone?

k. At what time do you leave school?

l. Do you have to queue up in the canteen?

Vocab Revision Workout 4

1. Match

Ich muss den Tisch abräumen.	I have to water the flowers.
Ich muss das Auto waschen.	I have to clear the table.
Ich mache normalerweise das Bett.	I have to mop the floor.
Ich muss den Boden wischen.	I usually make the bed.
Ich muss den Tisch decken.	I have to walk the dog.
Ich muss mit dem Hund spazieren gehen.	I have to help my brother.
Ich muss meinem Bruder helfen.	I have to lay the table.
Ich muss die Blumen gießen.	I have to wash the car.

2. Translate the sentences below into German using
Ich kann (nicht) + infinitive

a. I can go out with my friends.

b. I cannot play on my computer.

c. I can ride my bike in the park.

d. I can go to bed late.

e. I cannot have breakfast.

f. I can go to school by bike.

3. Split sentences

Ich habe ein Steak	im Fernsehen angesehen.
Ich habe mich beim	gegangen.
Ich habe nichts	aufgestanden.
Ich habe ein rosa	mit Pommes Frittes gegessen.
Ich habe mir ein Fußballspiel	gegangen.
	Kleid gekauft.
Ich bin ins	Lesen entspannt.
Ich bin Rad fahren	gespielt.
Ich bin früh	Einkaufszentrum gegangen.
Ich bin wandern	gemacht.
Ich habe Basketball	

4. Sentence puzzle: rewrite the sentences correctly

a. *Last weekend we went to the cinema together.*
zusammen Wochenende sind Letztes ins Kino gegangen wir.

b. *Yesterday I got up early and took many photos.*
bin Gestern ich früh und habe Fotos aufgestanden gemacht viele.

c. *I relaxed listening to music before going to bed.*
gegangen Bevor beim ich ins Bett bin, habe mich Musikhören entspannt ich.

d. *On Sunday we went hiking in the mountains.*
Berge Am Sonntag sind wir in gegangen wandern die.

5. Translate into English

a. Ich bin ins Schwimmbad gegangen.

b. Ich werde einkaufen gehen.

c. Wir sind aufs Land gefahren.

d. Wir haben Sport gemacht.

e. Wir werden Rad fahren gehen.

f. Ich bin schwimmen gegangen.

g. Ich werde ins Stadion gehen.

h. Gestern haben wir Basketball gespielt.

i. Wir sind Sightseeing gegangen.

j. Ich habe viele Fotos gemacht.

6. Complete the table below with the missing verb forms, as shown in the example

PAST (Perfect Tense)	PRESENT (Present Tense)	FUTURE (Future Tense)
*Ich **bin** ins Kino **gegangen.***	*Ich **gehe** ins Kino.*	*Ich **werde** ins Kino **gehen.***
1.	Wir gehen einkaufen.	Wir werden einkaufen gehen.
2.	3.	Ich werde meine Aufgaben machen.
Ich bin Rad fahren gegangen.	Ich gehe Rad fahren.	4.
5.	Ich gehe ins Stadion.	6.
7.	Ich reite.	8.
Ich bin auf eine Party gegangen.	Ich gehe auf eine Party.	9.
10.	11.	Ich werde ins Schwimmbad gehen.
12.	Ich gehe skateboarden.	Ich werde skateboarden gehen.

7. Faulty translation: correct the mistakes in the translations below

a. Morgen werde ich zu Hause bleiben. *Tomorrow I am going to do chores.*

b. Nächsten Samstag gehe ich ins Kino. *Next Friday I am going to watch a film.*

c. Nächsten Donnerstag gehen wir Rad fahren. *Next Thursday we are going to go horse riding.*

d. Nächsten Montag gehe ich joggen. *Next Tuesday I am going jogging.*

e. Freitags spielen meine Eltern Tennis. *On Fridays my parents play golf.*

f. Nächstes Wochenende werde ich wandern gehen. *Next weekend I will go skiing.*

g. Meine Schwester wird schwimmen gehen. *My brother is going to go to the beach.*

h. Nächste Woche werde ich spazieren gehen. *Next weekend I am going bike riding.*

8. Complete with the missing letters

a. M_ _ g_ _ _ _ _ _ m_ _ _ _ N_ _ _ _ _ _ _ _ _ _ _ _ _. *I like my neighbourhood.*

b. M_ _ k_ _ _ g_ _ e_ _ _ _ g_ _ _ _. *One can eat well.*

c. M_ _ k_ _ _ e_ _ _ _ _ _ _ _ _ g_ _ _ _. *One can go shopping.*

d. M_ _ k_ _ _ S_ _ _ _ m_ _ _ _ _. *One can do sports.*

e. M_ _ k_ _ _ R_ _ f_ _ _ _ _ g_ _ _ _. *One can ride a bike.*

f. G_ _ _ _ _ _ s_ _ _ w_ _ i_ _ K_ _ _ g_ _ _ _ _ _ _. *Yesterday we went to the cinema.*

Unit 9

Making after-school plans with a friend

In this unit you will learn:

- To suggest an activity to do with someone else
- To accept or refuse an invitation

Key sentence patterns:

- Question word + modal + infinitive
- *Ich würde gerne* + infinitive
- Modals *müssen* or *können* + infinitive

Grammar:

- Use of modal verbs
- Interjections

UNIT 9: Making after-school plans with a friend

Was willst du *[What do you want...]* **Was wollt ihr** *[What do you all want...]*	**heute Morgen** *[this morning]* **heute Nachmittag** *[this afternoon]* **dieses Wochenende** *[this weekend]*	**machen?** *[...to do?]* **unternehmen?** *[...to do?]*

Heute *[Today]*	**würde ich gerne** *[I would like to]* **will ich** *[I want to]*	**eine Radtour machen.** *[go for a bike ride]* **einkaufen gehen.** *[go shopping]*

Würdest du gerne *[Would you like to...]*	**mit mir** *[with me]* **gemeinsam** *[together]*	**im Stadtzentrum spazieren gehen?** *[...go for a walk in the city centre]* **zu Peter nach Hause gehen?** *[...go to Peter's house]*
Hast du Lust, *[Do you fancy to...]*		**in den Park zu gehen?** *[...go to the park]*

Tut mir leid, *[Sorry,]*	**ich habe keine Lust** *[I don't fancy it]* **ich will nicht** *[I don't want to]*

Na ja, *[Well,]*	**ich habe schon Lust, aber** *[I fancy it, but]* **ich würde schon gerne, aber** *[I would like to, but]*	**ich kann nicht** *[I can't]*	
		ich muss *[I have to]*	**bei der Hausarbeit helfen** *[help with the chores]* **meiner Mutter helfen** *[help my mum]* **zu meinen Großeltern gehen** *[go to my grandparents' house]*

Ja, (sehr) gerne *[Yes, I'd love to]*	**Super!** *[Great!]*

Schon gut, *[It's fine]* **Kein Problem/ Macht nichts,** *[No problem]* **OK,**	**wir können** *[we can]*	**Peter zu Hause besuchen** *[go to Peter's house]* **auf der Spielekonsole spielen** *[play on the games console]* **zu Hause bleiben** *[stay at home]*

Super! **Passt!** *[That suits me]*	**Um wie viel Uhr** *[At what time]* **Wo** *[Where]*	**sollen wir uns treffen?** *[shall we meet?]* **treffen wir uns?** *[do we meet]*

Treffen wir uns *[Let's meet]* **Wir treffen uns** *[We are going to meet]*	**um** *[at]*	**Viertel nach** **halb** **zehn nach**	**fünf** **sieben** **sechs**	**vor** *[in front of]*	**Peters Haus** **dem Einkaufszentrum** **der Schule**

Super, wir sehen uns dann später! *[Great, see you later!]*	**Bis später/dann!** *[See you later!]*

1. Match

eine Radtour machen Basketball spielen sich einen Film ansehen ins Stadion gehen nichts machen Gewichte heben schwimmen gehen mit meiner Freundin ausgehen zu Hause bleiben mit meinem besten Freund ausgehen lernen einen Freund zu Hause besuchen	to not do anything to go out with my best friend to go for a bike ride to go out with my girlfriend to study to play basketball to lift weights to stay at home to watch a film to go to a friend's house to go swimming to go to the stadium

2. Complete with the appropriate option

a. Ich will eine Radtour __________.

b. Ich will nichts __________.

c. Ich würde gerne mit meinen Freunden __________.

d. Ich muss heute den Boden __________.

e. Wir müssen Papas Auto __________.

f. Wir wollen Stefan zu Hause __________.

g. Wir hätten Lust, uns einen Film im Kino anzu ________.

h. Ich will meiner Mutter bei der Hausarbeit __________.

helfen	machen
machen	sehen
wischen	waschen
ausgehen	besuchen

3. Put these activities into the right categories below

1. Schach spielen
2. lernen
3. den Boden wischen
4. Hausaufgaben machen
5. ins Kino gehen
6. bummeln gehen
7. schwimmen gehen
8. Gewichte heben
9. einen Aufsatz schreiben
10. Gedichte auswendig lernen
11. den Tisch decken
12. für eine Prüfung lernen
13. Videospiele spielen
14. das Bett machen
15. sich ein Tennismatch ansehen
16. das Auto waschen

Hausarbeit *[chores]*	**Freizeit** *[free time]*	**Schule** *[school work]*

4. Sentence puzzle: rewrite the sentences in the correct order

a. wir treffen Wann uns?

b. Ich ins heute will Kino gehen Nachmittag.

c. Kino Wir vor uns dem treffen.

d. Heute Peter habe zu Lust, ich keine besuchen.

e. du willst Was machen?

f. nicht Ich ausgehen heute mit kann dir.

g. eine Ich Radtour mache.

5. Translate into English

a. Ich will heute Nachmittag eine Radtour machen.

b. Ich will morgen mit meinem Vater ins Stadion gehen.

c. Heute muss ich lernen, bevor ich mit meinem Freund ausgehe.

d. Ich habe heute keine Lust auf Sport.

e. Ich will mit meinem Bruder Schach spielen.

6. Multiple choice: choose the correct translation

	1	2	3
a. Wie geht es dir?	What?	What is it?	How are you?
b. Wo willst du hingehen?	Where are you?	Where shall we meet?	Where do you want to go?
c. Was willst du machen?	What do you want to do?	Where is it?	What do you want to see?
d. Wo sollen wir uns treffen?	Where are you?	Where shall we go?	Where shall we meet?
e. Hast du Lust?	Do you like it?	Do you fancy it?	Are you free?
f. Wie cool!	How cool!	How crazy!	How boring!
g. Wann sollen wir uns treffen?	Where are we going?	At what time shall we meet?	What time are you free?
h. Bis später!	Hello!	See you later!	See you tomorrow!
i. Kein Problem.	No problem.	I have nothing.	No big deal.
j. Ich habe keine Lust.	I'm not interested.	I don't have it.	I don't feel like it.

7. Match

Wie geht es dir?	What are we going to do?
Was willst du heute Abend machen?	Who are we going with?
Hast du Lust?	Where shall we meet?
Wo sollen wir uns treffen?	Do you fancy it?
Um wie viel Uhr sollen wir uns treffen?	How are you?
Mit wem gehen wir?	Why can't you come?
Warum kannst du nicht kommen?	At what time shall we meet?
Was werden wir machen?	What do you want to do this evening?

8. Match questions and answers

Wie geht es dir?	Nein, ich habe keine Lust, ich gehe lieber ins Kino.
Was willst du heute Nachmittag machen?	Vor der Bushaltestelle.
Hast du Lust?	Um halb acht.
Wo sollen wir uns treffen?	Mir geht es sehr gut, danke.
Um wie viel Uhr sollen wir uns treffen?	Weil ich für eine Prüfung lernen muss.
Warum kannst du nicht kommen?	Ich will in den Park gehen.
Was werden wir machen?	Wir werden Videospiele spielen und Musik hören.

9. Complete with the missing letters

a. H _ _ _ _! *Hello!*

b. W _ ? *Where?*

c. i _ _ h _ _ _ L _ _ _ *I fancy it*

d. i _ _ m _ _ _ *I have to*

e. bis d _ _ _ *see you*

f. s _ _ _ _ _ *later*

g. t_ _ m _ _ l_ _ _ *sorry*

h. ich k _ _ _ n _ _ _ _ *I can't*

i. ich w _ _ _ _ g _ _ _ _ *I would like to*

j. ich w _ _ _ n _ _ _ _ *I don't want*

k. k _ _ _ Problem *no problem*

l. U _ w _ _ v _ _ _ U _ _? *At what time?*

10a. Complete with the suitable option

Marcel: _________ Gert, wie geht es dir?

Gert: Hi Marcel. Gut, ___________.

Marcel: _______ willst du heute machen?

Gert: Heute würde ich gerne eine Radtour __________. Und du?

Marcel: Ach nein, darauf habe ich keine ________. Ich will lieber ins Kino gehen.

Gert: ________ Problem. Wir können ins Kino gehen.

Marcel: Super. _________ treffen wir uns?

Gert: __________ wir uns um sieben.

Marcel: _________, wo sollen wir uns treffen?

Gert: ________ dem Kino.

Marcel: OK, wir sehen uns __________.

Gert: Passt, __________ später.

bis	Hallo	treffen	vor
Lust	wann	danke	kein
was	machen	gut	später

10b. Complete with the suitable option

Manuel: _________ Robert, Wie geht's?

Robert: Hi Manuel. _______ gut, danke.

Manuel: Was ___________ wir heute?

Robert: Heute würde ich gerne ins Kino _______. Und du?

Manuel: Hm, darauf _________ ich keine Lust. Ich ________ Martin besuchen. Er gibt eine Party.

Robert: OK, kein ___________. Wir __________ zu Martins Party gehen.

Manuel: Super. ________ treffen wir uns?

Robert: ___________ wir uns um acht.

Manuel: Super, wir ________ uns später.

Robert: Passt, bis ________.

können	gehen	habe	wann
Problem	Hi	sehr	will
machen	sehen	treffen	dann

11. Faulty translation: correct the English

a. Wie geht's? *Who are you?*

b. Bis später. *See you tomorrow.*

c. Wann sollen wir uns treffen? *Why do we meet?*

d. Wir sehen uns später. *Nice to see you.*

e. Kein Problem. *There is a problem.*

f. Wir können los. *We not must go.*

g. Sehr gut. *Very badly.*

h. Ich habe keine Lust. *I really want to.*

i. Was willst du heute machen? *What do you want to do this evening?*

j. Ich würde gerne im Stadtzentrum spazieren gehen. *I'd like to go for a run in the city centre.*

Susanne: Hallo Marta, wie geht es dir?

Marta: Hallo Susanne. Gut, danke. Ich bin heute etwas müde.

Susanne: Was willst du heute Nachmittag machen?

Marta: Heute würde ich gerne im Einkaufszentrum bummeln gehen. Und du?

Susanne: Ich weiß nicht. Ich habe heute keine Lust, tut mir leid. Vielleicht morgen. Heute will ich Stefan zu Hause besuchen. Hast du Lust?

Marta: Okay. Macht nichts. Wir können natürlich Stefan besuchen.

Susanne: Super. Um wie viel Uhr treffen wir uns?

Marta: Um sechs?

Susanne: Nein, ich kann nicht um sechs, weil ich meiner Mutter bis sieben bei der Hausarbeit helfen muss.

Marta: Um halb sieben?

Susanne: Passt. Wo treffen wir uns?

Marta: Treffen wir uns im Café neben der Schule.

12. Find in the text the German equivalent

a. How are you?

b. What do you want to do this afternoon?

c. At what time shall we meet?

d. Where shall we meet?

e. No problem.

f. I would like to go window shopping today.

g. Let's meet in the café next to school

h. That suits me.

i. I am sorry.

j. I want to go to Stefan's house today.

k. I have to help my mother with the chores until seven o'clock.

13. Answer in English

a. How is Marta feeling today?

b. What does Marta want to do this evening?

c. What does Susanne want to do instead?

d. At what time does Marta want to meet?

e. Why can't Susanne meet at six?

f. Where are they going to meet?

14. Spot and correct the mistakes

a. Wann treffen wir?

b. Ich muss meine Mutter helfen.

c. OK. Macht nicht.

d. Ich habe kein Lust.

e. Bis spater.

f. Wo sollen wir uns trefen?

g. Was mochtest du heute Nachmittag machen?

h. An halb sieben?

Johann: Hallo Laura, wie geht es dir?

Laura: Hallo Johann. Gut, danke. Mir ist ein bisschen langweilig.

Johann: Was hast du letzten Samstag gemacht?

Laura: Nichts Besonderes. Ich habe meine Hausaufgaben gemacht, mein Zimmer aufgeräumt und bin mit dem Hund spazieren gegangen. Und du?

Johann: Ich war joggen, habe den Rasen gemäht und bin mit Peter im Park Rad fahren gegangen. Was willst du heute Nachmittag machen?

Laura: Heute würde ich gerne einkaufen gehen. Und du?

Johann: Ich weiß nicht, Schatz. Ich habe heute keine Lust zum Einkaufen, tut mir leid. Vielleicht morgen. Heute würde ich lieber ins Kino gehen. Hast du Lust?

Laura: Okay. Macht nichts. Ins Kino? Welchen Film willst du dir ansehen?

Johann: Den neuesten Star Wars-Film?

Laura: Super. Wann treffen wir uns?

Johann: Um vier?

Laura: Nein, ich kann nicht um vier, weil ich meinem Bruder bei den Hausaufgaben helfen muss.

Johann: Um fünf?

Laura: Nein, ich kann nicht um fünf, weil ich die Wäsche waschen und bügeln muss. Um halb sechs?

Johann: OK, sollen wir uns vor deinem Haus treffen?

Laura: Passt. Bis später.

15. Find the German equivalent in the conversation above

a. I am a bit bored.

b. I didn't do anything special.

c. I tidied my room.

d. I mowed the lawn.

e. I would like to go shopping today.

f. I don't know, darling.

g. Not a problem.

h. Which film would you like to see?

i. I have to do the laundry and iron.

j. Shall we meet in front of your house?

16. Answer in English

a. How is Laura feeling?

b. What three things did she do on Saturday?

c. What three things did Johann do?

d. What does Laura want to do this evening?

e. How about Johann?

f. Why can't Laura meet at four?

g. Why can't she meet at five?

h. At what time can she meet him?

17. Complete the table

Deutsch	English
Tut mir leid.	
	I am fine.
Ich kann nicht.	
Ich habe keine Lust.	
Heute Nachmittag.	
	In front of your house.
	At what time?
Wo treffen wir uns?	
Um wie viel Uhr treffen wir uns?	
Kein Problem.	

18. Complete with a suitable word

a. Was willst du _______________?

b. Wo _______________ wir uns?

c. Um ____________ fünf.

d. ____________ wir uns vor deinem Haus.

e. _________ treffen wir uns? Um acht?

f. Mir ist ein bisschen ______________.

g. Nein, ich habe keine _____________.

h. Ich will mit dir ins ____________ gehen.

i. Ich muss meiner Mutter beim Putzen ______________.

19. Complete

a. *Where shall we meet?* W___ s____________ w_____ u______ t___________?

b. *What do you want to do?* W____ w____________ d____ m_______________?

c. *OK. Not a problem.* OK. K_______ P_________________.

d. *I have to help my parents.* I______ m______ m__________ E____________ h_______.

e. *Sorry. I don't fancy it.* T____ m_____ l______. I_____ h______ k_______ L_______.

f. *Let's meet in front of the cinema.* T_________ w_____ u_____ v_____ d_____ K___________.

g. *I have to tidy my bedroom.* I______ m_____ m______ Z________ a_______________.

h. *We can go to the park.* W____ k___________ i__ d____ P_______ g__________.

i. *At what time shall we meet?* U___ w___ v____ U____ s________ w___ u___ t________?

j. *See you later.* B_____ s_____________.

20. Translate into German

a. Not a problem.

b. Do you want to go shopping?

c. I don't fancy it.

d. I can't because I have to study.

e. What do you want to do?

f. I have to help my mother.

g. I have to iron the clothes.

h. Where shall we meet?

i. Let's meet at the bus stop near my house.

j. At what time shall we meet?

k. I would like to go swimming.

l. I am sorry, I have to do my homework.

21. Answer each of the questions below with a full sentence, as in the example

e.g. Wie heißt du? – Ich heiße Mark.

a. Hallo, wie geht's?

b. Was hast du gestern gemacht?

c. Was willst du heute Nachmittag machen?

d. Willst du mit mir ins Einkaufszentrum gehen?

e. Wann treffen wir uns?

f. Wo treffen wir uns?

g. Was machst du morgen?

h. Willst du wieder mit mir ausgehen?

i. Würdest du gerne mit mir ins Kino gehen?

j. Was willst du nach dem Kino machen?

22. Write the questions for the answers below

e.g. Am Nachmittag gehe ich mit meinem Vater ins Stadion – Was machst du am Nachmittag?

a. Ich will PlayStation spielen.

b. Weil es langweilig ist.

c. Ich habe gestern nichts gemacht. Ich habe mich nur entspannt.

d. Wir treffen uns vor dem Schwimmbad.

e. Nein, ich habe keine Lust.

f. Ja, ich will ins Kino gehen.

g. Ich kann leider nicht am Freitag.

23. Translate 1 and 2 into English and 3 into German

1. Marina und Julian	2. Marcel und Elias	3. Anna und Christoph
M. Hallo Julian. Wie geht's? *J. Sehr gut, Marina. Und dir?* M. Gut, aber ich bin sehr müde. *J. Warum?* M. Gestern Nachmittag war ich joggen und dann schwimmen. Außerdem bin ich heute früh aufgestanden. *J. Oh. Du kannst heute Nachmittag also nicht ausgehen?* M. Doch, natürlich! Wo willst du hingehen? *J. Auf Oskars Party?* M. Cool! Wo treffen wir uns? *J. Treffen wir uns um sieben bei mir?* M. Super! Bis dann.	M. Hallo Elias. Wie geht's dir? *E. Sehr gut. Und dir?* M. Was hast du letzten Samstag gemacht? *E. Ich war mit meiner Mutter einkaufen. Und du?* M. Ich habe meinem Vater im Garten geholfen. Das war langweilig! *E. Willst du heute mit mir ins Stadion gehen?* M. Ja, passt. Wo wollen wir uns treffen und wann? *E. Treffen wir uns um drei an der Bushaltestelle vor meinem Haus.* M. OK, perfekt. Wir sehen uns dort um drei.	A. Hi Anna. Do you want to go out this afternoon? *C. Yes, but first I have to help my mother until 4:00 pm.* A. Ok. Do you want to go to the cinema this evening? *C. No. I am sorry, but I don't feel like it. I would like to go to the town centre and do some window-shopping.* A. OK, not a problem. At what time shall we meet? At 4:30? *C. I can't meet at 4:30. I have to help my brother with his homework. Let's meet at 5:00.* A. OK. At five. Where shall we meet? *C. Let's meet at your house.*

Question Skills Unit 9

English	German
What do you do in your free time?	**Was machst du in deiner Freizeit?**
What do you do to help your parents at home?	**Wie hilfst du deinen Eltern im Haushalt?**
What did you do yesterday to help your dad/mum?	**Was hast du gestern getan, um deinem Papa/deiner Mama zu helfen?**
What do you want to do this weekend with your friend?	**Was willst du dieses Wochenende mit deinem/r Freund/in unternehmen?**
What do you fancy doing this afternoon?	**Worauf hast du heute Nachmittag Lust?**
Do you want to go to the cinema with me?	**Willst du mit mir ins Kino gehen?**
Where shall we meet?	**Wo sollen wir uns treffen?**
At what time shall we meet?	**Um wie viel Uhr treffen wir uns?**
Do you fancy playing football in the park?	**Hast du Lust im Park Fußball zu spielen?**
Why can you not go out this afternoon/evening?	**Warum kannst du heute Nachmittag/Abend nicht ausgehen?**
What would you like to do this weekend?	**Was würdest du gerne dieses Wochenende machen?**
Are you going to meet up with your friends this weekend?	**Wirst du dich dieses Wochenende mit deinen Freunden treffen?**
Where are you going to go?	**Wo geht ihr hin?**

1. Match questions and answers

Was machst du, um im Haushalt zu helfen?	Ich habe Lust auf einen Spaziergang.
Was hast du gestern getan, um deinem Vater zu helfen?	Ich decke den Tisch und helfe meinen Eltern.
Worauf hast du heute Nachmittag Lust?	Ich habe Staub gesaugt und das Abendessen gemacht.
Wo treffen wir uns?	Treffen wir uns vor meinem Haus.
Um wie viel Uhr treffen wir uns?	Wir treffen uns mit Laura und Nico.
Warum kannst du heute Nachmittag nicht ausgehen?	Um fünf Uhr.
Mit wem treffen wir uns?	Weil ich viele Hausaufgaben und wenig Zeit habe.

2. Write the questions to the answers below

a.	Ja, ich will mit dir ins Kino gehen.
b.	Um halb acht.
c.	Vor dem Geschäft neben dem Kino.
d.	Wir gehen mit Sandra und Stefan ins Kino.
e.	Normalerweise gehe ich mit dem Hund spazieren.
f.	Gestern habe ich nichts gemacht, weil ich müde war.
g.	Ja, ich will mich mit meinen Freunden treffen.

3. Break the flow

a. Wiegehtesdirheute?

b. Waswillstduheutemachen?

c. WillstdumitmirinsStadtzentrumgehen?

d. JadaraufhätteichLust.

e. Wotreffenwiruns?

4. Spot and add in the one word missing from each sentence

a. Wie hilfst deinen Eltern im Haushalt?

b. Worauf du heute Nachmittag Lust?

c. Wo treffen wir?

d. Hast du Lust Kino zu gehen?

e. Warum du später nicht ausgehen?

f. Wo du dieses Wochenende hingehen?

5. Fill in the gaps with appropriate questions

Thomas: Hallo Valerie, (a.) ____________________ ?

Valerie: Hi Thomas. Mir geht's gut. (b.) ______________ ?

Thomas: Mir geht's auch gut, danke. (c.) ____________________________________ ?

Valerie: Heute würde ich gerne ins Stadion gehen. Bayern München spielen heute. (d.) ___________________ ?

Thomas: Ja, sehr! Bayern München ist super! (e.) ____________________________ ?

Valerie: Treffen wir uns vor dem Stadion. (f.) ________________________________ ?

Thomas: Gute Frage. Das Spiel ist um vier Uhr nachmittags. Treffen wir uns dann.

Valerie: Gut. (g.) ______________________________ ?

Thomas: Gehen wir mit Paul und Luca. Die beiden kommen aus München und lieben Fußball.

Valerie: Super, wir sehen uns später.

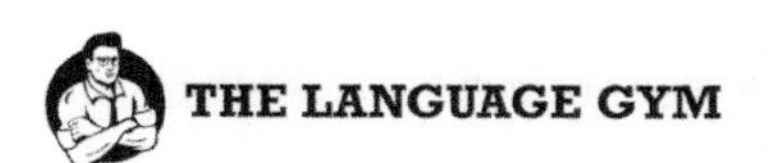

Unit 10

Describing a typical day in the past, present & future

In this unit you will learn:

- To describe a typical day in the past, present & future
- To say what you "had to" and "wanted to" do

Key sentence patterns:

- Time marker (*gestern/heute/morgen*) + verb in the present/perfect tense + noun or prepositional phrase
- Time marker + modal verb in the present/imperfect tense + infinitive
- Time marker + modal verb *wollen* / verb *werden* + infinitive

Grammar:

- Use of modal verbs across tenses
- First person singular of key verbs in present, future, perfect & imperfect tense

Gestern *[Yesterday]*	**Heute** *[Today]*	**Morgen** *[Tomorrow]*

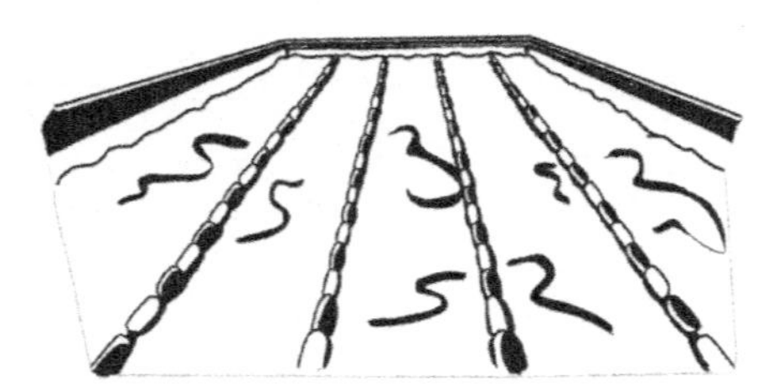

UNIT 10: Describing a typical day in the past, present & future

<table>
<tr><th colspan="4">PRESENT</th></tr>
<tr><td rowspan="7">Normalerweise
[Normally/ Usually]</td><td>esse ich [I eat]</td><td rowspan="7">unter der Woche
[during the week]</td><td>in einem italienischen Restaurant
[in an Italian restaurant]</td></tr>
<tr><td>gehe ich [I go]</td><td>in den Park [to the park]
ins Einkaufszentrum [to the shopping centre]
mit meinem Freund/meiner Freundin aus
[I go out with my boyfriend/girlfriend]
Rad fahren [bike riding]</td></tr>
<tr><td>helfe ich [I help]</td><td>meinen Eltern [my parents]</td></tr>
<tr><td>mache ich [I do]</td><td>meine Hausaufgaben [my homework]</td></tr>
<tr><td>spiele ich
[I play]</td><td>mit meinen Geschwistern [with my siblings]
Playstation</td></tr>
<tr><td>räume ich mein Zimmer
[I tidy my room]</td><td>auf</td></tr>
<tr><td>muss ich
[I have to]</td><td>meinem Bruder helfen [help my brother]</td></tr>
</table>

<table>
<tr><th colspan="3">PAST</th></tr>
<tr><td rowspan="3">Gestern
[Yesterday]
Letzten Freitag
[Last Friday]
Letzte Woche
[Last week]</td><td>habe ich [I]</td><td>das Wohnzimmer aufgeräumt [tidied the living room]
Gitarre gespielt [played guitar]
in einem chinesischen Restaurant gegessen
[ate at a Chinese restaurant]
meinem Bruder geholfen [helped my brother]</td></tr>
<tr><td>bin ich [I]</td><td>ins Stadion gegangen [went to the stadium]
bin ich mit meiner besten Freundin ausgegangen
[went out with my best friend -fem-]
im Park joggen gegangen [went jogging in the park]</td></tr>
<tr><td>konnte ich nicht
[I couldn't]
wollte ich nicht
[I didn't want to]
musste ich [I had to]</td><td>Sport machen [do sports]
Videospiele spielen [play videogames]
mit dem Hund spazieren gehen
[take the dog for a walk]
einkaufen gehen [go shopping]</td></tr>
</table>

<table>
<tr><th colspan="3">FUTURE</th></tr>
<tr><td>Nächstes Wochenende
[Next weekend]
Nächste Woche [Next week]
Morgen [Tomorrow]</td><td>will ich (nicht)
[I -don't- want to]
werde ich (nicht)
[I'm - not- going to]</td><td>im Haushalt helfen [help at home]
mein Zimmer aufräumen [tidy my room]
meine Freunde treffen [meet my friends]
meine Hausaufgaben machen
[do my homework]</td></tr>
</table>

1. Match: time markers

gestern	at the weekend
nächsten Samstag	tomorrow
morgen	last weekend
letzten Samstag	the day before yesterday
innerhalb von zwei Tagen	within two days
letzte Woche	two days ago
am Wochenende	yesterday
vorgestern	last week
vor zwei Tagen	last Saturday
letztes Wochenende	next Saturday

2. Complete the table

Deutsch	English
ich mache	
ich gehe	
	I have to
	I want
ich gehe aus	
ich stehe auf	
ich sehe	
	I read
	I write

3. Match: activities

Ich werde früh aufstehen.	I am going to go bike riding.
Ich werde ein Buch lesen.	I am going to study.
Ich werde lernen.	I am going to have fun.
Ich werde ausgehen.	I am going to get up early.
Ich werde Spaß haben.	I am going to help my brother.
Ich werde einkaufen gehen.	I am going to go out.
Ich werde meinem Bruder helfen.	I am going to read a book.
Ich werde Sport machen.	I am going to go shopping.
Ich werde Rad fahren gehen.	I am going to do sports.

4. Choose the correct translations

	1	2	3
I went	ich bin gegangen	ich bist gegangen	ich bin gesungen
I did	ich habe gespielt	er tat	ich habe getan
I helped	ich habe geholfen	ich hatte geholfen	ich helfe
I ate	ich habe essen	ich will essen	ich habe gegessen
I played	spielen	ich habe gespielt	wir spulen
I wanted	ich wollte	ich will	ich durfte
I drank	ich habe getrinken	ich habe getrunken	ich trinkte
I read	ich rette	ich habe gelest	ich habe gelesen
I saw	ich habe gesehen	ich hatte gesehen	ich sehe
I met	ich treffe	ich habe getroffen	ich habe treffen

5. Complete the table with the options provided below

Gestern	Heute	Morgen
		Ich werde Rad fahren gehen.
	Ich stehe auf.	
		Ich werde mit meinem Freund ausgehen.
	Ich trinke Kaffee.	
		Ich werde boxen gehen.
	Ich gehe ins Kino.	
		Ich werde Gitarre spielen.
	Ich esse viel.	

Ich werde viel essen.	Ich bin Rad gefahren.	Ich werde aufstehen.	Ich bin aufgestanden.
Ich habe viel gegessen.	Ich bin ins Kino gegangen.	Ich werde Kaffee trinken gehen.	Ich bin boxen gegangen.
Ich werde ins Kino gehen.	Ich habe Gitarre gespielt.	Ich habe Kaffee getrunken.	Ich bin mit meinem Freund ausgegangen.
Ich spiele Gitarre.	Ich gehe Rad fahren.	Ich gehe boxen.	Ich gehe mit meinem Freund aus.

6. Translate into English

a. Ich bin einkaufen gegangen.

b. Ich werde Schach spielen.

c. Ich habe Comics gelesen.

d. Ich trinke Almdudler.

e. Ich mache mein Bett.

f. Ich habe mir einen Film angesehen.

g. Ich werde aufstehen.

h. Ich habe Schach gespielt.

i. Ich helfe meinen Eltern.

j. Ich habe mich entspannt.

k. Ich muss lernen.

l. Ich gehe spät ins Bett.

m. Ich will feiern gehen.

n. Ich will ausgehen.

o. Ich habe Brezeln gegessen.

7. Sentence puzzle: rewrite the sentences in the correct order

a. gemacht Gestern ich Besonderes nichts habe. *Yesterday I didn't do anything special.*

b. Film habe ich einen angesehen mir Vorgestern. *The day before yesterday I watched a film.*

c. mache Am ich Hausarbeit Wochenende. *At the weekend I do chores.*

d. meiner Letzten ausgegangen bin ich mit Freundin Samstag. *Last Saturday I went out with my girlfriend.*

e. jeden aufstehen Ich Tag früh muss. *Every day I have to get up early.*

f. Schach Vor habe ich Tagen gespielt zwei. *Two days ago I played chess.*

g. an gehe Heute ich den Strand Nachmittag. *This afternoon I am going to go to the beach.*

8. Find the German for the verb phrases in the wordsearch

```
I C H B I N G E G A N G E N I X Z H I N
K C B A J M O K H G K A S C D N Z C C E
T R H G M U J A D E C E H M E K H H R H
I D K M O U F C H K S H I S T G F S D E
M S W B U F V J P Q A H S H E J R T F T
I Q C T H S N F R B P E C H V G H E Q S
U V V R X F S P E R G T E I M G I Z Q F
U G J D K R R G B E C N W N D O I V K U
X E Z N W X E G G R I T R J X N C A A A
Z B S F I M N E H E G E D R E W H C I E
V B E E A X B D C V N K S O V I S H L D
K U U C D A P U X M K Z J F B U P E Q R
T C H T H Q K Q M Y X Q L Y F T I L B E
I T A H L Y T J V W I H C Y A K E K C W
V V C S A C P H F I R D U R U F L E V H
P I S C F R R M K F H Z K O Q T E Q U C
R B S W L X R U M L C L H S J K G K G I
U H J A I W N E H C A M H C I B K A B F
N Y U J S E A Q Q E P R N R G U R S B G
S J P M A L T G A D O I V T C E U R A Y
```

e.g. I do — ***ich mache***

a. I did

b. I am going to go

c. I see

d. I am going to get up

e. I ate

f. I went

g. I have to

h. I play

i. I go

9. Complete with the correct option

a. Normalerweise ___________ ich meinem Papa im Garten am Wochenende.

b. Letztes Wochenende ______ ich PlayStation ______________ und ferngesehen.

c. Morgen _________ ich früh _________________, weil ich Fußball spielen werde.

d. Vorgestern _____ ich mit meiner Freundin ins Kino ______________.

e. Unter der Woche ________ ich normalerweise früh _____, um in die Schule zu gehen.

f. Heute Nachmittag __________ ich mit meiner Mama _________________ ____________.

g. Gestern ______ ich in der Stadt mit meinen Freundinnen ________________.

h. Heute _______ ich nicht mit meinem Freund _______________. Ich muss lernen.

i. Gestern _______ ich nichts Besonderes ______________. Ich habe nur Musik gehört.

bin	aufstehen	auf	bummeln	habe	gemacht
werde	werde	habe	stehe	gehen	muss
war	helfe	einkaufen	gegangen	gespielt	ausgehen

10. Guided translation (verbs only)

a. *I played*	ich h_ _ _ g_ _ _ _ _ _ _	e. *I eat*	ich e_ _ _
b. *I am going to go*	ich w_ _ _ _ g_ _ _ _	f. *I can't*	ich k_ _ _ n_ _ _ _
c. *I see*	ich s_ _ _	g. *I went*	ich b_ _ g_ _ _ _ _ _ _
d. *I did*	ich h_ _ _ g_ _ _ _ _ _	h. *I have to*	ich m_ _ _

11. Complete with the correct verb in the appropriate tense (perfect, present and future)

a. Gestern ____ ich mit meinem Freund ins Kino gegangen.	*Yesterday I went to the cinema with my friend.*
b. Vor zwei Tagen ______ ich ein Buch gelesen.	*Two days ago I read a book.*
c. Nächste Woche ______ ich ins Stadion______.	*Next week I am going to go to the stadium.*
d. Heute ____ ich für den Englischtest _________.	*Today I have to study for the English test.*
e. Sonntags _______ich normalerweise joggen.	*On Sundays I usually go jogging.*
f. Morgen ______ ich früh _______________.	*Tomorrow I am going to get up early.*
g. Letzten Freitag ____ ich mit meiner Freundin _________________.	*Last Friday I went out with my girlfriend.*
h. Vorgestern ____ ich in den Park ________.	*The day before yesterday I went to the park.*
i. Heute ______ ich nicht mit ihnen __________.	*Today I don't want to go out with them.*

Letztes Wochenende

Was hast du letztes Wochenende gemacht?

Martina: Ich habe nichts gemacht. Ich habe mich nur erholt und ein bisschen für den Deutschtest gelernt.

Sabine: Ich habe viel gegessen und mich beim Kartenspielen mit meinen Geschwistern erholt.

Felix: Ich hatte kein gutes Wochenende. es nicht gut verbracht. Ich war krank und es war sehr langweilig.

Regina: Ich war mit meiner Mama einkaufen und dann im Kino mit meinen Eltern. Das war sehr langweilig.

Beate: Ich habe meinen Eltern geholfen. Ich habe den Rasen gemäht, mein Zimmer aufgeräumt und den Boden im Wohnzimmer gewischt.

Paul: Normalerweise gehe ich mit meiner Freundin aus. Letztes Wochenende konnte sie aber nicht, weil sie für ihre Chemieprüfung lernen musste.

Alex: Ich habe ein sehr interessantes Buch gelesen. Ich war außerdem in der Kletterhalle klettern.

Leonie: Ich war in Graz mit meiner Familie. Wir haben Sightseeing gemacht und viele Fotos gemacht.

Tobias: Ich habe viel Sport gemacht. Ich war joggen und habe Gewichte gehoben. Tauchen war ich auch.

12. Answer the questions about the text on the left

a. Who did a lot of sports?

b. Who had a very boring time?

c. Who was ill?

d. Who went sightseeing?

e. Who couldn't go out with his girlfriend?

f. Who had a German test?

g. Who mopped the living-room floor?

h. Who had to study for a chemistry test?

i. Who went to the cinema?

j. Who relaxed by playing cards?

k. Who took a lot of pictures?

l. Who didn't do anything?

m. Who went rock climbing?

n. Who went shopping?

Was ich am Wochenende mache

Ich mache normalerweise sehr viel am Wochenende.

Am Samstag mache ich Sport. Morgens gehe ich mit meinem besten Freund Theo im Park joggen. Wir stehen sehr früh auf und joggen circa eine Stunde. Letzten Samstag waren wir bis halb neun unterwegs. Ich liebe es, laufen zu gehen. Danach gehe ich ins Fitnessstudio mit Theo und zwei anderen Freunden, Max und Thomas. Wir spielen Badminton, Tischtennis oder Tennis. Wir haben sehr viel Spaß, aber ich gewinne nie. Nachmittags gehe ich mit meinem Papa und meinem jüngeren Bruder klettern.

Am Sonntagmorgen gehe ich ebenfalls joggen, aber nur für eine halbe Stunde. Dann fahre ich mit meinen Eltern mit dem Auto nach Hause, mache meine Hausaufgaben und verbringe den Nachmittag mit Computerspielen oder Fernsehen. Ich mache nichts Besonderes. Normalerweise essen wir dann zu Abend bei meinen Großeltern, die sehr lustig und nett sind.

Für nächstes Wochenende ist etwas anderes geplant: ich werde mit meiner Klasse nach Berlin fahren. Wir werden uns das Brandenburger Tor und viele andere Sehenswürdigkeiten und historische Plätze ansehen. Außerdem gibt es in Berlin sehr viele ausgefallene Geschäfte. Ich freue mich schon auf die Kleidergeschäfte.

Letzes Jahr waren wir in Wien und es war Spitze. Wir haben morgens Sightseeing gemacht und nachmittags sind wir Souvenirs einkaufen gegangen. Es gab sehr viel zu sehen. Mein Freund Tom und ich haben zwei nette Mädchen in Wien kennengelernt, mit denen wir noch immer in Kontakt sind.

(Jakob, 15 Jahre. Dresden)

15. Correct the mistakes in the translation of the last two paragraphs of Jakob's text

Next weekend will be different because I am going to go on a trip to Hamburg with my family. We are going to visit the Berlin Wall and other sights and historic buildings of the city. There are many beautiful places in Berlin. I'm looking forward to the book shops. Last month we went to Wien and we had a boring time. We went hiking in the morning and in the afternoon we went clothes shopping. There was a lot to eat and drink. My friend Tom and I met two mean girls in Hamburg. We are no longer in touch with them.

13. Find in the text the German equivalent for:

a. I usually do a lot.

b. We got back at 8:30.

c. I go jogging with my best friend.

d. We have lots of fun.

e. I never win.

f. I love running.

g. On Sundays I jog for half an hour.

h. I spend the afternoon watching TV.

i. I don't do anything special.

j. I am going to go to Berlin.

k. I'm already looking forward to...

l. We went sightseeing.

m. We went shopping.

n. There was a lot to see.

14. Correct the statements

a. At the weekend Jakob doesn't do much.

b. On Saturdays he gets up late.

c. He always wins at racket sports.

d. In the afternoon he goes cycling with his father and older brother.

e. On Sundays he does more running than on Saturdays.

f. On Sunday mornings he spends time studying on his computer.

g. They usually have dinner with his grandparents, who are very strict.

h. Next weekend he is going to Berlin with his family.

i. He bought clothes.

j. He went sightseeing in the afternoon.

k. Jakob and Tom met two girls from Vienna but didn't get their contact details.

Am meisten gefällt mir an meiner Nachbarschaft, dass es viele Angebote für junge Leute gibt. Am Wochenende, wenn ich Zeit habe, mache ich viel mit meinen besten Freunden. Zuerst machen wir viel Sport. Letzten Samstag zum Beispiel, sind wir gemeinsam im Wald in der Nähe von meinem Haus Rad gefahren. Das war lustig. Ich bin einmal gestürzt, aber glücklicherweise ist nichts passiert. Dann haben wir Gewichte im Fitnessstudio in der Nähe von der Schule gehoben. Schließlich waren wir in der Kletterhalle klettern. Dort gibt es eine ziemlich hohe Wand. Glücklicherweise waren nicht viele Leute dort, sodass wir sehr oft hinaufklettern konnten, ohne lange zu warten. Das war anstrengend, aber wir hatten viel Spaß.

In meiner Nachbarschaft gibt es auch zwei große Einkaufszentren. Dort gibt es viele Kleidergeschäfte, Musik und Elektrogeschäfte sowie auch Restaurants und Fast Food Lokale. Obwohl ich weiß, dass Fast Food ungesund ist, schmeckt es mir.

Letzten Sonntag war ich mit meinem besten Freund Werner im Einkaufszentrum bummeln. Werner ist gutaussehend, sympathisch und witzig. Während unserer Einkaufstour haben wir ein paar Mädchen kennengelernt, mit denen wir den ganzen Nachmittag spazieren waren. Ein Mädchen, Laura, fand ich besonders sympathisch und wir haben nett geplaudert.

Nächstes Wochenende werde ich sie wieder treffen. Wir werden ins Kino gehen, um uns den neuesten Disney Film anzusehen. Danach werden wir noch ein Eis essen gehen. Das wird sicher lustig. **(Axel, 16 Jahre. Bern)**

16. Find in Axel's text the German equivalent for the following items

a. I like the most about

b. I do a lot

c. in the forest near my house

d. I crashed once

e. fortunately, nothing happened

f. there weren't many people

g. tiring

h. junk food is unhealthy

i. window shopping

j. a couple of girls

k. the whole afternoon

l. a nice chat

m. go and have ice-cream

17. Gapped sentences

a. At the weekend, when he has ____________, Axel and his friends do a lot of things.

b. First of all, they do ____________________.

c. Last weekend they ________________ in the __________________ near his house.

d. They ____________ a few times, but nothing ____________________.

e. They also ___________________ in the gym near the school.

f. Finally, they ____________________ on the climbing wall.

g. It was ___________ but they had lots of fun.

h. Last Sunday, Axel and his friend went _______________ in the shopping centre.

i. He met a couple of girls and they spent the whole afternoon _______________.

j. He enjoyed _________________ to Laura.

k. Next weekend he is going to ____________.

18. Answer the questions below in German

a. Was hat Axel letztes Wochenende mit seinen Freunden gemacht?

b. Wie war das Klettern?

c. Wie viele Einkaufszentren gibt es in Axels Nachbarschaft?

d. Beschreib Werner.

e. Was werden Axel und Laura nächstes Wochenende machen?

19. Complete with the correct option

Letzes Wochenende hat Axel sehr viel gemacht. Am Samstag ____ er im Wald _____________. Das hat ______________. Danach war er mit _________ Freunden im Fitnessstudio in der Nähe von seiner Schule. Dort hat er Gewichte _______________ und war dann noch ___________. In Axels Nachbarschaft ___________ zwei große Einkaufszentren. Letzen Sonntag war Axel mit seinem besten Freund Werner im Einkaufszentrum _____________. Während dem Einkaufen _______ Axel und Werner zwei Mädchen _________________, mit denen er und Werner den ganzen Nachmittag _______________ waren. Nächstes Wochenende werden sich Axel und Laura in der Stadt __________, um sich einen Film _____________. Danach wollen sie noch in die Eisdiele _________. Axel und Laura ________________ sich sehr gut.

gibt es	kennengelernt	seinen	Rad fahren	spazieren
Spaß gemacht	verstehen	war	gehoben	haben
treffen	klettern	bummeln	anzusehen	gehen

20. Complete the table using the perfect tense

Ich	Er / mein Bruder	Sie / meine Freunde und Freundinnen
Ich bin ins Kino gegangen.	1.	2.
3.	Er hat sich einen Film angesehen.	4.
5.	6.	Sie sind ausgegangen.
Ich habe meiner Mama geholfen.	7.	8.
9.	Er hat Fußball gespielt.	10.
Ich habe nichts gemacht.	11.	12.
13.	14.	Sie haben ein Buch gelesen.
Ich habe einen Spaziergang im Stadtzentrum gemacht.	15.	16.
17.	18.	Sie sind bummeln gegangen.
Ich habe einen Jungen kennengelernt.	19.	20.
21.	Er hat nicht gelernt.	22.

21. Guided translation

a. *Yesterday I went out with my friends.* G________ b_____ i_____ m_____ m______________ F_____________ a_______________.

b. *It was tiring but fun*. E_____ w______ a________________, a________ e______h_________ s________ v_________ S_____________ g_______________.

c. *Three days ago I went to a party.* V________ d________ T____________ w______ i______ a______ e______________ P_____________.

d. *Yesterday I washed my mum's car.* G__________ h_________ i______ d______ A________ m____________ M___________ g____________________.

e. *I usually get up at six thirty.* I_______ s__________ n________________ u____ h_________ s____________ a_____.

22. Translate into German

a. Yesterday I watched a film.

b. Two days ago I didn't do my homework.

c. This morning I didn't tidy my room.

d. Last Sunday I went to the park with my friends.

e. I have to make my bed and wash the car.

f. Tomorrow I am going to ride my bike.

g. Next week I am going to go to Munich.

h. This evening I am not going to do anything.

23. Translate into German

a. Two days ago we went jogging.

b. Last week my friends and I played golf.

c. Last Sunday I visited my grandparents.

d. Every day we have to lay and clear the table.

e. Today I can't go out with my girlfriend.

f. Next week we are going shopping.

g. The day before yesterday I studied a lot.

h. Once a week we have to take out the rubbish.

24. Translate into German

Usually, my family and I do a lot of things at the weekend. However, last weekend, we didn't do much.

I relaxed reading a book, did my homework and watched a film on TV. My parents went jogging, then did some chores and played cards. My older brother did his homework and then played the guitar all day. My younger brother spent the whole day on his computer and playing on the PlayStation.

It was a boring weekend, but I relaxed a lot. Next weekend I want to meet up with my friends and go to the cinema. I am going to play tennis with my friend Peter. Peter is 15 years old and very funny. He is my best friend.

25. Translate into German

In my family everyone has to help at home. For example, my mother has to look after the garden. My father cooks. My brother and I have to make our beds and tidy up our rooms. My sister looks after the dog.

We like to help our parents but we also do other things. For example, last weekend I washed my father's car and helped him in the garden. My brother cleaned the living room and did the laundry. My sister mowed the lawn and took the dog out. My parents were very happy.

26. Complete with a suitable word

a. Mir gefällt meine Stadt, weil sie ____________ ist.

b. In meiner Stadt gibt es viele _______________ für Jugendliche.

c. Meine Nachbarschaft ist am _________________.

d. Ich wohne in einer sehr _____________ Wohnung.

e. Was mir am besten an meiner Gegend gefällt, ist, dass sie sehr _____________ ist.

f. Was mir an meiner Nachbarschaft nicht gefällt, ist, dass sie ___________ ist.

g. In meiner Straße gibt es viele _________Geschäfte.

h. Neben meinem Haus gibt es einen _____________.

i. Meine Geschwister und ich helfen immer meinen ________________ im Haushalt.

j. Gestern zum Beispiel habe ich das __________________ aufgeräumt.

28. Answer the questions below in German and in full sentences

a. Wie heißt du?

b. Wie viele Familienmitglieder hat deine Familie?

c. Beschreib deinen Bruder / deine Schwester.

d. Beschreib deinen besten Freund / deine beste Freundin.

e. Was machst du im Haushalt?

f. Was gefällt dir am besten in deiner Gegend?

g. Welche Angebote gibt es für junge Leute in deiner Gegend?

h. Wie sieht ein typischer Schultag bei dir aus?

i. Was hast du gestern in der Mittagspause gemacht?

j. Was hast du gestern Nachmittag gemacht?

27. Complete the sentences below

a. Meine Stadt heißt…

b. Sie liegt in…

c. Mir gefällt meine Stadt (nicht), weil…

d. Meine Gegend liegt im…

e. In meiner Nachbarschaft gibt es…

f. Die Geschäfte in meiner Gegend sind…

g. In meiner Straße gibt es…

h. Neben meinem Haus ist ein…

i. Unter der Woche stehe ich um … auf.

j. Ich mache viel Sport, zum Beispiel…

k. Ich frühstücke normalerweise…

l. Normalerweise esse ich … zu Mittag.

m. Normalerweise esse ich … zu Abend.

n. Nächstes Wochenende habe ich viel vor, zum Beispiel…

29. Write a text including the points below (200 words minimum)

- Describe your neighbourhood saying what there is to see and do.
- Describe your house and bedroom and say what you like and dislike about it.
- Describe a typical day of yours saying what you normally do to help at home.
- Say what you did last weekend to help at home.
- Say what you did last weekend with your friends and family.
- Say what you are going to do next weekend with your friends and with your family.

Question Skills Unit 10

English	German
Where do you live?	**Wo wohnst du?**
Do you live in a house or in a flat?	**Wohnst du in einem Haus oder einer Wohnung?**
In your neighbourhood, what places are there?	**Was für Plätze gibt es in deiner Nachbarschaft?**
What shops are there in your neighbourhood?	**Welche Geschäfte gibt es in deiner Nachbarschaft?**
What can you do in your city?	**Was kann man in deiner Stadt unternehmen?**
What can you see in your city?	**Was kann man sich in deiner Stadt ansehen?**
What is your house like?	**Wie ist dein Haus?**
Since when have you lived there?	**Seit wann lebst du dort?**
What is there in your bedroom?	**Was gibt es in deinem Schlafzimmer?**
When do you wake up?	**Wann wachst du auf?**
How do you get to school?	**Wie kommst du in die Schule?**
What do you do to help your parents at home?	**Wie hilfst du deinen Eltern im Haushalt?**
Who helps more, your brother or you?	**Wer hilft mehr, dein Bruder oder du?**
What did you do yesterday to help at home?	**Was hast du gestern im Haushalt gemacht?**
How are you going to help at home this weekend?	**Was wirst du dieses Wochenende im Haushalt machen?**
Where are you going to go next weekend?	**Wo fährst du nächstes Wochenende hin?**
Where would you like to live in the future?	**Wo würdest du gerne in Zukunft wohnen?**

1. Complete with the missing words

a. ____________ wohnst du?

b. __________ historische Orte gibt es in deiner Gegend?

c. ___________ du in einer Wohnung oder in einem Haus?

d. _______ kann man in deiner Nachbarschaft machen?

e. Wie __________ du im Haushalt?

f. Wann __________ du auf?

g. Wie ____________ du in die Schule?

h.Wie ist deine ____________?

i. Seit wann ________ du dort?

j. Wie hast du gestern im Haushalt _____________?

wohnst	was	hilfst	was für	stehst
Nachbarschaft	wo	geholfen	kommst	wie

2. Match questions and answers

Wann stehst du auf?	Ja, ich liebe mein Haus.
Wohnst du in einer Wohnung oder in einem Haus?	Mein Haus ist klein, aber gemütlich.
Wie ist dein Haus?	Unter der Woche stehe ich um sieben Uhr auf.
Gefällt dir dein Haus?	Ich lebe dort, seitdem ich geboren bin.
Seit wann lebst du dort?	Ich wohne in einem Haus im Stadtzentrum.
Wie kommst du in die Schule?	In meiner Nachbarschaft gibt es viele Spielplätze.
Welche Angebote für Kinder gibt es in deiner Nachbarschaft?	Wenn ich groß bin, würde ich gerne einmal in Australien leben.
Was kann man in deiner Stadt machen?	Normalerweise reite ich in die Schule.
Wo würderst du gerne einmal leben?	Man kann ins Kino gehen, Sport machen und vieles mehr.
Wie hilfst du im Haushalt?	Ich sauge regelmäßig Staub und spüle das Geschirr.

3. Faulty translation: correct the English

a. Wie hilfst du deinen Eltern im Haushalt?	*What do you do to help your mum at home?*
b. Was kann man sich in deiner Stadt ansehen?	*What can you see in your neighbourhood?*
c. Was ist dein Lieblingsplatz in deiner Gegend?	*Which is your favourite place in your house?*
d. Wie ist dein Haus?	*What is your flat like?*
e. Warum gefällt dir dein Haus?	*Why do you hate your house?*
f. Seit wann lebst du dort?	*How long are you planning to live there?*
g. Wie hast du gestern im Haushalt geholfen?	*What did she do yesterday to help at home?*
h. Wer hilft mehr im Haushalt, dein Bruder oder du?	*Who helps more, your sister or yourself?*
i. Wann wachst du morgens auf?	*When do you get up in the morning?*

4. Translate into German

a. Where do you live?
b. Do you like your house?
c. Since when have you lived there?
d. In your neighbourhood, what places are there?
e. What can you do in your city?
f. What do you do to help at home?
g. Who helps more, your sister or you?
h. What did you do yesterday to help at home?

Vocab Revision Workout 5

1. Match

viele Angebote	in my street
in meinem Haus	old buildings
in meiner Stadt	many things
alte Gebäude	my ... hurt
im Norden	for young people
die Leute	in my house
für junge Leute	green spaces
mein ... tat weh	the people
Grünflächen	in my town
in meiner Straße	a lot to do
viele Dinge	in the north

2. Complete with suitable words

a. Ich lebe in einer __________ im Süden von _____________.

b. Meine Nachbarschaft ist am _____________.

c. Mir gefällt meine Nachbarschaft nicht, weil sie _____________ ist.

d. Es gibt keine ___________ oder Grünflächen.

e. Es gibt viel ______________ und deshalb ist es nicht sehr _____________.

f. Gestern habe ich nicht meine Hausaufgaben gemacht, weil mir mein Kopf _____________.

g. Ich wohne in einem _________und hässlichen Haus.

3. Translate into German

I live in a town in the south of Germany. My neighbourhood is on the outskirts of the town. My neighbourhood is big and beautiful. There are many green spaces and sports facilities. Also there is a huge shopping centre near my house with many good shops. In my street there is a gym, a small supermarket, a Chinese restaurant and a bar. Near my house there is a big park where I ride my bike, play with my friends and walk my dog. The best thing about my neighbourhood is that the people are friendly and polite. The worst thing is that there is not much to do for young people.

4. Sentence puzzle: write the sentences in the correct order

a. ich gegangen mit meiner Freundin bin ins Kino Gestern.

b. meinen bin ich mit Vorgestern Freunden im Park fahren gegangen Rad.

c. Sport Glücklicherweise man in kann Gegend viel meiner machen.

d. bin drei Vor Tagen gegangen ich mit Mama einkaufen meiner.

e. meiner gibt Kleidergeschäfte Es tolle in Gegend viele.

f. Nachbarschaft viele In meiner junge gibt es für Angebote Leute.

g. man In unserem eislaufen Park kann und gehen klettern.

h. am Letzte Woche ich Sportplatz habe gespielt Tennis.

i. Stadion bin ich mit meinem Fußballspiel Bruder ins gegangen, um ein anzusehen Gestern.

j. Burgtheater sehen Gestern war ich mit Familie meiner im Stück, um ein neues zu.

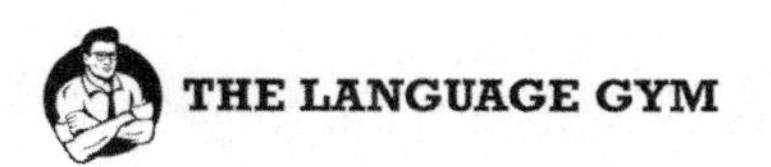

5. Complete with *gehen, ansehen* or *besichtigen* as appropriate

a. Man kann schwimmen ______________ .
b. Man kann sich Fußballspiele___________.
c. Man kann einkaufen ________________.
d. Man kann nicht auf Konzerte _________.
e. Man kann historische Schlösser _______.
f. Man kann Golf ____________.
g. Man kann sich Filme ________________.
h. Man kann wandern ______________.
i. Man kann Fußball spielen ____________.

6. Spot and correct the spelling errors

a. Glasgow ist in Schottenland.
b. In der Nähe von meinem House gibt es eine Fußgängerzone.
c. Mir gefellt meine Nachbarschaft gut.
d. Meine Gegend ist saub und sehr sicher.
e. In meiner Gegend gibt es fiel Verkehr.
f. In meiner Nachbarschaft kan man Fußball spülen.
g.Vorgestern war ich im Kieno.

7. Faulty translation: spot the mistakes in the English translations and correct them

a. In meiner Straße gibt es viele gute Geschäfte. *In my street there aren't many clothes shops.*
b. Der Tennisklub ist neben meiner Schule. *The tennis club is behind the cinema.*
c. Es gibt keine Sportgeschäfte in meiner Stadt. *There are no clothes shops in my city.*
d. Gibt es hier in der Nähe eine Bibliothek? *Is there a bakery nearby?*
e. Der Park ist gegenüber der Bushaltestelle. *The park is located behind the bus station.*
f. Es gibt einen Supermarkt hinter dem Sportzentrum. *There's a supermarket next to the sports centre.*
g. Das Restaurant ist zehn Minuten mit dem Auto entfernt. *The restaurant is a ten minute walk from here.*

8. Translate into English

a. Ich war im Schwimmbad.
b. Ich werde einkaufen gehen.
c. Wir waren auf dem Land.
d. Wir haben Sport gemacht.
e. Wir werden Rad fahren gehen.
f. Ich war schwimmen.
g. Ich werde ins Stadion gehen.
h. Wir haben Basketball gespielt.
i. Wir waren Sightseeing.
j. Wir haben Schnitzel gegessen.
k. Ich habe ein Buch gelesen.
l. Wir haben uns Filme angesehen.

9. Translate into German

a. I had a great time with my best friend.
b. I went to the cinema with my girlfriend.
c. We went sightseeing in the old town.
d. I am going to play basketball tomorrow.
e. I didn't do anything last Saturday.
f. We went shopping in the shopping centre near my house.
g. We are going to go to a party.
h. I went swimming and bike riding.
i. I didn't do my homework.
j. I didn't wash the car because I had to study.

Unit 11

Talking about a past holiday – where we went & where we stayed

In this unit you will learn:

- To describe a past holiday
- To say what you "had" to do and what you "wanted" to do

Key sentence patterns:

- Verb in the perfect tense + time marker + noun or prepositional phrase
- Verb phrase in the perfect tense + causal clause
- Local adverbial + verb in the past tense + prepositional phrase

Grammar:

- Perfect tense of *fahren, (an)reisen, wohnen*
- Preposition *in* + *Dativ* or *Akkusativ*
- Prepositions *auf, bei* and *nach* + *Dativ*

UNIT 11: Talking about a past holiday – where we went & where we stayed

Ich bin *[I...]* **Wir sind** *[We...]*	**letztes Jahr** *[last year]* **letzten Sommer** *[last summer]*	**vor einem Monat** *[one month ago]* **vor zwei Wochen** *[two weeks ago]*	***auf Urlaub gefahren** *[...went on holiday]*

Ich bin *[I...]* **Wir sind** *[We...]*	**nach** *[to]*	**China** *[China]* **Deutschland** *[Germany]* **Frankreich** *[France]*	**Irland** *[Ireland]* **Italien** *[Italy]* **Japan** *[Japan]*	**Österreich** *[Austria]* **Spanien** *[Spain]*	**gefahren** *[...went]*
	in *[to]*	**die Schweiz** *[Switzerland]* **die Vereinigten Staaten / die USA** *[the United States]*			

Ich bin *[I...]* **Wir sind** *[We...]*	**mit dem** *[by]*	**Auto** *[car]* **Bus** *[coach]* **Flugzeug** *[plane]* **Boot/Schiff** *[boat]* **Zug** *[train]*	**angereist** *[...travelled]* **gefahren** *[...went]*	**und die Fahrt** *[and the trip]*	**war angenehm** *[was comfy]* **war lang** *[was long]* **war lustig** *[was fun]* **war schnell** *[was quick]* **war toll** *[was great]*	
					dauerte *[took/lasted]*	**eine Stunde** **zwei Stunden**

Ich habe *[I...]* **Wir haben** *[We...]*	**in**	**einem Ferienappartment** *[a holiday apartment]* **einem günstigen Hotel** *[a cheap hotel]* **einem Hostel** **einer Jugendherberge** *[in a youth hostel]* **einem Luxushotel** *[a luxury hotel]*	**übernachtet** *[...stayed]*
	auf *[at]*	**einem Bauernhof** *[a farm]* **einem Campingplatz** *[a campsite]*	
	bei *[at]*	**meinen Großeltern** *[my grandparents' house]*	

Mir hat es gefallen, weil *[I liked it because]* **Ich hatte eine tolle Zeit, weil** *[I had a great time because]*	**das Hotel toll war** *[the hotel was great]* **die Leute nett waren** *[the people were nice]*	**es viele Angebote gab** *[there was a lot on offer]* **es schöne Strände gab** *[there were beautiful beaches]*

Im Hotel *[In the hotel]*	**gab es** *[there was/were]*	**ein Fitnessstudio** *[a gym]* **einen Pool** *[an outdoor swimming pool]* **einen Tennisplatz** *[a tennis court]*	**ein Spielzimmer für Kinder** *[a playroom for kids]* **einen Spabereich für meine Eltern** *[a spa area for my parents]*

***Author's note: due to regional differences, "auf Urlaub", "in Urlaub", and "in den Urlaub" are all acceptable ways of expressing "*on holiday*".**

1. Match

das Schiff das Auto die Fahrt das günstige Hotel das Luxushotel der Bauernhof bei meinen Großeltern das Flugzeug der Tennisplatz die Leute	the people at my grandparents' house the car the luxury hotel the farm the trip the plane the cheap hotel the ship the tennis court

2. Complete with the missing letter

a. Ich bin nach Fran__reich gefahren.

b. Ich bin nach Deut__chland gefahren.

c. Ich bin nach Jap__n gefahren.

d. Ich bin nach Spani__n gefahren.

e. Ich bin nach Itali__n gefahren.

f. Ich bin auf einen Ba__ernhof gefahren.

g. Ich bin in die Schwei__ gefahren.

h. Ich bin nach Ir__and gefahren.

3. Break the flow

a. LetztesJahrbinichnachDeutschlandgefahren.

b. IchbinmitmeinerFamiliedorthingefahren.

c. WirsindmitdemAutogereist.

d. DieReisewarlangundlangweilig.

e. IchhabeineinemLuxushotelnahedemStrandübernachtet.

f. DasHotelwargroßundmodern.

4. Complete with a suitable word

a. Letztes Jahr bin ich mit dem ____________ nach Italien gefahren.

b. Die Reise war sehr ______________.

c. Das Hotel war __________________.

d. Ich bin mit meiner ____________ nach England gefahren.

e. Es hat mir sehr _______________.

f. Die Leute waren ________________.

5. Faulty translation: correct the English

a. Vor zwei Wochen bin ich nach Österreich gefahren.
Two months ago, I went to Austria.

b. Die Reise mit dem Schiff war sehr lang.
The car trip was very fast.

c. Die letzte Woche war langweilig.
The last weekend was boring.

d. Ich hatte eine tolle Zeit.
I had a horrible time.

e. Es gab tolle Sehenswürdigkeiten.
There were great facilities.

f. Wir haben in einer Jugendherberge übernachtet.
We stayed in a luxury hotel.

g. Es gab viele Angebote für junge Leute.
There was a lot on offer for old people.

h. Es gab einen Tennisplatz.
We played tennis.

6. Sentence puzzle: rewrite the sentences

a. Monat gefahren wir nach sind Österreich Letzten.
Last month we went to Austria.

b. bin gefahren Ich mit besten Freund dorthin meinem.
I went there with my best friend.

c. Wir gemietet mit Zug und ein dann gefahren wir dem sind Auto haben.
We went by train and then we rented a car.

d. Die , aber sehr lang lustig war Fahrt.
The trip was very long but a lot of fun.

e. Ich Hotel in übernachtet einem im Stadtzentrum günstigen habe.
I stayed in a cheap hotel in the city centre.

7. Complete with the correct form of *sein*:

***ich bin, du bist, er/sie ist, wir sind, ihr seid, sie sind* gefahren**

a. Letztes Jahr ____ ich nach Italien gefahren.

b. Mein Bruder ____ nach Österreich gefahren.

c. Meine Eltern ____ nach Spanien gefahren.

d. Vor zwei Jahren ____ mein Freund und ich nach England gefahren.

e. Und du, wo ____ du hingefahren?

f. Und dein Bruder, wo ____ er hingefahren?

g. Mein bester Freund ____ nirgends hingefahren.

h. Meine Nachbarn ____ nach Wien gefahren.

i. Und ihr, wo ____ ihr hingefahren?

j. Wo ____ Sie hingefahren, Herr Meier?

8. Verb anagrams

a. Ich **tthae** eine tolle Zeit.
I had a great time.

b. Am ersten Tag **raw** das Wetter gut.
The weather was good on the first day.

c. Wir sind an den Strand **gangegen**.
We went to the beach.

d. Wir haben in einem Luxushotel **neracühbtet**. *We stayed in a luxury hotel.*

e. Im Hotel **abg** es einen tollen Swimmingpool.
In the hotel there was a great swimming pool.

f. Meine Eltern haben viel **sgeeseng**.
My parents ate a lot.

g. Mein Bruder hat jeden Tag Tennis **sgeieltp**.
My brother played tennis every day.

9. Gapped translation

a. Letzten Monat sind wir nach Zürich gefahren. *Last __________ we went to Zurich.*

b. Wir sind mit dem Flugzeug geflogen und haben ein Auto gemietet. *We took the plane and ___________ a car.*

c. Das Wetter war jeden Tag schön. *The weather was _________ every day.*

d. Wir haben in einem günstigen Hotel übernachtet. *We stayed in a ___________ hotel.*

e. Das Hotel war sehr weit vom Stadtzentrum entfernt. *The hotel was very __________ the city centre.*

f. Es gab viele Angebote für Jugendliche. *There was a lot on offer for ________________.*

g. An einem Tag habe wir einen Bootsausflug gemacht. *One day we went on a __________ trip.*

10. Translate into English

a. Wir sind mit dem Schiff gereist.

b. Wir sind nach Griechenland gefahren.

c. Ich bin nirgendwo hingefahren.

d. Es gab tolle Strände.

e. Meine Eltern hatten viel Spaß.

f. Wir haben oft Sightseeing gemacht.

g. Wir haben in einer Jugendherberge übernachtet.

h. Es gab viele Angebote für Jugendliche.

i. Wir hatten viel Spaß.

j. Wir waren fast jeden Tag wandern.

k. Die Leute waren sehr nett.

l. Wir haben viele tolle Orte gesehen.

11. Wordsearch: find the German translation of the sentences below and write them as shown in the example

```
L Z L T F V K T C U Y E L D Z L Q U N H E A S V F
T K V O O H T K P N K Q I E U J P L K D Q A T M V
Z I G A H Y H N C Y T Y U N T C E W K Z L D V N Z
N B X W N D A K E A D G V I T T L T B T G T B J X
B Q Z I R S V U N M G P G K O E E Q Q Y P H O U Y
L A W Z E F M L P P T A L H A Q N K M W S C J O O
Y M R U U C B Z C T P R M I J O E N T P I Y G P B
D O D K A S V L E Z O E A M P B Z B I Y Q F M N U
B F Y G B V R L L Q N Y V P U L U E Z S U X D I O
W J Y L N R E M M I Z L E I P S N I E K P B H L A
Z G F H I D O P E K L X F Q M A J Q R V O L A N L
O Q J R E X O N T O U U I A I V N A T S S F A F G
Q Y Q E Y S I W O S K E L Z Z G M E S I S I R T L
B H N I V P A D L G W Z W D N U V B I U C D J K Z
F X T E C A Y D L M S X J B I C L X Z R L C L J O
H C I E R E B A P S N I E H I G S C J K E O A F U
Y E G U U W Q W I C H B I N G E R E I S T F F N X
```

e.g. a spa area — ***ein Spabereich***

a. *a play room*

b. *a farm*

c. *I travelled*

d. *great*

e. *holiday apartment*

f. *in a hotel*

g. *a tennis court*

12. Categorise the sentences below with a T for "means of transport", an A for "accommodation" or a W for "weather"

a. Das Hotel war sehr schön.
b. Wir sind mit dem Schiff gereist.
c. Wir haben in einer Jugendherberge übernachtet.
d. Wir hatten schönes Wetter.
e. Wir haben eine Radtour gemacht.
f. Der Bus war schmutzig und hat gestunken.
g. Wir waren auf einem Campingplatz.
h. Mein Bruder ist nach Japan geflogen.
i. Mein Zimmer hat mir sehr gut gefallen.
j. Meine Eltern haben bei meinem Onkel übernachtet.
k. An einem Tag hat es am Morgen geregnet.
l. Wir haben ein Chalet im Grünen gemietet.

13. Slalom writing

e.g. We travelled by plane, and then by car.
a. The trip was long, boring and tiring.
b. Our hotel was near the city centre.
c. In the hotel there was a playroom for kids.
d. My parents went shopping.
e. My sister went sightseeing with her boyfriend.
f. My brother and I went to the beach.
g. We had a great time. I want to go back there.

Wir sind	eine tolle	sind	Strand	gegangen.
Die Fahrt	**mit dem**	mit ihrem Freund	**und dann**	gegangen.
Unser	Eltern	**Flugzeug gereist,**	einkaufen	**mit dem Auto.**
Im Hotel	Hotel	sind an den	Spielzimmer	vom Stadtzentrum.
Meine	gab es	lang,	in der Nähe	gemacht.
Meine Schwester	und ich	war	dorthin	anstrengend.
Mein Bruder	war	ein	langweilig und	für Kinder.
Wir hatten	hat	Zeit. Ich will	Sightseeing	zurückkehren.

Letztes Jahr bin ich nach Österreich gefahren. Wir sind mit dem Zug gefahren und haben dann ein Auto gemietet. Die Fahrt war ziemlich lang und langweilig. Wir haben in einem sehr guten Hotel in Wien übernachtet. Das Hotel war sehr nahe dem Stadtzentrum. Es war toll. Es gab einen fantastischen Pool, ein Spielzimmer für Kinder und auch einen Spabereich für meine Eltern. Das Essen im Restaurant war köstlich, also haben wir viel gegessen. Das Wetter war jeden Tag gut und so konnten wir schwimmen gehen. Abends ist mein älterer Bruder in die Klubs gegangen. **(Rita, 13 Jahre. Ulm)**

Letztes Jahr bin ich nach Österreich gefahren. Wir sind mit dem Flugzeug angereist und haben uns dann ein Auto gemietet. Der Flug war kurz, aber ziemlich langweilig. Wir haben in einem günstigen Hotel übernachtet. Das Hotel war sehr weit vom Stadtzentrum entfernt (drei Kilometer), sodass wir viel laufen mussten. Das Hotel hat mir nicht so gut gefallen. Es gab einen kleinen Pool ohne Wasser und keinen Fitnessraum. Im Restaurant gab es nur ungesundes und fettiges Essen, daher habe ich nicht viel gegessen. Zum Glück war das Wetter fast jeden Tag schön, sodass wir sehr oft in einem nahen See schwimmen gehen konnten. Es gab viele gute Geschäfte und ich habe viel Kleidung und Ohrringe gekauft. Meine Eltern sind jeden Abend in Restaurants gegangen. Das Beste war, dass viele junge Leute im Hotel waren. **(Alice, 14 Jahre. Mainz)**

15. Answer the following questions about Alice

a. How did she travel to Austria?

b. What was the flight like? (2 details)

c. Where did they stay?

d. How far was the hotel from the city centre?

e. How often did Alice go swimming?

f. What did her parents do in the evenings?

g. What did Alice buy there?

h. What was wrong with the swimming pool?

i. What was the best thing about the hotel?

Letztes Jahr war ich mit meinen Eltern, meinen Onkeln und Cousins auf Sylt. Wir sind mit einem Schiff angereist und haben dann ein Auto gemietet. Die Reise war sehr lang, hat aber viel Spaß gemacht. Auf dem Schiff gab es viele Angebote für junge Leute. Ich hatte eine fantastische Zeit. Auf Sylt haben wir in einem Vier-Sterne-Hotel am Meer übernachtet. Ich habe das Hotel geliebt. Es gab einen Tennisplatz, ein riesiges Fitnessstudio und drei Restaurants. Das Essen war gut, also haben wir viel gegessen. Es war sonnig und heiß, also sind wir jeden Tag an den Strand gegangen. Nachmittags habe ich mich im Hotel ausgeruht und gelesen, aber mein Bruder und meine Cousine sind jeden Tag ausgegangen.
(Chiara, 12 Jahre. Stuttgart)

14. Find the German equivalent in Rita's text

a. we rented	j. therefore
b. the trip	k. good weather
c. quite long	l. we were able to swim
d. we stayed	m. every day
e. was very near	n. in the evening
f. there was	o. it was great
g. a playroom	p. in the afternoon
h. a spa area	q. my older brother
i. the food	r. went clubbing

16. Find someone who…

a. …stayed in a cheap hotel

b. …stayed in a four-star hotel

c. …went on holiday with their cousins

d. …rented a car

e. …stayed in a hotel without a gym

f. …went swimming in a lake

g. …bought lots of earrings

h. …loved the hotel

i. …had a fantastic pool in their hotel

j. …travelled on a ship

k. …didn't like their hotel much

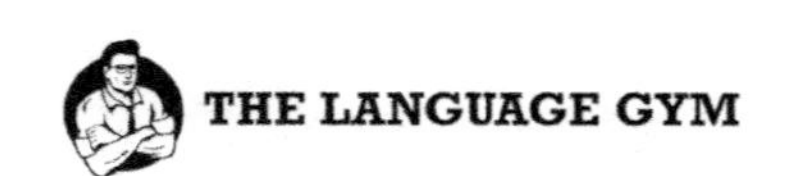

17. Complete with the options provided in the box below

Letztes Jahr bin ich nach ___________ gereist. Wir sind mit dem ________ geflogen und dann haben wir ein Auto gemietet. Die Reise war ziemlich ___________ und langweilig. Wir waren in einem sehr _____________ (aber guten) Hotel in Bremen. Das Hotel war nicht weit vom ___________ entfernt. Das war _____________. Es gab einen sehr _________ Pool, ein Spielzimmer für die Kinder und auch einen Spabereich für meine Eltern. Im Restaurant gab es sehr ____________ Essen, also haben wir viel gegessen. Es war jeden Tag _____________, also sind wir oft schwimmen gegangen. Abends bin ich nicht _____________, aber mein älterer Bruder schon. **(Johanna, 13. Linz)**

ausgegangen	lang	toll	großen	Flugzeug
günstigen	heiß	Deutschland	Stadtzentrum	leckeres

18. Jigsaw reading: arrange in the correct order

Letztes Jahr bin ich nach Deutschland gefahren. Wir sind mit dem Flugzeug angereist und	1
dann haben wir ein Auto gemietet. Die Reise war	
übernachtet. Das Hotel	
Pool und einen super Fitnessraum.	
war weit vom Stadtzentrum entfernt, sodass wir	
Das Hotel war toll. Es gab einen großen, sauberen	
ziemlich langweilig. Wir haben in einem sehr schönen Hotel in Stralsund	
lange laufen mussten.	

19. Correct the following sentences from Alice's text at page 140

a. Letztes Jahr bist ich nach Österreich gefahren.

b. Das Flug war kurz, aber ziemlich langweilig.

c. Wir hast in einem günstigen Hotel übernachtet.

d. Das Hotel war sehr weit Stadtzentrum entfernt, sodass wir lange laufen mussten.

e. Das Hotel hat nicht so gut gefallen.

f. Im Restaurant gab es nur ungesundes und fettiges Essen, daher habe nicht viel gegessen.

20. Complete the sentences below with any suitable word

a. Letztes Jahr bin ich nach ______________ gefahren.

b. Ich bin mit dem ____________ gereist.

c. Die Reise war ziemlich ____________ und ____________.

d. Wir haben in einem ______________ Hotel übernachtet.

e. Das Hotel war in der Nähe vom ____________.

f. Das Hotel war toll, weil es ____________ war.

g. Das Essen war _______________.

h. Am Nachmittag bin ich im Hotel ________________.

i. In der Stadt gab es viele Geschäfte, sodass ich viel ________________ habe.

<table>
<tr><td colspan="6">Im Hotel</td></tr>
<tr><td rowspan="3">*Mir hat
[I...]</td><td rowspan="3">mein Zimmer
[my room]</td><td rowspan="3">gefallen,
[...liked]

nicht gefallen,
[...didn't like]</td><td rowspan="2">weil es
[because it]</td><td>gut ausgestattet [well furnished]
schlecht ausgestattet [badly furnished]
sauber [clean]
schmutzig [dirty]</td><td>war
[was]</td></tr>
<tr><td>einen Meerblick [sea views]</td><td>hatte</td></tr>
<tr><td></td><td>alte Möbel [old furniture]
einen neuen Fernseher [a new TV]
ein bequemes Bett [a comfortable bed]
saubere Kissen [clean pillows]</td><td>gab</td></tr>
<tr><td rowspan="2">Es gab
[There was /were]</td><td colspan="3">schmutzige Kissen [dirty pillows]
saubere Bettlaken [clean sheets]
Kakerlaken [cockroaches]</td><td colspan="2">im Hotelzimmer
[in the room]</td></tr>
<tr><td colspan="3">keine Seife [no soap]
keine sauberen Handtücher [no clean towels]</td><td colspan="2">im Badezimmer
[in the bathroom]</td></tr>
<tr><td colspan="2">Der Aufzug [lift]
Der Fernseher
Der Kühlschrank
[fridge]</td><td colspan="2">Die Dusche [shower]
Die Klimaanlage
[air conditioning]</td><td>Das WiFi</td><td>hat gut funktioniert
[worked well]
hat nicht gut funktioniert
[did not work well]</td></tr>
<tr><td colspan="6">*Author's note: The personal pronoun "mir" is the dative case of "ich" and serves as the indirect object of the sentence. It translates into English as "to me" or "for me".</td></tr>
</table>

21. Gapped translation

a. saubere Handtücher *clean* ________________
b. gut ausgestattet *well-*________________
c. keine Seife *no* __________
d. im Badezimmer *in the*_______________.
e. mit Meerblick *with* ___________.
f. nichts hat funktioniert *nothing* ___________.
g. viele Kakerlaken *many* ____________
h. alte Möbel *old* _______________
i. schmutzige Kissen *dirty* ___________
j. saubere Bettlaken *clean* ______________
k. eine Klimaanlage *air* ______________
l. eine neuer Fernseher *a* _____________ *TV*
m. ein bequemes Bett *a* _____________ *bed*
n. ein Kühlschrank *a* _____________

22. Match

sauber	sea views
schmutzig	fridge
hat funktioniert	furniture
Kühlschrank	towels
gut ausgestattet	it worked
Möbel	sheets
Meerblick	well-furnished
Handtücher	dirty
Bettlaken	soap
Seife	clean

23. Complete with the missing letters

a. mein Z _ _ _ _ _ *my room*
b. ein b _ _ _ _ _ _ _ _ Bett *a comfy bed*
c. nichts hat f _ _ _ _ _ _ _ _ _ _ _ *nothing worked*
d. saubere K _ _ _ _ _ *clean pillows*
e. es gab K _ _ _ _ _ _ _ _ _ *there were cockroaches*
f. schlecht a _ _ _ _ _ _ _ _ _ _ _ *badly-furnished*

24. Match questions and answers

Wo warst du auf Urlaub?	Es gab ein Bett, einen Schreibtisch und einen Fernseher.
Wann warst du dort?	Wir haben in einem Hotel übernachtet.
Wie bist du gereist?	Mit dem Flugzeug natürlich.
Mit wem warst du dort?	Einen sehr großen Pool, ein Fitnessstudio und ein Restaurant.
Wo hast du übernachtet?	Zwei Wochen.
Wo war das Hotel?	Sehr sauber und gemütlich.
Wie war das Hotel?	Letzen Sommer.
Was gab es im Hotel?	In Stralsund in Deutschland.
Wie lang hast du dort übernachtet?	Es war in der Nähe vom Stadtzentrum.
Wie war dein Zimmer?	Mit meiner Familie.
Wie war dein Zimmer ausgestattet?	Es war ein Luxushotel, sehr groß und modern.

25. Complete with the missing letters

a. V _ _ zwei Jahren. *Two years ago.*

b. Wir sind nach Deutschland g _ _ _ _ _ _ _ _. *We went to Germany.*

c. Ich bin mit dem Flugzeug g _ _ _ _ _ _ _. *I travelled by plane.*

d. Es w _ _ sehr entspannend. *It was very relaxing.*

e. Wir haben auf einem Campingplatz ü _ _ _ _ _ _ _ _ _ _. *I stayed at a campsite.*

f. Ich habe viele Sehenswürdigkeiten g _ _ _ _ _ _ _. *I saw many monuments.*

26. Translate into German

a. last year
b. we travelled by car
c. I stayed
d. in a cheap hotel
e. near the city centre
f. there was a big swimming pool
g. delicious food
h. the weather was nice
i. nearly every day
j. fortunately
k. it was great

27. Complete

a. I___ b__ n_____ D_____________ a___ U________ g________. *I went on holiday to Germany.*

b. I___ b___ m___ d____ A________ g_____________. *I travelled by car.*

c. I___ b___ m___ m______ F________ d________ g________. *I went there with my family.*

d. D___ F_______ w____ l_______. *The journey was long.*

e. W_____ h______ i_ e____ J_____________ ü_____________. *We stayed in a youth hostel.*

f. M__ h___ d__ H_______ s______ g___ g_____________. *I liked the hotel a lot.*

g. W__ h_______ e______ t_______ Z______. *We had a great time.*

h. I___ H_______ g_____ e__ v____ A_____________. *In the hotel there was a lot on offer.*

Letztes Jahr war ich mit meinem besten Freund Leo in Italien. Wir sind mit dem Flugzeug angereist und haben uns dann ein Auto gemietet. Die Fahrt war ziemlich lang und langweilig. Wir haben in einem sehr guten Hotel in Sorrento übernachtet, einer sehr touristischen Stadt im Süden des Landes. Das Hotel war sehr nahe dem Strand. Es hat mir sehr gut gefallen, weil es modern und komfortabel war. Es gab einen Pool, ein Spielzimmer für Kinder und auch einen Spabereich. Das Essen im Restaurant war großartig, also haben wir viel gegessen. Das Wetter war jeden Tag gut, sodass wir oft an den Strand gehen konnten.

(Jürgen, 18 Jahre. Hamburg)

28a. Answer the questions as if you were Jürgen (using answers from the text where possible)

a. Wo warst du auf Urlaub?

b. Wann bist du gefahren?

c. Wie bist du angereist?

d. Mit wem bist du gefahren?

e. Wo hast du übernachtet?

f. Wo liegt die Stadt?

g. Wo war das Hotel?

h. Wie war das Hotel?

i. Was gab es im Hotel?

j. Wie war das Essen?

k. Wie war das Wetter?

l. Was hast du oft gemacht?

28b. Cast your mind back to a recent holiday of yours and answer the questions in 28a Please answer with full sentences

29. Translate into German

a. Last year I went on holiday to Germany. I travelled by plane. We stayed in a luxury hotel in Munich. The hotel was very beautiful and modern. There were a lot of sports facilities. Moreover, there was a nice restaurant and some very nice clothes shops.

b. Fortunately, the weather was good, therefore we were able to go to the Isar every day. The Isar was only 300 metres on foot from the hotel. Every day we sunbathed, swam, played volleyball and went for long walks along the river. The people there were very nice and friendly.

c. I really liked the hotel. There were many things on offer for young people like me, and also a spa area for my parents. The swimming pool and the gym were phenomenal. In the evening there were live concerts *[Live-Konzerte]* and other shows. My room was big and well furnished. There was a big TV and a big balcony with a view of the city. Everything worked perfectly.

d. My friend Paul went on holiday to Germany too, but he went to Berlin. He was there with his mother and his sister. The weather wasn't good, so he couldn't do much sightseeing every day. He loves to walk around the city, so he was very disappointed. Fortunately, there were many good shops, so he bought a lot of things for himself and his girlfriend.

Question Skills Unit 11

English	German
Where did you go on holidays last year?	**Wo warst du letztes Jahr auf Urlaub?**
When did you go?	**Wann bist du gefahren?**
How did you travel? How was the trip?	**Wie bist du angereist? Wie war die Fahrt?**
How long did the trip take?	**Wie lange hat die Fahrt gedauert?**
Who did you go with?	**Mit wem bist du gefahren?**
Where did you stay? What was it like?	**Wo hast du übernachtet? Wie war es?**
Did you like the hotel? Why? Why not?	**Hat dir das Hotel gefallen? Warum? Warum nicht?**
What did you do during the holidays?	**Was hast du im Urlaub gemacht/unternommen?**
What shops were there? What did you buy?	**Welche Geschäfte gab es? Was hast du gekauft?**
What was the food like?	**Wie war das Essen?**
Did you try any typical dish?	**Hast du ein typisches Gericht probiert?**
What was the weather like?	**Wie war das Wetter?**
What places did you visit?	**Welche Orte hast du besucht?**
What tourist attractions were there?	**Welche Sehenswürdigkeiten gab es?**
What was the best/worst about your holidays?	**Was war das Beste/Schlechteste an deinem Urlaub?**
Did you have any problem in your hotel?	**Hattest du irgendein Problem im Hotel?**
Would you like to go back next year?	**Würdest du nächstes Jahr gerne wieder dorthin fahren?**

1. Complete the sentences using the words provided

a. Wo ______ du letztes Jahr auf Urlaub?

b. Wie bist du ________________ und _________ war die Fahrt?

c. Mit _______________ bist du gefahren?

d. _______________ hast du übernachtet? Hat es dir _______________?

e. Was hast du im Urlaub _______________?

f. Hast du ein typisches Gericht _______________?

g. ________________ Sehenswürdigkeiten gab es?

h. ________________ du irgendein Problem im Hotel?

wem
wie
welche
wo
hattest
unternommen
gefallen
angereist
warst
probiert

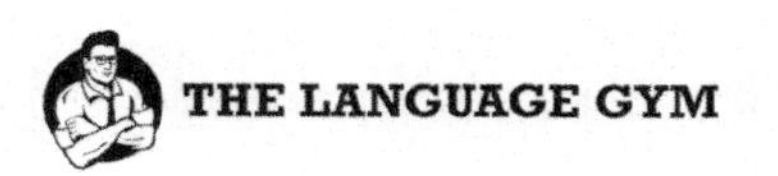

2. Write a question for each of the answers

Question	Answer
a. ______________________________?	Ich bin nach Hamburg gefahren.
b. ______________________________?	Ich bin bin dem Bus angereist und habe mir dann ein Auto gemietet.
c. ______________________________?	Ich bin mit meinem Freund Nico gefahren.
d. ______________________________?	Ich habe in einem günstigen Hotel übernachtet.
e. ______________________________?	Mir hat das Hotel gefallen, weil es sehr gemütlich war.
f. ______________________________?	Es war jeden Tag sonnig.
g. ______________________________?	Ich war einkaufen und habe mich entspannt.
h. ______________________________?	Das Beste war das Essen.
i. ______________________________?	Es gab Kakerlaken in meinem Zimmer.

3. Rewrite the questions in correct German

a. Wo wast du leztes Jahr auv Urlaup?	*Where did you go on holiday last year?*
b. Wie bisst du amgeriest?	*How did you travel?*
c. Wo hasst du ubernachtet?	*Where did you stay?*
d. Wie war dass Weter?	*What was the weather like?*
e. Wass hast du im Urlaup undernomen?	*What did you do during the holiday?*
f. Wurdesst du nähstes Jar gerrne wider dorthin faren?	*Would you like to go back next year?*
g. Wie wahr de Farrt? Wi longe hat sie gedrauert?	*What was the trip like? How long did it take?*

4. Translate into German

a. Where did you go on holiday last year?

b. Who did you go with?

c. How did you travel?

d. Where did you stay?

e. How was the hotel?

f. Did you have any problem in the hotel?

g. What did you do during the holidays?

h. Did you try any typical dish?

i. What was the best thing about the holidays?

j. Would you like to go back next year?

Unit 12

Talking about a past holiday – what we did and our opinion of it

In this unit you will learn:

- To talk about what your family, friends and you did during a holiday
- To give your opinion about what you liked & disliked

Key sentence patterns:

- Time marker + perfect tense + noun phrase
- Time marker + perfect tense of *fahren* and *(an)reisen* + noun phrase + *um ... zu* + infinitive
- *Das Beste war, als* + perfect tense + prepositional phrase
- *Meiner Meinung nach* + *war es ein* + adjective + *Urlaub* + adversative clause

Grammar:

- First person perfect tense
- Use of *um ... zu* to indicate "in order to"
- Use of Konjunktiv II to indicate "I would like"

Unit 12: Talking about a past holiday – what we did and our opinion of it

Im Urlaub *[During the holidays]* **Am ersten Tag** *[On the first day]*	**habe ich viel gemacht/unternommen** *[I did many things]* **habe ich fast nichts gemacht** *[I did hardly anything]* **habe ich viel Zeit mit meiner Familie verbracht** *[I spent a lot of time with my family]* **habe ich einige Zeit allein verbracht** *[I spent quite a bit of time alone]*

<table>
<tr><td rowspan="5">Am ersten Tag [On the first day]
Am zweiten Tag [On the second day]
Am Morgen [In the morning]
Am Nachmittag [In the afternoon]
Am Abend [In the evening]</td><td>habe ich [I]
haben wir [we]</td><td colspan="4">einen Ausflug gemacht [went on a day trip]
einen netten Jungen/ein nettes Mädchen kennengelernt [met a nice boy/girl]
einen Spaziergang gemacht [went for a walk]
ein Rad gemietet [rented a bike]
historische Orte besucht [visited historic places]
leckeres Essen gegessen [ate delicious food]
typische Gerichte probiert [tried typical dishes]</td></tr>
<tr><td>habe ich mich [I]
haben wir uns [we]</td><td colspan="4">am Strand entspannt [relaxed on the beach]
gesonnt [sunbathed]</td></tr>
<tr><td rowspan="3">bin ich [I...]
sind wir [we...]</td><td colspan="4">spät aufgestanden [got up late]
spät schlafen gegangen [went to bed late]</td></tr>
<tr><td>an den See [to the lake]
auf den Berg [to the mountain]
in den Klub [to the club]
ins Stadtzentrum [to the city centre]</td><td>gegangen, [...went]
gefahren, [...went]</td><td>um</td><td>einkaufen zu gehen [to go shopping]
schwimmen zu gehen [to go swimming]
zu wandern [to hike]
zu feiern [to party]</td></tr>
<tr><td>tauchen [scuba diving]
in ein Restaurant</td><td colspan="3">gegangen [...went]</td></tr>
</table>

Das Beste war, *[The best thing was]*	**dass ich** *[that I]*	**mit meinem besten Freund** **mit meiner besten Freundin** *[with my best friend]* **mit meinen Cousins** **mit meinen Großeltern** *[with my grandparents]* **mit meiner Familie**	**ein Fußballspiel gesehen habe** *[saw a football match]* **in einem Restaurant zu Abend gegessen habe** *[had dinner in a restaurant]* **Zeit verbracht habe** *[spent time with]*

Meiner Meinung nach *[In my opinion]*	**war es ein** *[it was a]*	**echt toller** *[really great]* **langweiliger** *[boring]* **phänomenaler** *[phenomenal]*	**schrecklicher** *[terrible]* **unvergesslicher** *[unforgettable]*	**Urlaub** *[holiday]*

und *[and]* **, aber** *[but]*	**ich würde** *[I would...]*	**nächstes Jahr** *[next year]*	**gerne** *[...like]* **nicht** *[...not like]*	**wieder dorthin fahren** *[to go back]*

1. Match

Am ersten Tag...	*On the first day...*
habe ich ein Fahrrad gemietet.	I sunbathed.
habe ich typische Gerichte probiert.	I went scuba diving.
habe ich Souvenirs gekauft.	I rented a bike.
habe ich mich gesonnt.	I relaxed on the beach.
bin ich tauchen gegangen.	I bought souvenirs.
habe mich am Strand entspannt.	I tried typical dishes.

2. Missing letters

a. Ich habe ein Rad gem__etet.
b. Ich habe Souvenirs ge__auft.
c. Ich habe mich ge__onnt.
d. Ich bin ta__chen gegangen.
e. Ich habe einen netten Jun__en kennengelernt.
f. Ich habe einen Spa__iergang im Stadtzentrum gemacht.
g. Ich habe typische __erichte probiert.
h. Ich war auf dem Land w__ndern.
i. Ich habe viele Fotos ge__acht.
j. Ich bin sp__t schlafen gegangen.

3. Faulty translation

a. Ich bin spät aufgestanden *I got up early.*
b. Ich bin wandern gegangen. *I relaxed.*
c. Ich hab einen Spaziergang gemacht. *I went for a run.*
d. Ich habe mich entspannt. *I danced.*
e. Ich habe einen Jungen kennengelernt. *I met a girl.*
f. Ich habe typische Gerichte probiert. *I avoived typical dishes.*
g. Ich habe fast nichts gemacht. *I did a lot.*
h. Ich habe mit meiner Familie Zeit verbracht. *I spent time with my friends.*

4. Spot and add the missing word

a. Es ein toller Urlaub. *It was a great holiday.*
b. Ich habe einen kennengelernt. *I met a boy.*
c. Ich habe gesonnt. *I sunbathed.*
d. Ich habe ein Rad. *I rented a bike.*
e. Ich habe Ausflug gemacht. *I went on a trip.*
f. Ich habe einen gemacht. *I went for a walk.*
g. Ich mit meinen Cousins gespielt. *I played with my cousins.*
h. Ich bin im Meer. *I swam in the sea.*
i. Ich bin tauchen. *I went diving.*

5. Sentence puzzle: rewrite the sentences in the correct order

a. Am Tag ich fast ersten gemacht habe nichts. *On the first day I did nearly nothing.*
b. Am bin Pool ich zum Morgen gegangen. *In the morning I went to the pool.*
c. gesonnt Ich mich gehört und dabei habe Musik. *I sunbathed listening to music.*
d. spät Eltern sind aufgestanden Meine. *My parents got up late.*
e. Mein seinem Bruder hat jüngerer die Zeit mit gespielt ganze Handy. *My younger brother spent all the time playing on his mobile phone.*
f. etwa gegessen 12:30 Um haben Mittag im Restaurant wir zu. *At around 12:30 we had lunch in the hotel restaurant.*
g. meinem Nach bin dort ich zum Strand niemand nahe Hotel gegangen Nickerchen dem, aber war. *After my nap I went to the beach near the hotel, but there was nobody there.*

6. Wordsearch: find the German translation of the sentences below and write them as shown in the example

E	H	E	B	F	D	W	H	T	K	G	Q	A	L	Y	B	X	H	R	H
I	N	V	T	F	S	E	I	S	U	S	M	J	S	K	V	P	E	H	C
X	B	R	Q	H	N	U	C	X	R	V	P	D	K	F	C	X	E	H	A
M	W	A	E	J	C	Z	G	M	L	M	D	P	J	N	B	G	L	S	N
R	P	Y	U	G	X	I	Z	J	A	S	Z	D	V	X	Y	O	A	M	G
X	X	E	L	F	E	B	R	Z	U	Y	M	S	D	Z	W	S	N	C	N
A	J	N	S	J	D	D	C	E	B	T	W	F	Z	X	J	M	W	P	U
C	E	U	S	T	N	E	R	I	G	K	H	R	U	U	J	P	D	S	N
T	S	V	E	E	D	M	N	Ü	M	E	S	E	D	Y	L	W	I	M	I
E	E	S	N	E	D	N	A	B	W	O	H	V	C	I	B	C	L	B	E
M	W	W	D	G	M	Q	K	I	E	H	M	C	I	U	H	V	Y	B	M
E	N	W	O	E	E	F	J	Q	Q	R	C	L	S	S	K	F	N	E	R
C	V	L	B	J	M	W	M	J	O	Q	G	I	O	I	H	C	N	G	E
B	X	F	Z	C	R	N	V	R	X	M	N	N	Y	R	P	O	G	X	N
C	J	W	T	Q	L	N	G	J	D	D	N	K	Z	P	S	Y	N	P	I
N	D	G	U	L	G	A	Q	Y	O	E	M	W	J	P	V	M	T	Z	E
Q	K	F	U	E	U	M	X	W	N	P	L	Z	Z	X	V	K	Y	N	M
I	C	H	H	A	B	E	I	N	R	A	D	G	E	M	I	E	T	E	T
K	X	T	J	A	G	X	A	A	E	A	U	C	G	E	F	T	M	S	R
R	H	A	J	S	E	T	S	H	C	Ä	N	T	M	Z	X	A	S	N	A

e.g. to the lake — ***an den See***

a. I would like to

b. typical dishes

c. in my opinion

d. I rented a bike

e. to the mountain

f. holidays

g. to sunbathe

h. next year

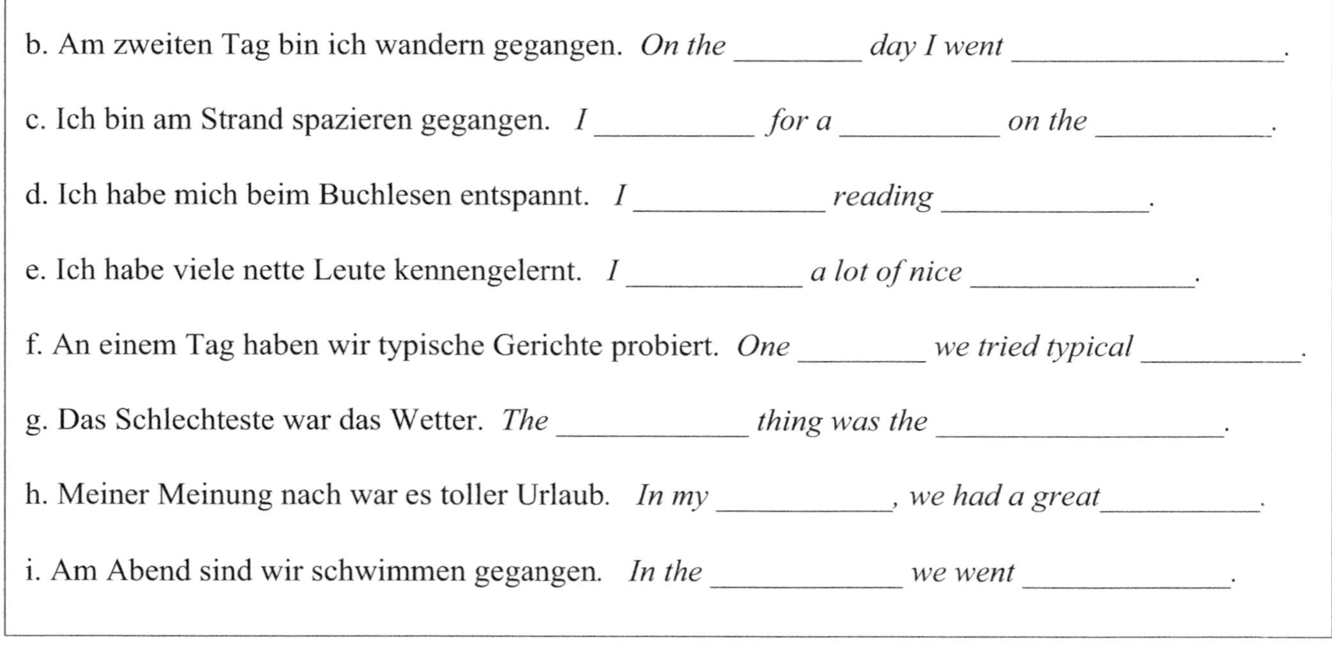

7. Gapped translation

a. Am ersten Tag habe ich fast nichts gemacht. *On the* ____________ *day, I did hardly* ___________.

b. Am zweiten Tag bin ich wandern gegangen. *On the* _________ *day I went* ________________.

c. Ich bin am Strand spazieren gegangen. *I* ___________ *for a* ___________ *on the* ____________.

d. Ich habe mich beim Buchlesen entspannt. *I* _____________ *reading* ______________.

e. Ich habe viele nette Leute kennengelernt. *I* ____________ *a lot of nice* _______________.

f. An einem Tag haben wir typische Gerichte probiert. *One* _________ *we tried typical* ___________.

g. Das Schlechteste war das Wetter. *The* _____________ *thing was the* ___________________.

h. Meiner Meinung nach war es toller Urlaub. *In my* ____________, *we had a great* ___________.

i. Am Abend sind wir schwimmen gegangen. *In the* _____________ *we went* ______________.

8. Complete with the correct option

a. Ich habe ______________ gemietet.

b. Ich habe _______________ durch das Stadtzentrum gemacht.

c. Ich habe __________________ gemacht.

d. Ich bin ___________________ geschwommen.

e. Ich habe viel ______________ mit meiner Familie verbracht.

f. Am ________________ war ich im Klub feiern.

g. Ich habe ________________________ probiert.

h. Ich war in der _________________.

i. Ich habe viele ____________ gekauft.

j. Ich habe viele ______________ gemacht.

Fotos	Abend	Zeit
fast nichts	ein Rad	im Meer
einen Spaziergang		Souvenirs
typische Gerichte		Altstadt

9. Complete the table

Deutsch	English
Ich bin wandern gegangen.	
Ich bin spät aufgestanden.	
	I took photos.
Ich habe in einem Restaurant gegessen.	
	I tried typical dishes.
Ich habe Zeit verbracht.	
Ich habe mich gesonnt.	
	I visited historic places.
	I went clubbing.

Paul: Das Beste war, dass wir einen Ausflug in eine historische Stadt gemacht haben. Es gab viele alte Gebäude und sogar ein Schloss. Es war sehr interessant.

Erika: Das Beste war, dass wir bis drei Uhr morgens tanzen gegangen sind.

Marta: Das Beste war, dass wir in das Restaurant in der Nähe von meinem Hotel gegangen sind und viele typische Gerichte probiert haben. Das Essen war so lecker!

Oskar: Das Beste war, dass wir mit meinen Cousins Skifahren waren. Es hat Spaß gemacht.

Anton: Das Beste war, dass wir ein Konzert in Wien besucht haben. Es war phänomenal.

Gabriel: Das Beste war, dass mein Bruder und ich zwei Mädchen aus Berlin getroffen haben. Sie waren so cool! Wir hatten viel Spaß mit ihnen.

Lisa: Das Beste war, dass wir ein Motorrad gemietet und die Stadt besichtigt haben.

Vera: Das Beste war, dass wir einkaufen gegangen sind und ich viele schöne Kleidung gekauft habe.

10. Find someone who...

a. ...rented a means of transport

b. ...went skiing with relatives

c. ...saw a concert

d. ...saw a castle

e. ...tried lots of typical dishes

f. ...went shopping and bought clothes

g. ...went dancing until late

h. ...met two cool girls

11. Find the German equivalent

a. the best thing was
b. a motorbike
c. pretty clothes
d. shopping
e. near my hotel
f. typical dishes
g. a concert
h. old buildings

i. a trip.
j. a lot of fun.
k. a castle
l. so delicious
m. phenomenal
n. a historic town
o. even
p. when we rented

12. Translate into English

a. Am ersten Tag habe ich nicht viel gemacht.

b. Ich habe viel Zeit mit meiner Familie verbracht.

c. Ich habe typische Gerichte probiert.

d. Wir haben einen Spaziergang durch die Altstadt gemacht.

e. Wir haben historische Orte besucht.

f. Ich bin spät schlafen gegangen.

g. Ich bin früh aufgestanden.

13. Anagrams: rewrite the word in bold correctly

Ich bin im Meer **gmecnhwsome**. *e.g.* **geschwommen**

a. Ich habe ein Motorrad **tgeietme**. ____________

b. Wie haben eine Radtour **eacmght**. ____________

c. Mein Bruder ist zum Strand **ngeagegn**. ________

d. Ich habe mich **gensnot**. ____________

e. Ich habe fast nichts **egmcaht**. ____________

f. Ich habe typische Gerichte **ropierbt**. __________

14. Insert *ich*, *du*, *er/sie/es*, *wir*, *ihr* or *sie* as appropriate

a. Und _______, seid _______ ausgegangen?

b. _________ habe historische Orte besucht.

c. _________ sind im Meer geschwommen.

d. _________ habe mich am Strand gesonnt.

e. _________ (Kai+Mia) haben im Café gegessen .

f. _____________ haben Sightseeing gemacht.

g. ___________ sind viel tauchen gegangen.

h. ____________ hast leckeres Essen gegessen.

i. _____________ habe ein Rad gemietet.

j. ___________ (ich+Tom) haben einen Spaziergang gemacht.

15. Complete the table

verb	perfect tense – ich	perfect tense – er/sie/es	perfect tense – sie/Sie
mieten *[to rent]*			haben gemietet
verbringen *[to spend time]*	habe verbracht		
sich sonnen *[to sunbathe]*		hat sich gesonnt	
kennenlernen *[to know]*	habe kennengelernt	hat kennengelernt	
machen *[to do]*		hat gemacht	haben gemacht
gehen *[to go]*		ist gegangen	sind gegangen
geben *[to give]*		hat gegeben	
sehen *[to see]*	habe gesehen		haben gesehen

16. Complete with the correct verb

a. Am ersten Tag haben wir einen Ausflug g _ _ _ _ _ _ _. *On the first day we went on a trip.*

b. Meine Eltern sind jeden Tag w _ _ _ _ _ _ _ gegangen. *My parents went hiking every day.*

c. Mein Bruder hat mit seinen Freunden Fußball g _ _ _ _ _ _ _ _. *My brother played football with his friends.*

d. Wir haben Zeit mit unseren Großeltern v _ _ _ _ _ _ _ _ _. *We spent time with our grandparents.*

e. Ich bin jeden Tag spät a _ _ _ _ _ _ _ _ _ _ _. *I woke up late every day.*

f. Ich habe historische Orte b _ _ _ _ _ _ _. *I visited historic places.*

g. Mein Vater hat ein kleines Boot g _ _ _ _ _ _ _ _. *My father rented a small boat.*

h. Ich habe viele Fotos g _ _ _ _ _ _ _. *I took many photos.*

17. Rock-climbing translation

e.g. On the first day I did hardly anything.

a. One day we rented a bike and went for a bike ride.

b. In the afternoon I relaxed listening to music and reading.

c. They were unforgettable holidays and I would love to go back.

d. The best thing was when we went clubbing.

e. The day before going back we met two girls from Vienna.

sind.	**gemacht.**	gemacht.	kennengelernt.	entspannt.	fahren.
nichts	gegangen	wieder dorthin	eine Radtour	zwei Mädchen aus Wien	und Lesen
haben wir	ich würde gerne	Musikhören	die Klubs	**fast**	gemietet und
ein Rad	mich beim	Urlaub und	**habe ich**	wir in	Abreise
war, als	**Tag**	habe ich	haben wir	unvergesslicher	unserer
Am ersten	An einem Tag	Am Nachmittag	Es war ein	Das Beste	Am Tag vor

18. Guided translation

a. A__ M_______ b___ i___ a__ d__ S_____ g________. *In the morning I went to the beach.*

b. I__ h_____ f____ n______ g___________. *I did hardly anything.*

c. I___ h_____ v____ Z____ m____ m_______ E________ v____________. *I spent a lot of time with my parents.*

d. E___ w______ e____ u______________ U_________. *They were unforgettable holidays.*

e. M_____ B_________ h____ e___ M________ k________________. *My brother met a girl.*

f. M______ E________ s_____ w_______ g__________. *My parents went hiking.*

Letzten Sommer war ich mit meiner Familie in Deutschland. Wir sind mit dem Zug angereist und haben uns dann ein Auto gemietet. Wir waren in einem sehr guten Hotel in der Nähe von Konstanz. Das Hotel lag direkt am Bodensee. Es war toll. Das Wetter war jeden Tag gut, sodass wir oft an den See gehen konnten. Am Morgen haben wir uns am See gesonnt, sind getaucht, geschnorchelt und geschwommen. Am Nachmittag haben wir uns im Hotel entspannt.
Am Tag vor der Abreise haben wir einen Ausflug nach Ulm gemacht. Es war sehr interessant, weil es eine sehr historische Stadt ist. Wir haben das Münster besucht und viele Fotos gemacht. Das Beste war, als mein Bruder und ich zwei nette englische Mädchen getroffen haben und mit ihnen essen gegangen sind. Es war großartig!
Jeden Tag sind wir früh aufgestanden und spät ins Bett gegangen. Daher waren wir am Ende des Urlaubs alle müde. Es war ein ausgezeichneter Urlaub.
(Marcel, 15 Jahre. Bern)

Letzten Winter, im Dezember, war ich in Innsbruck in Österreich. Wir sind mit dem Auto dorthin gefahren. Wir haben in einem sehr schönen Hotel in den Bergen übernachtet. Es hat mir sehr gut gefallen, weil es so gemütlich war und das Essen lecker war.
Es hat jeden Tag geschneit und wir konnten Ski fahren. Die Pisten waren großartig, aber es waren viele Leute da. Den Morgen haben wir mit Skifahren verbracht. Am Nachmittag haben wir uns im Hotel entspannt oder sind einkaufen gegangen. Meine Eltern haben viele Souvenirs gekauft und meine Schwester und ich habe viel schöne Kleidung gekauft.
Zwei Tage vor der Abreise nach Schottland haben wir einen Ausflug nach Wien gemacht. Es war sehr interessant, weil es eine sehr historische Stadt ist. Wir haben einen alten Palast, Museen und die Oper besucht. Wir haben viele Fotos gemacht. Außerdem haben wir typisch österreichische Gerichte probiert. Mein Bruder und ich haben viele Einheimische kennengelernt. Es war ein unvergesslicher Urlaub.
(Ross, 14. Glasgow)

19. Answer in English

a. How did Marcel travel to Germany?

b. How far was his hotel from Konstanz?

c. Where was the hotel?

d. What was the weather like?

e. How did they spend the mornings?

f. What did they do in the afternoons?

g. When did they go on a trip to Ulm?

h. What is the name of the cathedral they visited?

i. Where were the two girls they met from?

j. Why were they tired by the end of the holidays?

20. Tick the items that you can find (in German) in Marcel's text

a. summer	f. we took many photos
b. car	g. the best was
c. near	h. to eat Sushi
d. by the lake	i. we went to bed late
e. we were able to	j. first of all

21. Ross' text: find the German equivalent

a. last winter	g. we went shopping
b. we stayed	h. many souvenirs
c. I liked it a lot	i. nice clothes
d. there were	j. two days before
e. many people	k. Austrian dishes
f. we relaxed	l. local people

22. Find the German in Ross's text

a. a season starting with 'W': ____________

b. a means of transport with 'A': ____________

c. an adjective with 'g': ____________

d. a verb with 'e': ____________

e. a verb with 'p': ____________

f. an adjective with 'a': ____________

g. a noun with 'G': ____________

23. Jigsaw reading: arrange the text in the correct order

Letzten Sommer habe ich Urlaub in	1
der Nähe vom Zentrum übernachtet. Es hat mir	
gegangen sind. Es gab viele Angebote	
Restaurant war köstlich. Das Wetter war	
für junge Leute und es gab viele gute Geschäfte.	
Deutschland gemacht. Wir sind mit dem Flugzeug angereist und haben dann	
Wir haben viel gekauft. Ich habe	
gut gefallen, weil es groß und modern war. Es gab ein tolles Schwimmbad und das Fitnessstudio	
viel Kleidung und Souvenirs gekauft.	
jeden Tag gut, sodass wir jeden Tag schwimmen	
war sehr gut ausgestattet. Das Essen im	
ein Auto gemietet. Wir haben in einem Hotel in	

24. Complete with a suitable word

a. Wir sind nach ________________ gefahren.

b. Die Reise war sehr ______________.

c. Wir haben in einem günstigen Hotel __________.

d. Das Wetter war jeden Tag __________.

e. Am Morgen sind wir schwimmen __________.

f. Ich habe mich am See _________ und mich beim Musikhören __________.

g. Außerdem habe ich ein Buch __________.

h. Es gab viele _________ für junge Leute.

i. Es gab viele tolle __________, sodass ich viel ______________ gekauft habe.

25. Tangled translation: rewrite in German

a. Am ersten **day** haben wir einen **day trip** in die **mountains** gemacht.

b. Wir **have** in einem Hotel in der Nähe vom **city centre stayed**.

c. Im Hotel **there were** viel **on offer** für **young people**.

d. Wir haben sehr **delicious food** gegessen.

e. Zum Glück war das **weather** jeden **day nice**.

f. Wir sind oft **swimming went**.

g. Wir haben uns **sunbathed** und Volleyball **played**.

26. Translate into German

a. *I went hiking.* I _ _ b _ _ w _ _ _ _ _ _ _ g _ _ _ _ _ _ _ _.

b. *I rented a bike.* I _ _ h _ _ _ e _ _ R _ _ g _ _ _ _ _ _ _ _.

c. *We had dinner.* W _ _ h _ _ _ _ z _ A _ _ _ _ g _ _ _ _ _ _ _.

d. *He played tennis.* E _ h_ _ T _ _ _ _ _ _ g _ _ _ _ _ _ _ _.

e. *He got up late.* E _ _ i _ _ s _ _ _ a _ _ _ _ _ _ _ _ _ _ _ _ _.

27. Translate into German

a. On the 1st day I visited the old town.

b. On the 2nd day I rented a bike.

c. On the 3rd day we went sightseeing.

d. In the morning I got up late.

e. I sunbathed until noon.

f. We went hiking every day.

g. Yesterday I went for a walk.

h. We swam in the lake.

i. We stayed in a cheap hotel.

j. At night my parents went clubbing.

k. We tried typical dishes.

l. The weather was nice every day.

28. Complete the following sentences creatively

a. Letzten Sommer bin ich mit meiner ______________________________ nach ____________ ____________ gefahren.

b. Wir sind mit dem _____________ angereist und die Reise war ____________________

c. Während der Fahrt ____

d. Wir haben in einem ________________________ übernachtet, das ______________________ _____________ war.

e. Am ersten Tag ____

f. Am zweiten Tag ____

g. Am dritten Tag haben wir einen Ausflug gemacht. Wir sind ___________________________ ____ gefahren.

h. Nächstes Jahr würde ich gerne ____

29. Translate the paragraphs into German

1. Writing in the first person singular (*ich*), include the following points:

Last week I came back from Italy. I spent a week in Rome with my family.

I stayed in a cheap hotel near the train station. My room was small but cozy.

I visited the city centre, many museums, Roman ruins and saw many ancient monuments, churches and palaces.

The best thing was that I met a nice boy from Argentina. We had a great time together.

I also went to the beach. The beach was an hour from Rome by car.

2. Writing in the third person singular (*er/sie*), include the following points:

Two months ago, my older brother went to Germany on his own.

He stayed in a small village in the Black Forest *[Schwarzwald]*, half an hour away from Freiburg.

He rented a small apartment.

The apartment was clean and cozy but there was neither *[weder]* TV nor [*noch*] Internet.

The lake near the village was great, so he went swimming every day and went for long walks.

In the evenings he tried typical local dishes and afterwards went clubbing in Freiburg.

3. Writing in the third person plural (*sie*), include the following points:

Last winter your parents went to France.

They spent two weeks in Chamonix in the French Alps.

They stayed in a four-star hotel very near a fantastic ski slope *[Skipiste]*. The view was magnificent. It snowed every day, so there was a lot of snow.

They got up early and skied every morning and afternoon for one hour.

There were not a lot of people, so it was a lot of fun.

In the evening they ate French food. It was delicious.

Question Skills Unit 12

English	German
Where did you go on holiday last year?	**Wo warst du letztes Jahr auf Urlaub?**
How did you travel?	**Wie bist du (an)gereist?**
How long did the trip take? What was it like?	**Wie lange war die Fahrt? Wie war die Fahrt?**
Where did you stay?	**Wo hast du übernachtet?**
Did you like the hotel? Why? Why not?	**Hat dir das Hotel gefallen? Warum? Warum nicht?**
How long did you stay there?	**Wie lange warst du dort?**
What did you do on the first day in the morning?	**Was hast du am ersten Tag am Morgen gemacht?**
What did you do in the afternoon?	**Was hast du am Nachmittag unternommen?**
What was the weather like?	**Wie war das Wetter?**
What was the best thing about your holidays?	**Was war das Beste an deinem Urlaub?**
Did you like the holidays?	**Hat dir der Urlaub gefallen?**
How did the holidays go?	**Wie ist der Urlaub gelaufen?**
Would you like to go back next year?	**Würdest du nächstes Jahr gerne wieder dorthin fahren?**
Do you prefer to travel by car or by plane?	**Reist du lieber mit dem Auto oder dem Flugzeug?**
Who do you prefer to travel with, your friends or your parents?	**Mit wem reist du lieber, mit deinen Freunden oder deinen Eltern?**

1. Match questions and answers

Wo warst du letztes Jahr auf Urlaub?	Am besten hat mir das Tauchen gefallen.
Wie bist du gereist?	Ich habe auf einem Campingplatz übernachtet.
Wie war die Fahrt?	Ich bin mit dem Flugzeug angereist.
Wo hast du übernachtet?	Ich reise gerne mit dem Zug. Es ist so bequem.
Wie lange warst du dort?	Ich bin früh aufgestanden und habe gefrühstückt.
Was hast du am ersten Tag gemacht?	Die Fahrt war kurz und entspannt.
Was hast du am Nachmittag gemacht?	Ich war in Bremen.
Hat dir der Urlaub gefallen?	Ich war eineinhalb Wochen dort.
Was war das Beste an deinem Urlaub?	Nach dem Mittagessen war ich am See.
Wie reist du gerne?	Ja, sehr. Es war ein toller Urlaub.

2. Write in the missing word

a. Wo _________ du auf Urlaub?	*Where did you go on holiday?*
b. Wie bist du _________ und wie war die Fahrt?	*How did you travel and how did the trip go?*
c. __________ reist du lieber?	*How do you prefer to travel?*
d. Wo hast du _________?	*Where did you stay?*
e. _________ hast du am Morgen gemacht?	*What did you do in the morning?*
f. Wie war das __________ am Nachmittag?	*What was the weather like in the afternoon?*
g.Wie __________ warst du dort?	*How long did you stay there?*
h. Was hast du am Nachmittag ___________?	*What did you do in the afternoon?*
i. Was war das ________ an deinem Urlaub?	*What was the best thing about your holidays?*
j. Hat dir der Urlaub ____________?	*Did you like the holidays?*
k. ____________ du gerne wieder dorthin fahren?	*Would you like to go back?*

3. Write the questions to the answers below

a.	Ich war in Griechenland auf Urlaub.
b.	Ich bin mit dem Flugzeug gereist.
c.	Ich habe in einer Jugendherberge übernachtet.
d.	Nach dem Frühstück bin ich an den Strand gegangen.
e.	Am ersten Tag war es sehr sonnig.
f.	Ich war fünf Tage dort.
g.	Ja, die Jugendherberge hat mir sehr gut gefallen.
h.	Das Beste war das griechische Essen.
i.	Ja, ich würde gerne wieder dorthin fahren.

4. Translate the following questions into German

a. Where did you go on holiday last year?	____________________________?
b. How did you travel?	____________________________?
c. Who did you travel with?	____________________________?
d. Where did you stay?	____________________________?
e. How long did you stay there?	____________________________?
f. What was the best thing about your holiday?	____________________________?
g. Would you like to go back again next year?	____________________________?

Vocab Revision Workout 6

1. Faulty translation

a. Ich habe den Tisch nicht abgeräumt. *I didn't throw the table.*

b. Ich habe nichts gemacht. *I didn't want anything.*

c. Ich habe nicht Staub gesaugt. *I didn't dust.*

d. Ich habe das Auto gewaschen. *I washed the coach.*

e. Ich habe mein Schlafzimmer aufgeräumt. *I tidied my dog's bones.*

f. Ich habe das Geschirr nicht gespült. *I didn't wash the dog.*

2. Complete with a suitable word
Please ensure no word is repeated

a. Gestern _________ ich keine Lust zu helfen.

b. Mir ___________ der Kopf weh.

c. Ich _____________ beschäftigt.

d. Ich konnte _______.

e. _____ tat der Rücken weh.

f. Ich _________ viele Hausaufgaben.

g. Ich ___________ nicht.

h. Ich hatte keine _____________.

i. Mir tat ______ Arm weh.

3. Translate

a. Ich konnte meine Hausaufgaben nicht machen.
______________________________________.

b. Ich habe meinem Vater nicht geholfen.
______________________________________.

c. Ich war beschäftigt. ____________________.

d. Ich habe den Tisch nicht gedeckt.
______________________________________.

e. Normalerweise wasche ich das Auto
______________________________________.

f. Ich bin nicht mit dem Hund spazieren gegangen.
______________________________________.

4. Complete with a suitable word

Marcel: _________ Peter, wie geht's?

Peter: Hallo Marcel. Gut, und __________?

Marcel: Mir geht's gut. _______ willst du heute machen?

Peter: Ich würde gerne eine Radtour _______. Und du?

Marcel: Hm, das ______________ ich nicht. Ich will ins Kino gehen.

Peter: ______ Problem. Wir können ins Kino gehen.

Marcel: Super. ________ treffen wir uns?

Peter: __________ wir uns um sieben.

Marcel: Sehr gut, und ____________?

Peter: Treffen wir uns gegenüber ________ Kino.

5. Complete with the missing letters

a. ich k _ _ _ nicht — *I can't*

b. ich m _ _ _ — *I have to*

c. bis s _ _ _ _ _ _ — *see you later*

d. ich w _ _ _ _ g _ _ _ _ — *I would like*

e. ich w _ _ _ nicht — *I don't want*

f. k _ _ _ Problem — *no problem*

g. T _ _ _ _ _ _ _ wir uns? — *Shall we meet?*

6. Acro-translation: write out the acronym in full

e.g. *I don't fancy it* — **IHKL*: ich habe keine Lust***

a. *see you later* — **BS:**

b. *opposite the cinema* — **GDK:**

7. Complete

a. *Where do we meet this evening?* W______ t___________ w______ u_____ h_____ A______?

b. *What do you want to do?* W____ w______________ d____ m___________?

c. *OK. No problem.* OK. K________ P___________.

d. *I can't. I have to help my parents.* I__ k_______ n________. I______ m______ m__________ E__________ h________.

e. *Sorry. I don't fancy it.* T___ m____ l_____. I___ h______ k_______ L_______.

f. *I have to tidy my room.* I___ m____ m_______ Z_________ a_________________.

g. *We can go to the park with them.* W____ k________ m_____ i______ i__ d__ P____ g______.

h. *At what time shall we meet?* U____ w__ v___ U____ s______ w___ u___ t________?

8. Sentence puzzle: rewrite the sentences in the correct order

a. ich Besonderes Gestern nichts gemacht habe. — *Yesterday I didn't do anything special.*

b. habe mir Vorgestern angesehen ich Film einen. — *The day before yesterday I saw a film.*

c. Am Hausaufgaben mache meine ich Wochenende. — *At the weekend I usually do my homework.*

d. bin meiner ausgegangen Letzten mit Samstag ich Freundin. — *Last Saturday I went out with my girlfriend.*

e. jeden Ich aufstehen Tag muss früh. — *Every day I have to get up early.*

f. mit zwei Vor habe ich meinem gespielt Tagen Papa Schach. — *Two days ago I played chess with my dad.*

g. werde zum Abend gehen ich Heute Strand. — *This evening I am going to go to the beach.*

h. entspannt Gestern mich Abend habe ich. — *Yesterday evening I relaxed.*

9. Complete with the correct verb in the appropriate tense (perfect, present or future)

a. Gestern ______ ich ins Kino __________. — *Yesterday I went to the cinema.*

b. Vor zwei Tagen ________ ich ein sehr gutes Buch _________. — *Two days ago I read a very good book.*

c. Nächstes Wochenende _______ ich ins Stadion ______. — *Next weekend I am going go to the stadium.*

d. Heute ___________ ich Englisch ___________. — *Today I have to study English.*

e. Am Sonntag ___________ ich normalerweise __________. — *On Sundays I usually go jogging.*

f. Morgen ____________ ich früh __________. — *Tomorrow I am going to get up early.*

g. Letzten Freitag _____ ich mit meiner Freundin _________. — *Last Friday I went out with my girlfriend.*

h. Vorgestern _______ ich in den Park __________. — *The day before yesterday I went to the park.*

i. Heute ______ ich nicht _____ ihnen ausgehen. — *Today I don't want to go out with them.*

j. Normalerweise _______ ich keinen Sport. — *Usually I don't do sports.*

k. Morgen ________ ich spät ins Bett _______. — *Tomorrow I am going to go to bed late.*

Unit 13

Talking about a recent day trip

In this unit you will learn:

- To say what you did from the morning until you went to bed
- To talk about travel routines
- To say what activities you did in the past

Key sentence patterns:

- Time marker + *war/waren* + locative adverbial + prepositional phrase
- *hatte/hatten* + food
- Time marker + *war* + weather
- Prepositional phrase with *vor/während* + perfect tense
- *Es war* + noun phrase

Grammar:

- All persons of the perfect and imperfect tense
- Various time markers

UNIT 13: Talking about a recent day trip

Gestern Morgen *[Yesterday morning]*	**war ich** *[I was]* **waren wir** *[we were]*	**mit meinen Eltern** **mit meinen Freunden**	**auf dem Land** **am See**	**im Schwimmbad** **am Strand**

Ich bin früh aufgewacht *[I woke up early]*	**Ich bin um acht aufgestanden** *[I got up at 8]*	**Meine Mama ist spät aufgestanden** *[My mum got up late]*	**Meine Eltern haben lange geschlafen** *[My parents slept until late]*

Ich habe in der Küche gefrühstückt *[I had breakfast in the kitchen]*	**Meine Eltern haben gemeinsam gefrühstückt** *[My parents had breakfast together]*	**Zum Frühstück** *[For breakfast]*	**hatte ich** *[I had]* **hatten wir** *[we had]* **hatten sie** *[they had]*	**Cornflakes** **ein weiches Ei** *[a soft-boiled egg]* **einen Toast mit Butter** *[buttered toast]*

Um neun *[At 9]* **Nach dem Frühstück** *[After having breakfast]*	**habe ich** *[I]* **haben wir** *[we]*	**das Haus verlassen** *[left home]*	**und**	**den Ausflug** *[the day trip]*	**begonnen** *[started]*

Ich bin zuerst *[First, I...]* **Wir sind zuerst** *[First, we...]*	**mit dem Auto** **mit dem Zug**	**und dann** *[and then]*	**mit dem Bus** ***mit dem Schiff**	**gefahren** *[...travelled]*

Die Fahrt *[The trip]*	**hat**	**eine Stunde** *[one hour]* **zwei Stunden** *[two hours]*	**gedauert** *[...took]*	**und war** *[and was]*	**angenehm** *[pleasant]* **kurz** *[short]* **lang** *[long]* **langweilig** *[boring]*

Morgens *[In the morning]* **Nachmittags** *[In the afternoon]*	**war das Wetter** *[the weather was]*	**schön** *[nice]* **schlecht** *[bad]*	**und dann** *[and then]*	**war es etwas windig** *[it was a bit windy]*
	war es *[it was]*	**kalt/heiß** *[cold/hot]* **sonnig** *[sunny]*		**hat es ein wenig geregnet** *[it rained a bit]*

Ich habe *[I]* **Wir haben** *[We]*	**viel gemacht,** *[did a lot]*	**wie zum Beispiel** *[for example]*	**einen Spaziergang** *[a walk]* **eine Führung** *[a guided tour]*	**auf dem Land** *[in the countryside]* **am Strand** *[at the beach]* **in der Altstadt** *[in the old town]*

und dann *[and then]*	**habe ich** **haben wir**	**Musik gehört,**	**mich** **uns**	**gesonnt** *[sunbathed]*	**und**	**bin** **sind**	**im Meer geschwommen**

Ich bin **Wir sind**	**mit dem Auto nach Hause gefahren** *[returned home by car]*	**und**	**während der Fahrt** *[during the trip]*	**habe ich** **haben wir**	**mit dem Handy gespielt** *[played on the phone]*

Vor dem Schlafengehen *[Before bedtime]*	**habe ich zu Abend gegessen** *[I had dinner]*	**Es war** *[It was]*	**ein spannender** *[an exciting]* **ein langweiliger** *[a boring]*	**Tag** *[day]* **Ausflug** *[trip]*

***Author's note: for traveling by most means of transport one uses "fahren", e.g. "Bus fahren", "Zug fahren", etc. For air travel however we must use "fliegen", "Ich bin mit dem Flugzeug geflogen".**

1. Match

Gestern Morgen war ich auf dem Land.	I got up late.
Ich bin mit meinen Eltern gereist.	I travelled with my parents.
Ich bin früh aufgewacht.	Yesterday morning I went to the countryside.
Ich bin spät aufgestanden.	I left the house.
Ich habe das Haus verlassen.	I woke up early.
Ich bin mit dem Auto gefahren.	I travelled by car.

2. Complete

a. Die F_ _ _ _ hat eine Stunde gedauert.

b. Ich bin um sieben a_ _ _ _ _ _ _ _ _ _ _ _.

c. Wir haben gemeinsam g_ _ _ _ _ _ _ _ _ _ _ _.

d. Wir haben uns am Strand g_ _ _ _ _ _.

e. Ich habe Musik g_ _ _ _ _ .

f. Ich habe einen S_ _ _ _ _ _ _ _ _ _ _ am Strand gemacht.

3. Gapped translation

a. Gestern Morgen war ich am Strand. ___________ *morning I* ________ *to the beach.*

b. Meine Eltern haben jeden Tag lange geschlafen. *My* ___________ *slept in every* _____.

c. Wir sind ausgegangen. *We* __________.

d. Wir waren im Schwimmbad. *We went to the* ____________.

e. Wir sind mit dem Flugzeug geflogen. *We travelled by* ___________.

f. Die Fahrt war lang. *The journey was* __________.

g. Ich bin am Strand angekommen. *I* ___________ *at the beach.*

h. Ich habe viel gemacht. *I did a lot of* __________.

4. Arrange in chronological order

Ich bin um sechs Uhr aufgestanden.	1
Dann habe ich mit meinem Bruder gefrühstückt.	
Der Strand war traumhaft.	
Zuerst waren wir schwimmen.	
zum Strand gefahren.	
Um fünf sind wir wieder nach Hause	
Dann haben wir uns gesonnt und ein Picknick gemacht.	
gefahren. Die Fahrt hat circa eine Stunde gedauert.	
Um acht sind wir mit dem Auto	

5. Break the flow

a. Ichbinfrühaufgestanden.

b. Ichbingleichaufgestanden.

c. DannhabeichmitmeinemBrudergefrühstückt.

d. MeineElternhabenspätgefrühstückt.

e. IchbinmitdemMietautogefahren.

f. GlücklicherweisewardasWetterschön.

g. DieFahrtwarlang.

6. Verb anagrams

a. Ich bin früh **tanaufgesden**.

b. Wir sind mit dem Auto **gefrenah.**

c. Wir sind so gegen neun am Strand **anmengekom**.

d. Der Strand **rwa** traumhauft.

e. Glücklicherweise **arw** es sehr sonnig.

f. Ich war **chetaun**.

g. Meine Eltern sind am Strand **ierspazen** gegangen.

i. Mein Bruder hat Postkarten **geschenrieb**.

7. Likely or unlikely?

a. Ich bin gestern Morgen früh aufgestanden, so gegen sieben.
b. Dann habe ich die Cornflakes mit Milch rasiert.
c. Ich habe mich in der Küche geduscht.
d. Um neun haben wir das Haus verlassen, um an den See zu fahren.
e. Der See war nicht weit entfernt, so circa hundert Kilometer.
f. Wir sind mit dem Raumschiff hingefahren.
g. Die Fahrt war sehr langweilig.
h. Wir sind um drei Uhr nachmittags angekommen.
i. Glücklicherweise war das Wetter gut. Es war sonnig und warm.
j. Wir waren im See schwimmen, Wasserskifahren und dann haben wir uns am Ufer gesonnt.
k. Mittags haben wir dann ein Picknick gemacht. Das Essen war köstlich.

8. Multiple choice quiz

	1	2	3
Ich bin aufgewacht.	I got up.	I woke up.	I went to bed.
Ich war am See.	I went to the sea.	I can see you.	I was at the lake.
Ich muss früh schlafen gehen.	I have to go to bed early.	I have to get up early.	I go to bed very early.
Wir sind spät zurückgekommen.	We went out late.	We got there late.	We came back late.
Wir sind früh losgefahren.	We left early.	We arrived early.	We woke up early.
Die Fahrt war lang.	The trip took long.	There were lentils.	The trip was fun.
Wir waren wandern.	We went running.	We swam.	We went hiking.
Wir waren fischen.	We fished in Brazil.	We went fishing.	We fished in the lake.

9. Complete with the options in the box

a. Ich bin um sechs Uhr ______________.
b. Ich _____ Cornflakes gegessen.
c. Mein Eltern ____ spät aufgestanden.
d. Wir haben um acht das _____verlassen.
e. Wir haben einen Ausflug an einen ____ gemacht.
f. Es ______ ein großer See.
g. Viele Leute waren _______.
h. Das Wetter war schön. Es war ________.
i. Ich _____ im See geschwommen
j. Wir haben Volleyball ___________.
k. Meine ____________ war Wasserskifahren.

sonnig
aufgestanden
habe
bin
dort
Schwester
gespielt
Haus
war
See
sind

10. Write *Ich, Er/Sie, Wir, Sie* as appropriate

a. ______ bin geschwommen.
b. ______ haben einen Ausflug gemacht (ich+Tim).
c. ______ ist klettern gegangen.
d. ______ haben ein Auto gemietet (Sabine+Katja).
e. ______ sind ausgegangen (ich+Irene).
f. _______ sind spazieren gegangen (Lukas+Anna)
g. _____ habe mich geduscht.

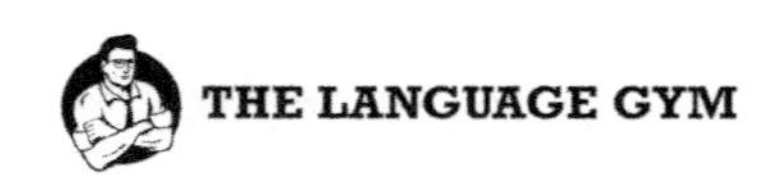

11. Categories: match the activities to the appropriate pronoun

1. bin aufgestanden	2. sind aufgestanden (ich+ Mama)	3. haben einen Ausflug gemacht (Tim+Karin)	4. ist aufs Land gefahren
5. haben gegessen (ich+Pia)	6. ist im See geschwommen	7. war sonnig	8. war heiß
9. haben geschlafen (ich+Peter)	10. hat geschlafen	11. haben Volleyball gespielt (Bernd+Sabine)	12. bin gewandert

ich	mein Bruder	wir	sie (plural)	das Wetter
1				

12. Sentence puzzle: rewrite the sentences in the correct order

a. wir einen Gestern Ausflug ans haben Meer gemacht.

b. Wir aufgestanden sind früh.

c. Hotel Wir um das sieben verlassen haben.

d. langweilig Die Fahrt lang und war.

e. angekommen Strand Um halb sind wir am neun.

f. traumhaft Der Strand dort viele war, aber es waren Leute.

g. Meine haben sich Eltern gesonnt.

h. Volleyball war und meine schwimmen gespielt Geschwister Ich haben.

i. mussten Um vier Uhr wir begonnen wieder regnen zurück, ins Hotel weil es zu hat.

13. Translate into English

a. Ich bin früh aufgestanden.

b. Wir sind um sieben am See angekommen.

c. Bis um vier Uhr war es sonnig, dann hat es zu regnen begonnen.

d. Das Wasser war klar.

e. Meine Eltern sind Wasserski gefahren.

f. Ich war am Strand spazieren.

g. Das war sehr entspannend.

14. Tangled translation: rewrite in German

a. Ich war im **pool with** meinem **best** Freund.

b. Ich bin **early** aufgestanden.

c. Ich habe mit meiner **family had breakfast.**

d. **I** habe das **house** um **seven left**.

e. Wir sind im **car** mit meinem **dad** hingefahren.

f. Die Fahrt **was** lang, **but fun**.

g. Gestern **morning** bin ich **at six** Uhr aufgestanden.

h. Wir sind um zehn am **beach arrived**.

i. **The** Strand **was** traumhaft.

j. **We** haben viele **things** gemeinsam **made**.

k. Das Wetter war **nice in the morning.**

l. Mein Bruder is im **sea swam**.

m. Ich war **in the sea** tauchen.

n. Ich habe mich gesonnt **and music listened.**

15. Collocation challenge: put each item where it fits best (using each number only once)

1. heiß	2. nette Leute	3. mit dem Zug	4. einen Ausflug	5. Berlin
6. ein Haus	7. einem Café	8. eine Reise	9. Volleyball	10. ein Auto
11. Pommes	12. Comics	13. sonnig	14. mit einem Schiff	15. Schach
16. mit dem Auto	17. sympathische Mädchen	18. einen Engländer		

Wir haben				gemietet.
Wir haben				gegessen.
Wir haben				kennengelernt.
Wir waren in				
Wir haben				gemacht.
Es war	1			
Wir haben				gespielt.
Wir haben				gelesen.
Wir sind				gefahren.

16. Spot and add in the missing words

e.g. ***Ich*** bin früh aufgestanden.

a. Wir um sieben gefrühstückt.

b. Wir sind mit Bus gefahren.

c. Die war lang und langweilig.

d. Morgens es kalt.

e. Nachmittags wir im Meer geschwommen.

f. Ich mich gesonnt.

g. Meine Eltern am Strand spazieren.

h. Mein Bruder ist schwimmen.

i. Meine Schwester hat Buch gelesen.

18. Translate the following sentences into German

a. I got up early.

b. I had breakfast.

c. I ate toast with butter.

d. We left the hotel.

e. We travelled by car.

f. We arrived at nine.

g. The journey was long.

h. The weather was nice.

i. It was hot.

j. We swam in the sea.

k. We did scuba diving.

l. My brother sunbathed.

m. He played volleyball.

n. My parents relaxed.

o. They read a book.

p. They slept.

17. Complete with a suitable word

e.g. Gestern haben wir einen **Ausflug** gemacht.

a. Wir sind früh _______________.

b. Zum Frühstück habe ich __________ gegessen.

c. Meine Eltern haben einen ___________ gegessen.

d. Wir haben um _________ das Hotel verlassen.

e. Wir sind mit dem ________ gefahren.

f. Die Fahrt hat ____________ gedauert.

g. Um neun ______ wir am Strand angekommen.

h. Glücklicherweise ______ es sonnig.

i. Ich bin im ________ geschwommen.

j. Meine Eltern__________ sich gesonnt

k. Zum Mittagessen haben wir ein Picknick ______________.

l. Um vier Uhr sind wir zurück ins _________ gefahren, weil es zu regnen begonnen hat.

Hallo! Ich heiße Georg und komme aus Hamburg. Ich wohne in einem kleinen, aber modernen Haus am Stadtrand. Gestern habe ich einen tollen Tag mit meiner Familie verbracht. Wir sind an einen Strand auf Sylt gefahren. Sylt ist eine Insel in der Nordsee, die für ihre schönen Strände und Strandkörbe bekannt ist. Von Hamburg ist man in drei Stunden mit dem Zug auf Sylt, wo es vor allem erstklassige Restaurants und frische Meeresfrüchte gibt.

Morgens sind wir alle früh aufgewacht und haben dann in der Küche gefrühstückt. Ich habe einen Toast mit Butter gegessen, aber mein Bruder Leo hat nichts gegessen, sondern nur einen Tee getrunken. Meine Eltern hatten Cornflakes mit einem Orangensaft.

Nach dem Frühstück sind wir gleich mit dem Auto zum Bahnhof gefahren. Ich liebe es mit dem Auto zu fahren, weil mein Papa die Musik aufdreht und wir dann Sportfreunde Stiller hören. Mein Bruder fährt nicht gern mit dem Auto, weil ihm oft übel wird und er sich übergeben muss.

Den ganzen Tag war es sonnig. Im Sommer ist meistens schönes Wetter auf Sylt. Als wir angekommen sind, haben wir einen Spaziergang am Strand gemacht und sind anschließend im Meer schwimmen gegangen. Das Wasser war sauber und erfrischend. Dann habe ich mit meinem Bruder Volleyball gespielt. Auch wenn er viel besser spielt als ich, hat es trotzdem Spaß gemacht.

Mittags haben wir in einem Restaurant auf der Strandpromenade gegessen. Ich hatte Nordseekrabben und einen Friesentee. Das war sehr lecker.

Auf der Rückfahrt haben wir im Zug geschlafen, weil der Tag so aufregend war. Zuhause angekommen, habe ich mich noch geduscht, etwas gegessen und mich dann ins Bett gelegt. Das war ein wunderbarer Tag, den ich bald wiederholen will. **(Georg, 13 Jahre. Hamburg)**

19. Find the German equivalent

a. I spent a day

b. an island

c. ate nothing

d. fresh seafood

e. we all woke up

f. a piece of toast

g. after breakfast

h. promenade

i. because my dad puts on music

j. because he often feels nauseous

k. it was however fun

20. Gapped translation

a. I live in a _______________ but modern _______________ on the _______________ of the city.

b. My parents had _______________ and an _______________ _______________.

c. I love ____________________ by _________ because my dad puts on _________________ that I ___________.

d. We went for a _____________ along the ____________ and then we __________ in the ______.

e. We ____________ to a restaurant and had _______________ and __________________.

21. Answer the questions in English

a. Where does Georg live?

b. What did his brother have for breakfast?

c. Why does Georg like travelling by car?

d. Why is his brother not a good traveller?

e. What did they do when they got to the beach?

f. What was the water like?

g. Where did they have lunch?

h. What did he do on the return trip?

1) Hallo! Ich bin Leo, der kleine Bruder von Georg. Gestern hatte ich einen tollen Tag mit meiner Familie am Strand. Ich war mit meinen Eltern und meinem Bruder auf Sylt. Sylt ist eine Insel in der Nordsee, die drei Stunden von Hamburg mit dem Zug entfernt ist. Auf Sylt gibt es tolle Strände und hervorragende Restaurants, wo man frische Meeresfrüchte essen kann.

(2) Morgens bin ich früh aufgewacht und in die Küche gegangen. Ich habe nur einen Tee getrunken, aber mein Bruder hat einen Toast mit Butter gegessen. Meine Eltern haben Cornflakes gegessen und einen Orangensaft getrunken.

(3) Um neun Uhr sind wir nach dem Frühstück mit dem Auto losgefahren. Ich fahre nicht gerne mit dem Auto, weil mir sehr oft übel wird. Manchmal muss ich mich übergeben, dieses Mal aber nicht. Georg hingegen liebt es, mit dem Auto zu fahren, weil er mit meinem Papa im Auto Sportfreunde Stiller hört, was die Lieblingsband von Georg ist.

(4) Es war den ganzen Tag über sonnig. Normalerweise ist das Wetter auf Sylt immer gut, vor allem im Sommer. Als wir auf Sylt angekommen sind, haben wir einen Spaziergang am Strand gemacht und dann sind wir schwimmen gegangen. Das Wasser war sauber und sehr erfrischend. Anschließend haben wir Volleyball gespielt. Ich spiele etwas besser als mein Bruder, aber auf das kommt es nicht an. Das Wichtigste ist, dass wir Spaß haben. Danach habe ich ein Buch gelesen und mich entspannt.

(5) Zu Mittag haben wir in einem Restaurant auf der Strandpromenade gegessen. Wir hatten Nordseekrabben mit Friesentee. Das war sehr lecker.

(6) Auf der Heimfahrt haben wir im Zug geschlafen. Zuhause habe ich noch Musik gehört. Ich hatte einen super Tag, den ich gerne wiederholen will. **(Leo, 12 Jahre. Hamburg)**

22. Correct the wrong statements (not all are wrong)

a. Sylt is located in the Baltic Sea.

b. It has many dirty beaches and average restaurants.

c. Leo threw up while in the car.

d. Georg loves travelling by car because his dad plays his favourite music.

e. In the summer, the weather is sometimes good on the Sylt.

f. The water was clean and refreshing.

g. When playing volleyball, the most important thing for Leo is winning.

h. Later on, Leo relaxed reading comics and listening to music.

i. They returned home by train and the siblings slept for the whole trip.

j. Leo watched TV before going to bed.

23. Tick or cross? Tick the phrases below that are contained in Leo's text and cross out the ones that are not

a. einen tollen Tag.	f. ich fahre nicht gerne	k. sehr erfrischend
b. eine Insel in der Nordsee	g. Georg hingegen	l. dass wir Spaß haben
c. alte Meeresfrüchte	h. Sportfreunde Stiller	m. kein Buch gelesen
d. nur einen Kaffee getrunken	i. einen Spaziergang	n. in einem Café
e. Toast mit Butter gegessen	j. ich spiele schlechter	o. das war lecker

24. Translate Part 4 of the text into English

25. Wordsearch: find the German translation of the sentences below and write them as shown in the example

E X I U Z Q E O P I U T H C W C D I T G A O N E W
J M E H I A C L K L M I D S M U F C G R G B E I I
A C K Z B H U C C R U P Q Y W C Z Z G N Z H G N R
O T H X H P D L C S O B A Z Q U K G V E N S N K S
D F M E Y F T E H Y U V S P Q C N E T L C W A A I
N E D N A T S E G F U A H Ü R F N I B H C I G F N
W W H Y H N B S L X V Q C G E F R A T W M X E F D
V Z I W N T K Z Q K G Q N F Y G X L H C C W G E M
D P I L U J H N D G V S Y L O A E U N R G T N E I
U J Y K D R B T Y F T J N B H I L A I L G J R E T
Z A A K F E M A O F Y S T L P Z F Z C Z V Q E I D
U T L K H W T R W H D B C S B Z T B B M G G D V E
A S Q I O M J I O M W D E G B B V I B H D F N A M
R K C N J Y V C E I I G N B B U Z V V Y N X A G B
I G I C J E X Y E R Y K B L X S Z N Z O O U W Z U
L K C P N U J L Q D E O D K C B U Y V W S Q D S S
I P B I X Y I X N Z G Z F U A F S P C T R P N L G
M W B S K X U A R A Y W N X D C U C Z B H F I M E
G I D L K Q H N R Z L D Z O Y Y W K L K L T S U F
T Y Q T H M R L S I K D E E R P O U D L L Q E F A
I S E R E G S M O W J C P L I A M O I T Q B I W H
B O E D I Q T M I H N E D E I E Z N R G Q U S N R
B Y T G L J U I L I F L K H N N R J C R B B B J E
B I P L O P L C U J W M F A A N N P L W O H T Y N
M W I R S I N D I M M E E R G E S C H W O M M E N

e.g. I got up early.
— Ich bin früh aufgestanden

a. they went hiking

b. played with the phone

c. we swam in the sea

d. wild animals

e. a coffee

f. we travelled by coach

g. flowers

26. Guided translation

a. V_ _ z_ _ _ T_ _ _ _ h_ _ _ i_ _ e_ _ _ _ A_ _ _ _ _ _ g_ _ _ _ _ _.	*Two days ago I went on a trip.*
b. W_ _ s_ _ _ f_ _ _ l_ _ _ _ _ _ _ _ _ _ _.	*We left home early.*
c. W_ _ s_ _ _ m_ _ d_ _ A_ _ _ g_ _ _ _ _ _ _ _.	*We travelled by car.*
d. D_ _ F_ _ _ _ w_ _ l_ _ _ u_ _ l_ _ _ _ _ _ _ _ _ _.	*The trip was long and boring.*
e. W_ _ s_ _ _ u_ a_ _ _ a_ S_ _ _ _ _ a_ _ _ _ _ _ _ _ _ _.	*We got to the beach at eight.*
f. D_ _ S_ _ _ _ _ w_ _ s_ _ _ _ .	*The beach was beautiful.*
g. M_ _ _ _ M_ _ _ w_ _ W_ _ _ _ _ _ _ _ _ _ _ _ _ _ _.	*My mum did water skiing.*
h. I_ _ h_ _ _ m_ _ _ g_ _ _ _ _ _ u_ _ e_ _ B_ _ _ g_ _ _ _ _ _.	*I sunbathed and read a book.*
i. W_ _ h_ _ _ _ _ v_ _ _ S_ _ _.	*We had a lot of fun.*

27. Complete with the correct option

Letztes Wochenende hat mein Freund Timo einen _________ aufs Land gemacht. Er ist früh _________, so gegen sieben. Dann hat er sich geduscht, sich ____________ und mit seiner Familie gefrühstückt. Zum ___________ hatte er einen _____________ und einen Orangensaft. Nele, seine Schwester, ist später ____________und _________ daher nicht mehr frühstücken. Um halb neun sind sie mit dem Auto ___________. Die Fahrt hat ungefähr eine Stunde ____________. Als Timo und seine Familie angekommen sind, haben sie gleich einen ____________ auf dem Land gemacht. Sie sind bei einem schönen _______ vorbeigekommen. Timo ist gleich ins Wasser gehüpft und hat sich anschließend gesonnt. Nele hat am Ufer Musik _________. Nach dem Schwimmen hat Timo ein Buch _________. Das Beste an ihrem Ausflug war, dass sie eine Schar Wildgänse im See ________ haben. Timo liebt es, _______ zu beobachten. Außerdem hat Timo viele Fotos gemacht. Es war ein sehr entspannter Tag.

Toast	aufgestanden	gelesen	aufgestanden	gedauert
angezogen	losgefahren	Ausflug	konnte	Spaziergang
See	Frühstück	gehört	gesehen	Tiere

Letzten Samstag ist mein Bruder Michael mit seinen Freunden an den Strand gefahren. Ich musste leider zu Hause bleiben, weil ich krank war.
Michael ist um fünf Uhr aufgestanden. Er hat sich geduscht, sich angezogen und einen Kaffee getrunken. Dann ist er mit dem Bus nach Rostock gefahren. Die Fahrt hat ungefähr eine Stunde gedauert, weil unser Haus relativ weit vom Meer entfernt ist.
Als Michael angekommen ist, ist er eine Runde am Strand spazieren gegangen. Dann hat er mit seinen Freunden Volleyall gespielt. Sie sind oft ins Wasser gegangen, um sich abzukühlen. Mittags sind sie in ein Standcafé essen gegangen.
Den Nachmittag haben sie dann entspannt am Strand verbracht, viel geplaudert und Gitarre gespielt. Ein Freund von Michael spielt wahnsinnig gut Gitarre.
Um vier sind sie dann alle mit dem Bus nach Hause gefahren. Mein Bruder meinte, dass er einen super Tag am Strand hatte und dass ich das nächste Mal unbedingt mitkommen müsse.

(Karoline, 13 Jahre. Schwerin)

28. Find the German equivalent in Karoline's text

a. I had to stay at home.

b. Michael got up at five.

c. He showered, got changed...

d. ...and had a coffee.

e. Then he took the bus.

f. The trip took about an hour.

g. When Michael arrived...

h. ...he went for a walk on the beach.

i. Then he played volleyball.

j. They often went into the water.

k. At noon they went for lunch.

l. They spent the afternoon at the beach.

m. His friend plays the guitar exremely well.

n. They went home at four.

o. I should come along next time.

29. Complete the table

ich	er/sie	sie/Sie
habe ein Brötchen gegessen	hat ein Brötchen gegessen	
bin im Meer geschwommen		sind im Meer geschwommen
	hat ein Auto gemietet	
habe mich gesonnt		
	ist am Strand spazieren gegangen	
	hat Volleyball gespielt	haben Volleyball gespielt
		haben Fotos gemacht
bin wandern gegangen	ist wandern gegangen	
		sind aufs Land gefahren
bin um 8 nach Hause gefahren		

30. Write two texts in German, one in the first person (*ich*) and one in third person (*er/sie*)

- Two days ago I went on a day trip to the countryside with my family.
- I woke up very early, around five.
- I showered, got dressed and had breakfast with my brother.
- I ate a banana and drank coffee with milk.
- My parents got up later.
- We left home at 7:30.
- We travelled by car.
- The journey lasted about an hour.
- We arrived at my uncle's farm at 8.30.
- My brother and I went to the lake with my cousins.
- My parents went hiking with my uncle.
- The weather was very nice, so I swam in the lake and then sunbathed.
- My parents came to the lake later. They sunbathed reading and chatting with my uncle and aunt.
- We had a picnic by the lake.
- After lunch I went hiking alone.
- I saw wild animals *[wilde Tiere]* and took pictures of insects and flowers. It was very relaxing.

- Yesterday, my friend Michael went on a day trip to the seaside.
- He woke up very early, around 6.
- He showered, got dressed and had breakfast with his family.
- He ate two eggs and drank coffee.
- His brother and sister got up later.
- They left home at around 8:15.
- They travelled by coach.
- The journey lasted about 45 minutes.
- They reached the beach at around 9:00.
- Michael and his siblings played volleyball.
- His parents went for a walk on the beach.
- It was a very hot day. So, after playing volleyball, they all swam in the sea.
- His parents met nice people and chatted with them.
- At noon they all ate sandwiches and drank coffee.
- Then Michael sunbathed listening to music. It was very relaxing.
- It was a great day. They all had a blast.

Question Skills Unit 13

English	German
Tell me about a recent day trip.	**Erzähl mir etwas über einem Ausflug, den du vor Kurzem gemacht hast.**
Where did you go?	**Wo bist du hingefahren? / Wo warst du?**
When did you wake up?	**Wann bist du aufgewacht?**
At what time did you get up?	**Um wie viel Uhr bist du aufgestanden?**
How did you travel?	**Wie bist du hingefahren?**
How did the trip go?	**Wie war die Fahrt?**
What did you do in the morning?	**Was hast du am Morgen gemacht?**
What did you do in the afternoon?	**Was hast du am Nachmittag gemacht?**
At what time did you get back home?	**Um wie viel Uhr bist du nach Hause gekommen?**
What did you do before going to bed?	**Was hast du vor dem Schlafengehen gemacht?**
What was the best thing about the day trip?	**Was hat dir an deinem Ausflug am besten gefallen? Was war das Beste an deinem Ausflug?**
What did you see?	**Was hast du dir angesehen?**
Who did you meet?	**Wen hast du kennengelernt?**

1. Match questions and answers

Questions	Answers
Wo bist du hingefahren?	Sehr früh, so gegen halb sechs.
Um wie viel Uhr bist du aufgewacht?	Eine mittelalterliche Burg und ein Jagdschloss.
Wie bist du hingefahren?	Mit dem Auto zum Bahnhof und dann mit dem Zug.
Wie war die Fahrt?	Ich war um zehn zu Hause.
Was hast du am Morgen gemacht?	Nur zwei Tage insgesamt.
Welche Sehenswürdigkeiten hast du dir angesehen?	Ich habe mich geduscht und bin dann ins Bett gegangen.
Wie viele Tage hast du dort verbracht?	Definitiv der Strand.
Wann bist du nach Hause gekommen?	Ich habe gefrühstückt und dann bin ich zum Strand gegangen.
Was hat dir an deinem Ausflug am besten gefallen?	Ich war auf Rügen.
Was hast du vor dem Schlafengehen gemacht?	Ein bisschen langweilig, aber bequem.

2. Complete with a suitable question word

a. ___________bist du aufgestanden?

b. __________ war das Beste an deinem Tag?

c. ___________hast du vor dem Schlafengehen gemacht?

d. _________ bist du hingefahren?

e. ________ viele Tage bist du dort geblieben?

f. ____________ war die Fahrt?

g. Mit _________ bist du hingefahren?

h. _____ viel Zeit hast du am Strand verbracht?

3. Translate into English

a. Wie bist du hingefahren?

b. Wo bist du hingefahren?

c. Hattest du Spaß?

d. Wen hast du kennengelernt?

e. Was hast du gesehen?

f. Was war das Beste an deinem Ausflug?

g. Hast du Sightseeing gemacht?

h. Wie war das Wetter?

4. Sentence puzzle: rewrite the sentences

a. hast Was du vor Schlafengehen gemacht dem?

b. Wie gereist bist du?

c. war Wie Fahrt die?

d. Was du am hast gemacht Morgen?

e. Nachmittag Was hast du am gemacht?

f. Um Uhr wie viel bist aufgestanden du?

g. gefahren Um du bist wie viel nach Hause Uhr?

h. war Beste das an deinem Was Ausflug?

5. Spot and correct the mistakes

a. W bist du hingefahren?

b. Was hat du vor dem Schlafengehen gemacht?

c. Welche Sehenswükeiten hast du dir angesehen?

d. Um wie viel Ohr bist du aufgestanden?

e. Wie war der Fahrt?

f. Wie bist du hingefahrt?

g. Wann bist du aufgestinden?

h. Was war das Beste an deines Ausflug?

6. Write a question for each of the answers below

Fragen	Antworten
a.	Ich war in Wien.
b.	Mit dem Flugzeug.
c.	Den Stephansdom.
d.	Ich bin früh aufgestanden, so um fünf.
e.	Dass ich einen sympathischen Jungen kennengelernt habe.
f.	Sie war sehr langweilig.
g.	Drei Tage.
h.	Ich bin spät nach Hause gekommen.
j.	Wir waren am Morgen Sightseeing.

Unit 14

Talking about when I went to the *Rosenmontagszug* in Cologne

In this unit you will learn:

- To talk about a trip to a festival
- To say what you "have to" do
- What is customary and advisable
- To say what activities you did in the past

Key sentence patterns:

- Time marker + *war ich/waren wir* + locative adverbial + *um ... zu* + infinitive
- Perfect tense + noun phrase or prepositional phrase
- *Man muss* + noun phrase + infinitive
- Time marker + expression of weather with *war es*

Grammar:

- All persons of the perfect tense
- *Man muss* + infinitive

UNIT 14: Talking about when I went to the *Rosenmontagszug* in Cologne

Letztes Jahr *[Last year]* **Letzten Monat** *[Last month]*	**war ich** *[I was]* **waren wir** *[we were]*	**in Köln,** *[in Cologne]*	**um am** *[to]* **um den** *[to]*	**Rosenmontagszug** *[Rose Monday parade]*	**teilzunehmen** *[participate]* **zu sehen** *[see]*

Ich bin *[I]* **Wir sind** *[We]*	**alleine hingefahren.** *[went alone]* **mit meinem/-r besten Freund/ Freundin hingefahren.** *[went with my best friend]*	**Ich bin** **Er/Sie ist** *[He/She]* **Wir sind** *[We]*	**um acht Uhr** *[at 8 o'clock]*	**aufgestanden** *[got up]*

Ich bin *[I]* **Wir sind** *[We]*	**mit dem Flugzeug geflogen** *[went by plane]* **mit dem Auto** *[took the car]*	**und dann** *[and then]*	**mit dem Zug** *[by train]*	**gefahren.** *[went]*	**Die Fahrt war** *[The trip was]*	**lang** *[long]*	**, aber** *[but]* **und** *[and]*	**aufregend** *[exciting]* **anstrengend** *[exhausting]*
Ich habe *[I]*	**Wir haben** *[We]*		**ein Auto** *[a car]*		**gemietet** *[rented]*			

Am Rosenmontag	**war ich** *[I was]* **waren wir** *[we were]*	**früh** *[early]*	**in der Innenstadt** *[in the city centre]*	**, um einen guten Platz zu ergattern** *[to get a good spot]*

Es gibt einige Regeln zu beachten *[There are some rules to follow]*	
Es ist üblich, dass *[It is customary that]*	**man sich verkleidet** *[one wears a costume]* **die Damen den Herrn die Krawatten abschneiden** *[ladies cut off the men's ties]*
Man muss *[One has to]*	**Getränke aus Plastikflaschen trinken** *[use plastic bottles]* **die öffentlichen Toiletten benutzen** *[use public toilets]* **rechtzeitig ein Hotel buchen** *[book a hotel on time]*
Es empfiehlt sich, *[It's advisable]*	**mit dem Zug anzureisen** *[to travel by train]* **Wertgegenstände zu Hause zu lassen** *[to leave valuables at home]*

Am Morgen	**war es bewölkt** *[it was cloudy]* **war es sonnig** *[it was sunny]* **hat es geschneit** *[it snowed]*	**, aber am Nachmittag**	**war es kalt** *[it was cold]* **hat es geregnet** *[it rained]* **war es angenehm** *[it was pleasant]*

Während des Rosenmontagszugs *[During the parade]*	**habe ich** **haben wir**	**nette Leute kennengelernt** *[met friendly people]* **viel gelacht** *[we laughed a lot]* **viele Bonbons gefangen** *[caught lots of sweets]*
	habe ich mir **haben wir uns**	**viele Wagen angesehen** *[watched many carnival floats]*

Am Nachmittag *[In the afternoon]*	**bin ich** **sind wir**	**ins Hotel zurückgekehrt**	**und**	**habe** **haben**	**einen Krapfen gegessen** *[ate a doughnut]* **ein Nickerchen gemacht** *[had a nap]*

Abends *[In the evening]*	**bin ich** **sind wir**	**um zehn** *[at ten]*	**schlafen gegangen.**	**Es war eine**	**einzigartige** *[unique]* **tolle** *[great]*	**kulturelle** *[cultural]*	**Erfahrung.** *[experience]*

1. Match

Ich war in Köln, um an der Parade teilzunehmen	She woke up.
Sie ist aufgewacht.	The trip was exhausting.
Wir haben ein Auto gemietet.	I was in Cologne to participate in the parade.
Die Fahrt war anstrengend.	We rented a car.
Man muss die öffentlichen Toiletten benutzen.	One has to use the public toilets.
Es empfiehlt sich, mit dem Zug anzureisen.	It's advisable to travel by train.

2. Missing letters

a. Letztes J_hr wa_ ich in Köln.

b. Ich b_n früh aufgestanden.

c. Am Ro_enmontag w_r es sonnig.

d. Es gibt e_nige Regeln.

e. Wir si_d mit dem Z_g fahren

f. Man muss die _ffentlichen Toiletten benutzen.

g. Am M_rgen sind wir in die I_ _enstadt geg_ngen.

h. Während des Rosenmontags_ugs ha_e ich viel gel_cht.

i. Ich habe viele Bon_ons gefangen.

3. Faulty translation

a. mein bester Freund	*my boyfriend*
b. um acht Uhr aufgewacht	*woke up at nine*
c. früh ankommen	*to arrive late*
d. die Regeln beachten	*ignore the rules*
e. Plastikflaschen benutzen	*use glass bottles*
f. ein Kostüm	two costumes
g. es war kalt	*it was sunny*
h. einen Krapfen essen	*to eat an apple*
i. viel gelacht	*I cried a lot*
j. ins Hotel zurückkehren	*to return home*
k. ein Nickerchen	*a run*

4. Spot and add in the missing word

a. Ich bin mit Auto gefahren.	*I travelled by car.*
b. Die Fahrt lang.	*The trip was long.*
c. Wir früh angekommen.	*We arrived early.*
d. Es anstrengend.	*It was exhausting.*
e. Man verkleidet.	*One wears a costume.*
f. Es geregnet.	*It rained a bit.*
g. Ich habe gelacht.	*I laughed a lot.*
h. Ich bin ins Hotel.	*I returned to the hotel.*
i. Ich habe ein gemacht.	*I had a nap.*
j. Es viele Regeln.	*There are many rules.*

5. Sentence puzzle: rewrite the sentences in the correct order

a. ich in Letztes war Köln Jahr ...	*Last year I went to Cologne...*
b. …, Rosenmontagszug um teilzunehmen am.	*…to take part in the Rose Monday parade.*
c. Innenstadt Ich in war früh der ...	*I was in the city centre early...*
d. …, einen Platz um zu ergattern guten.	*…to get a good spot.*
e. öffentlichen Man die benutzen Toiletten muss.	*One has to use public toilets.*
f. bewölkt Am war es Morgen.	*In the morning it was cloudy.*
g. Während Rosenmontagszugs des ...	*During the Rose Monday parade...*
h. … kennengelernt ich Leute habe nette.	*…I met nice people.*

6. Complete with the verb in the imperfect/perfect tense

a. Letztes Jahr _________ ich in Köln. *sein*

b. Ich ____ mit meinem besten Freund _____________. *hinfahren*

c. Ich ___ früh ______________. *aufstehen*

d. Wir _______ früh in der Innenstadt. *sein*

e. Wir _____ nette Leute _____________. *kennenlernen*

f. Wir _____ um vier ins Hotel ___________. *zurückkehren*

g. Ich ______ einen Krapfen _____________. *essen*

h. Ich ______ viel ___________. *lachen*

i. Es _____ eine einzigartige Erfahrung. *sein*

7. Ist es eine gute (G) oder schlechte (S) Idee?
***e.g. Man muss die öffentlichen Toiletten benutzen*: G (gute Idee)**

a. Man muss keine Regeln beachten:

b. Man muss kein Hotel buchen:

c. Man muss mit dem Auto fahren:

d. Es empfiehlt sich, ein Kostüm zu tragen:

e. Man soll Wertgegenstände mitnehmen:

f. Man soll aus Plastikflaschen trinken:

8. Gapped translation

a. Letztes Jahr war ich in Köln.	*Last __________ I was in Cologne.*
b. Ich war beim Rosenmontagszug.	*I _______ at the Rose Monday parade.*
c. Ich bin mit meiner besten Freundin hingefahren.	*I went there with my _________friend.*
d. Wir sind mit dem Zug hingefahren.	*We _____________ by train.*
e. Es gibt einige Regeln zu beachten.	*There are some ________ to follow.*
f. Man muss die öffentlichen Toiletten benutzen.	*One has to use public ___________.*
g. Am Morgen war es sonnig...	*In the morning it was __________...*
h. ...aber am Nachmittag hat es geregnet.	*...but in the afternoon it ___________.*
i. Während des Rosenmontagszugs...	*During the Rose Monday ____________...*
j. ...habe ich viel gelacht.	*...I laughed _______.*

9. Translate into English

a. am Morgen

b. es war kalt

c. aber am Nachmittag

d. war es angenehm

e. einen Krapfen essen

f. Regeln beachten

g. die Damen schneiden den Herrn…

h. …die Krawatten ab

i. ein Auto mieten

j. ein Nickerchen machen

k. dann bin ich ins Hotel zurückgekehrt

l. eine kulturelle Erfahrung

10. Sentence puzzle: rewrite the sentences in the correct order

a. habe Ich am teilgenommen Rosenmontagszug.	*I participated in the Rose Monday parade.*
b. Ich mit dem bin geflogen Flugzeug	*I travelled by plane.*
c. lang Die war Fahrt.	*The trip was long but fun.*
d. gibt Es einige beachten Regeln zu.	*There are some rules to follow.*
e. Man trinken muss Plastikflaschen aus.	*One has to use plastic bottles.*
f. Man rechtzeitig muss buchen ein Hotel.	*One has to book a hotel room on time.*
g. kennengelernt Ich Leute habe nette.	*I met nice people.*
h. gegangen Abends schlafen bin ich um zehn.	*In the evening I went to bed at ten.*

Anna: Ich war beim Rosenmontagszug und fand es toll. Ich habe viele Bonbons gefangen. Es war eine einzigartige Erfahrung.

Thea: Ich war vor zehn Jahren in Köln und mir hat der Rosenmontagszug sehr gut gefallen.

Karl: Es gibt zu viele Regeln. Man darf nur aus Plastikflaschen trinken. Das nervt, weil es schädlich für die Umwelt ist.

Max: Was mir am besten gefallen hat, war, dass ich viele nette und lustige Leute kennengelernt habe. Außerdem war das Wetter gut.

Steffi: Ich habe viel gelacht. Es war eine unvergessliche Erfahrung. Am Nachmittag hat es allerdings geregnet.

Matthias: Ich bin ins Hotel zurückgefahren und habe ein Nickerchen gemacht. Das hat mir am besten gefallen.

Vera: Nach dem Rosenmontagszug habe ich mit meinen Freunden einen Krapfen gegessen.

David: Es gibt viele Regeln, aber die sind wichtig, damit das Festival sicher ist.

11. Find someone who…

…thinks there are too many rules

…laughed a lot

…went to Cologne a long time ago

…experienced some rain in the afternoon

…thinks the rules are important for safety

…thought that drinking out of plastic bottles was annoying

…had really good weather all day

…had a doughnut

…had a unique experience

…loves that they could meet new people

…had a nap at the hotel

12. Gapped translation

a. Vor einem Jahr war ich mit meinem besten Freund beim Rosenmontagszug.

Last year I ________ to the Rose Monday parade __________________ friend.

b. Wir sind mit dem Flugzeug geflogen, weil das am Schnellsten geht.

We went _____________ because it is the fastest way of getting there.

c. Die Fahrt war lang und langweilig. Mir war sehr langweilig und meiner Freundin auch.

The ___________ was _______ and boring. I got ______ bored and so did _______ .

d. Am Rosenmontag sind wir früh losgefahren, um einen guten Platz zu ergattern.

_____ Rose Monday we _______________ to _________ a good spot.

e. Es empfiehlt sich, rechtzeitig ein Hotel zu buchen.

It is _______________ to book a _________________ on time.

f. Man muss aus Plastiskflaschen trinken.

One has to drink from __________ bottles.

g. Ich habe nette Leute kennengelernt und viel Spaß gehabt.

I met lots of nice _____________ and had lots of _________.

13a. Complete the grid with the appropriate auxiliary verb HABEN in the perfect tense

Ich	Wir
Ich habe gelacht.	
	Wir haben gesehen.
Ich habe mich verkleidet.	
	Wir haben Bonbons gefangen.

13b. Complete the grid with the appropriate auxilary verb SEIN in the perfect tense

Ich	Wir
Ich bin hingefahren.	
	Wir sind ins Bett gegangen.
Ich bin gereist.	
	Wir sind gefahren.

14. Complete with a suitable word

a. Ich war in Köln, um am Rosenmontagszug ___________________.

b. Ich ___ mit meiner Freundin __________.

c. Wir haben ein ___________ gemietet.

d. Die Fahrt war sehr ___________.

e. Wir sind früh _____________, um einen guten Platz zu bekommen.

f. Ich habe viele Leute ________________.

g. Ich ___________ mich verkleidet.

h. Wir haben viele ____________ gefangen.

i. Ich habe im Hotel ein _______________ gemacht.

j. Dann habe ich einen Krapfen ____________ und einen Tee getrunken.

Hallo! Ich bin Julian. Letztes Wochenende war super.

Ich bin mit meinem besten Freund nach Köln gefahren, um mir den Rosenmontagszug anzusehen. Mein bester Freund heißt Franz. Er ist sehr sportlich und witzig. Er liebt alle Wassersportarten, wie zum Beispiel das Windsurfen.

Am Tag unserer Abreise mussten wir sehr früh aufstehen, um das Flugzeug zu erwischen. Anschließend sind wir mit dem Zug gefahren. Die Fahrt war lang, aber sehr witzig. Ich habe Musik gehört und mir die Landschaft angesehen. Am Rosenmontag sind wir dann früh losgefahren, um einen guten Platz in der Innenstadt zu ergattern.

Während der Parade gibt es einige wichtige Regeln zu beachten. Man muss zum Beispiel die öffentlichen Toiletten benutzen und darf nur aus Plastikfaschen trinken.

Außerdem empfielt es sich, Wertgegenstände zu Hause oder im Hotel zu lassen, damit sie in den Menschenmassen nicht gestohlen werden. Was das Wetter betrifft, war es am Morgen kalt, aber am Nachmittag angenehm.

Nachmittags sind wir ins Hotel zurückgefahren, um ein Nickerchen zu machen und einen Krapfen zu essen. Um zehn sind wir ins Bett gegangen. Der Rosenmontagszug war eine tolle kulturelle Erfahrung, die ich gerne wiederholen will.

(Julian, 18 Jahre. Tulln)

15. Find the German equivalent in Julian's text

a. was amazing

b. to see

c. to get up

d. we took the train

e. we left early

f. during the parade

g. important rules to follow

h. use public toilets

i. to leave valuables at home or at the hotel

j. it was cold in the morning

k. to have a nap

l. return to the hotel

m. …that I want to repeat

16. Answer the questions in German in full sentences, as if you were Julian.

a. Wann warst du beim Rosenmontagszug?

b. Mit wem bist du hingefahren?

c. Wie bist du hingefahren?

d. Welche Regeln findest du dort wichtig?

e. Warum soll man Wertgegenstände nicht mitnehmen?

f. Wie war das Wetter in Köln?

g. Willst du noch einmal zum Rosenmontagszug nach Köln fahren?

17. Complete the sentences

a. *My best friend is called Franz and he is very* ____________ *and* _______________.

b. *On the day of our departure we had to leave* ________ *to catch a* _____________.

c. The trip was ______ *but* _____.

d. *During the parade* _______________ *some* ___________ *to follow.*

e. *It's also advisable to leave* _______________ ____ _____________.

f. *The Rose Monday parade* _______ *a* ________ ____________ *experience.*

Hallo, ich bin Franz. Letztes Wochenende war ich bei einem berühmten Festival in Köln. Köln liegt am Rhein und ist weltweit bekannt für seine Kultur und Kulinarik. Ich bin mit meinem besten Freund Julian zur bekannten Kölner Karneval Parade gefahren, dem Rosenmontagszug, gefahren. Julian ist sehr intelligent, aber ein bisschen faul. Er spielt gerne Gitarre, aber macht wenig Sport.

Am Tag unserer Abreise sind wir um fünf Uhr aufgestanden. Das war vielleicht früh! Danach sind wir mit dem Flugzeug geflogen und anschließend mit dem Zug weitergefahren. Die Fahrt hat insgesamt vier Stunden gedauert. Ehrlich gesagt, war die Fahrt ziemlich anstrengend. Am Tag der Parade sind wir früh in die Innenstadt gefahren, um einen guten Platz zu ergattern.

Während des Rosenmontagszugs musste man einige Regeln beachten. Erstens durfte man nicht aus Glasflaschen trinken. Das war ein Problem, weil ich mir aus dem Hotel eine große Flasche Cola mitgenommen hatte. Zweitens musste man die öffentlichen Toiletten benutzen. Das Wetter war am Morgen sehr kalt, was mir nicht gefallen hat.

Persönlich haben mir die Menschenmassen nicht gefallen. Mir war die Musik zu laut und die Bonbons haben mich am Kopf getroffen (*the sweets hit me on the head*).

Am Nachmittag sind wir glücklicherweise wieder ins Hotel zurückgekehrt. Wir haben Krapfen gegessen und ein Nickerchen gemacht. Ich war froh, dass dieser schreckliche Tag endlich vorbei war. Ich habe keine Lust, noch einmal am Rosenmontagszug teilzunehmen.

(Franz, 18 Jahre. Tulln)

18. Find the German equivalent

a. at a famous festival

b. worldwide

c. culinary art

d. on the day of the trip

e. exhausting

f. to get a good spot

g. that was a problem

h. a big bottle of Coke

i. public toilets

j. crowds

k. I am not keen

19. Translate into English the following phrases from the text above

a. Köln liegt am Rhein

b. Julian ist sehr intelligent

c. ehrlich gesagt

d. einen guten Platz zu ergattern

e. nicht aus Glasflaschen trinken

f. was mir nicht gefallen hat

g. die Musik war zu laut

h. dieser schreckliche Tag

20. Write R (Richtig), F (Falsch) or NE (Nicht erwähnt) and correct the wrong statements

a. He got up at five o'clock.

b. He thought it was a fun trip.

c. They arrived late on the day of the festival.

d. He had brought a plastic bottle.

e. There was a big storm in the afternoon.

f. He liked the weather.

g. He hates crowds.

h. He is keen to return next year.

21. Complete the text with the options below

Letzen Monat _____ ich nach Köln ___________, um den Rosenmontagszug zu sehen. Am Tag der Abreise bin ich ____ aufgestanden, um den Flug nicht zu verpassen. Danach ging es mit dem ______ weiter. Die Fahrt war lang, aber _________. Ich habe mit meinem Cousin Musik ____________.

Am Tag des Rosenmontagszugs ________ wir früh losgefahren, um einen guten _________ zu ergattern. Während der Parade gibt es einige _________ zu beachten. Das Wichtigste ist, aus Plastikflaschen zu ____________, um Unfälle (*accidents*) zu vermeiden. Während des Rosenmontagszugs haben wir ______ Leute kennengelernt. Nachmittags sind ____ wieder ins Hotel zurückgekehrt. Wir haben einen Krapfen ______________. Ich würde gerne __________ zum Rosenmontagszug fahren.

wieder	früh	Zug	bin	witzig	Platz	nette
trinken	sind	gegessen	gefahren	Regeln	gehört	wir

22. Jigsaw: arrange the text in the correct order

Ich bin mit meiner Freundin hingefahren.	
und ein Nickerchen gemacht.	
Letztes Jahr war ich am Rosenmontagszug	1
Dort haben wir einen Krapfen gegessen	
am Nachmittag wieder ins Hotel	
Nächstes Jahr will ich wieder hinfahren.	
Wir sind früh losgefahren,	
zurückgekehrt.	
um einen guten Platz zu ergattern.	
in Köln.	
Wir haben nette Leute getroffen und sind	

23. Translate the sentences below into German using:

Man muss* + _________ + *infinitve

a. One has to book a hotel on time.

b. One has to use public toilets.

c. One has to take the train.

d. One has to catch sweets.

e. One has to follow rules.

f. One has to leave early.

24. Translate the sentences below into German using the perfect or imperfect (where indicated) tense

a. I woke up.

b. I was. (Imp)

c. I travelled.

d. I arrived.

e. I met.

f. I caught sweets.

g. I had a nap.

h. I had fun. (Imp)

i. I ate a doughnut.

j. I returned.

k. I left.

l. I used.

25. Translate the sentences below into German using the perfect tense

a. We got up very early.

b. We took a plane.

c. We arrived early in the city centre.

d. We had a nap.

e. We met nice people.

f. We went to bed.

26. Guided translation

a. L__________ S____________ w____ i_____ i__ K________.
Last summer I went to Cologne.

b. I___ b____ m____ m___________ b_________ F________ J___________ g___________.
I went with my best friend Johannes.

c. W_____ h_____________ a___ R__________________ t_________________.
We participated in the Rose Monday carneval.

d. E__ g_____ e____________ R_____________ z____ b________________.
There are some rules to follow.

e. M_____ m________ d ____ ö_________________ T_________________ b_________________.
One has to use public toilets.

f. A___ M_________ w_____ e____ s____________.
In the morning it was sunny.

g. W__________ d____ R__________________ h_______ i____ B____________ g__________.
During the Rose Monday carneval, I caught sweets.

h. I_____ h________ n______ L____________ k__________________.
I met nice people.

27. Translate the following text into German

Hi. My name is Paul. Last year I went to Cologne, which is well known for its culture and culinary art.

I wanted to take part in the Rosenmontagszug. I went with my best friend Theo. He is intelligent and funny. We travelled by plane and then by train. The trip was very long but quite fun.

On the day of the carneval, we arrived early to get a good spot. In this carneval, there are some rules to follow. One has to use public toilets and only use plastic bottles. In general, it is recommended to take the train.

In the morning, it was sunny but in the afternoon it was cloudy.

We met nice people and caught a lot of sweets. We laughed a lot.

In the evening we returned to the hotel, had a doughnut and watched TV.

It was an unforgettable experience and I would like to return again next year.

28. Write a 150 to 250 words paragraph in which you talk about a make-believe trip to the Rosenmontagszug. Mention:

- When you went.
- Who you went with.
- What they are like.
- How you travelled.
- How the trip was.
- Some of the main rules of the Rosenmontagszug.
- Three things you did during the parade.
- What you did afterwards.
- Your impressions of the experience.
- Whether you would like to return again one day.

Question Skills Unit 14

Imagine you have just come back from the Rosenmontagszug

English	German
Tell me about your trip to the Rosenmontagszug in Cologne.	**Erzähl mir von deinem Ausflug zum Rosenmontagszug in Köln.**
Where did you go?	**Wo bist du hingefahren?**
How did you travel? How was the trip?	**Wie bist du hingefahren? Wie war die Fahrt?**
What did you do on the day of the parade?	**Was hast du am Tag des Umzugs gemacht?**
What are some rules you have to follow during the Rosenmontagszug?	**Welche Regeln muss man während des Rosenmontagszugs beachten?**
What was the weather like in the morning/afternoon?	**Wie war das Wetter am Morgen/Nachmittag?**
How was the Rosenmontagszug? What did you see there?	**Wie war der Rosenmontagszug? Was hast du dort gesehen?**
What did you do after the parade?	**Was hast du nach dem Umzug gemacht?**
What was the best thing about the festival?	**Was hat dir an dem Fest am besten gefallen?**
How did you find the cultural experience?	**Wie war die kulturelle Erfahrung?**
Would you like to return some day?	**Würdest du gerne noch einmal hinfahren?**

1. Match questions and answers

Wo bist du hingefahren?	Der Rosenmontagszug war fantastisch.
Mit wem bist du hingefahren?	Wir sind mit dem Flugzeug geflogen.
Wie bist du hingefahren?	Ich würde sehr gerne noch einmal am Rosenmontagszug teilnehmen. Es war eine einzigartige kulturelle Erfahrung.
Wie war die Fahrt?	Ich war mit meinem Cousin.
Wo hast du übernachtet?	Am Morgen war es kalt, aber sonnig.
Was genau hast du am Tag der Parade gemacht?	Ich habe mir die bunten Wägen angesehen und Bonbons gefangen.
Wie war der Rosenmontagszug?	Ich war in Köln beim Rosenmontagszug.
Was hast du nach dem Umzug gemacht?	Die Fahrt war lang, aber wir hatten Spaß.
Wie war das Wetter?	Ich bin mit meinem Cousin ins Hotel gefahren.
Würdest du gerne noch einmal am Rosenmontagszug teilnehmen?	Wir haben in einem Hotel übernachtet.

2. Sentence puzzle: rewrite the sentences in the correct order

a. deiner Erzähl mir von Reise letzten.	*Tell me about your most recent trip.*
b. du entschlossen, teilzunehmen Warum hast dich Rosenmontagszug am.	*Why did you decide to go to the Rosenmontagszug?*
c. bist du und wie war die hingefahren. Wie Fahrt?	*How did you travel and what was the trip like?*
d. Parade Was hast am Tag der du gemacht?	*What did you do on the day of the parade?*
e. Wie das Morgen Wetter war am?	*What was the weather like in the morning?*
f. angekommen Wann bist du Innenstadt in der?	*At what time did you arrive in the centre?*
g. Nachmittag hast du am Was gemacht?	*What did you do in the evening?*
h. besten Was hat gefallen dir am?	*What was the best thing?*

3. Guided translation

a. W_ _ _ w_ _ _ _ d_ i_ K_ _ _? W_ _ b_ _ _ d_ h_ _ _ _ _ _ _ _ _ _ _?

When did you go to Cologne? How did you travel?

b. M_ _ w_ _ b_ _ _ d_ h_ _ _ _ _ _ _ _ _ _ _?

Who did you go with?

c. W_ _ w_ _ d_ _ W_ _ _ _ _ a_ M_ _ _ _ _?

What was the weather like in the morning?

d. W_ h_ _ _ d_ ü_ _ _ _ _ _ _ _ _ _ _? H_ _ e_ d_ _ g_ _ _ _ _ _ _?

Where did you stay? Did you like it?

e. W_ _ w_ _ e_ _ _ w_ _ _ _ _ _ _ _ R_ _ _ _?

What was an important rule?

f. W_ _ h_ _ _ d_ w_ _ _ _ _ _ _ d_ _ R_ _ _ _ _ _ _ _ _ _ _ _ _ _ _ _ g_ _ _ _ _ _?

What did you do during the Rose Monday parade?

g. W_ _ h_ _ d_ _ a_ b_ _ _ _ _ a_ d_ _ P_ _ _ _ _ g_ _ _ _ _ _ _?

What did you like best about the parade?

4. Answer the following questions in your own words, using full sentences

Wann bist du nach Köln gefahren?

Wie bist du hingefahren?

Wo hast du übernachtet?

Welche Regel hast du am wichtigsten gefunden?

Was hast du während des Rosenmontagszugs gemacht?

Was hast du danach gemacht?

Würdest du gerne noch einmal hinfahren?

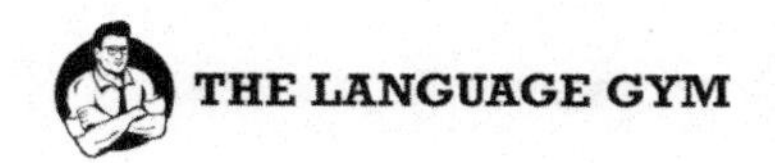

Vocab Revision Workout 7

1. Gapped translation

a. Letzten Monat sind wir in die Schweiz gefahren.

Last ___________ we went to Switzerland.

b. Wir sind mit dem Flugzeug geflogen.

We travelled by ___________.

c. Das Wetter war jeden Tag gut.

The weather was __________ every day.

d. Wir haben in einem Hotel übernachtet.

We __________ in a hotel.

e. Das Hotel war in der Innenstadt von Bern.

The hotel was in the _______ _______ of Bern.

f. Mir hat das Hotel sehr gut gefallen.

I __________ the hotel a lot.

2. Verb anagrams

a. Ich **thate** viel Spaß.
I had a blast.

b. Das Wetter **raw** gut.
The weather was good.

c. Wir **renwa** am Strand.
We were at the beach.

d. Wir haben in einem Luxushotel **tenaübercht**.
We stayed in a luxury hotel.

e. Im Hotel **bga** es ein tolles Schwimmbad.
In the hotel there was a great swimming pool.

f. Meine Eltern haben viel **eessngeg**.
My parents ate a lot.

g. Mein Bruder hat jeden Tag Tennis **iepgeslt**.
My brother played tennis every day.

3. Select the correct auxiliary verb

a. Mark und Tom **haben/sind/hat** ihre Aufgaben gemacht.

b. Ich **habe/hat/hast** ein Auto gemietet.

c. Mein Papa **hat/ist/hast** das Haus geputzt.

d. Meine Geschwister **sind/haben/ist** ausgegangen.

e. Meine Cousine **hat/ist/hast** mich besucht.

f. Meine Freunde **ist/sind/hat** gekommen.

g. Mein Bruder **hat/ist/sind** etwas gefangen.

h. Er **ist/hast/hat** es gewußt.

i. Ich **bin/habe/ist** zu Hause geblieben.

j. Er **hast/bist/hat** Pizza gegessen.

k. Wir **sind/sein/haben** ins Kino gegangen.

l.Ich **habe/bin/hat** Sightseeing. gemacht.

4. Complete with any suitable verb, using the third person singular and plural of the perfect tense (e.g. *er ist gefahren, sie sind gefahren , etc.*) to talk about Peter's last weekend

Peter und sein Papa waren letztes Wochenende im Sportzentrum. Sie ________ mit dem Auto ____________ und ______________ den ganzen Vormittag Tennis __________________. Danach _______________ sie in der Cafeteria Mittag __________________. Petter hatte Schnitzel mit Pommes. Das war sehr lecker. Pommes sind zwar nicht sehr gesund, aber schmecken sehr gut. Nach dem Mittagessen ____ Peters Papa eine Runde joggen ____________. Peter ___ alleine schwimmen ________________. Danach _____ Peter auf einer Sonnenliege *(sun lounger)* ein Nickerchen ______________. Anschließend _____________ Peter und sein Papa noch ein Eis _______________. Vanille und Pistazie sind Peters Lieblingssorten *(favourite flavours)*. Um fünf _______ sie wieder nach Hause ____________________. Zu Hause ________ sie für Mama ein Abendessen __________. Peter liebt es, für seine Mama etwas zu kochen.

5. Match questions and answers

Wo bist du hingefahren?	Sehr gemütlich, es gab ein großen Bett.
Wann bist du hingefahren?	In einem teuren Hotel.
Wie bist du hingefahren?	Mit dem Mietauto.
Mit wem bist du hingefahren?	Es gab einen Pool und einen großen Tennisplatz.
Wo hast du übernachtet?	Sehr modern und luxuriös.
Wo war das Hotel?	Nach Travemünde.
Wie war das Hotel?	Direkt am Strand.
Wie war das Hotel ausgestattet?	Mit meiner Familie.
Wie lange bist du geblieben?	Eine Woche.
Wie war dein Zimmer?	Im August.
Würdest du noch einmal hinfahren?	Selbstverständlich. Der Urlaub war super.

6. Complete

a. I____ b____ n_____ D_______________ a____ U_________ g___________.
I went on holiday to Germany.

b. I____ b____ m____ d__ B____ g___________. *I travelled by coach.*

c. I____ b____ m____ m_____ F________ h___________. *I went there with my family.*

d. D__ F______ w____ l______________. *The journey was boring.*

e. D__ H_______ h___ m___ n______ s______ g__ g_________. *I didn't like the hotel much.*

f. W__ h______ e______ t______ Z______. *We had a very good time.*

g. W___ h______ i__e______ J______________ ü___________. *We stayed in a youth hostel.*

h. E__ g___ e____ P_____ u____ e__ F________________. *There was a pool and a gym.*

7. Translate into German

a. *On the 1st day we visited the museum.*

b. *On the 2nd day we rented a bike.*

c. *On the 3rd day they went sightseeing.*

d. *In the morning she got up late.*

e. *I sunbathed on the beach until noon.*

f. *We went hiking every day.*

g. *Yesterday he went for a walk.*

h. *We swam in the sea.*

i. *We stayed in a cheap hotel.*

j. *In the evenings my parents went clubbing.*

k. *They tried many typical dishes.*

8. Translate into German

- Last summer, my older brother went to Switzerland with his girlfriend.
- They stayed in the city centre of Bern.
- They rented an apartment not far from the train station.
- The apartment was clean and cosy. There was a television, but there was no Internet.
- The old town was beautiful, so they spent every day sightseeing and going for long walks in the city centre.
- In the evening they went to restaurants and tried typical dishes.
- The best thing was when they went to the museum.

Unit 15

Talking about a trip to Berlin and Vienna – past & future

In this unit you will learn:

- To talk about what you did on a recent trip
- To talk about an upcoming trip
- Key places to visit and things to do in *Berlin* and *Vienna*

Key sentence patterns:

- Time marker + *war ich* / *waren wir* + noun phrase/prepositional phrase
- What I liked the most about + place + *war als* + perfect tense
- *Es war* + adjective + however + noun + *war* + adjective
- Time marker + *werde ich* + noun phrase / prepositional phrase + infinitive

Grammar:

- All persons of the perfect tense
- All persons of the near future
- Some uses of the imperfect tense

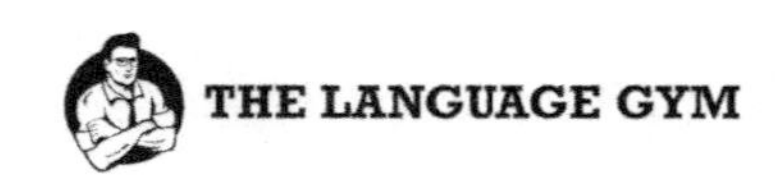

Unit 15: Talking about a trip to Berlin & Vienna – past & future

Mein letzter Ausflug nach Berlin

Vor zwei Tagen [Two days ago]	war ich waren wir	in Berlin.	Ich bin [I...] Wir sind [We...]	mit dem [by]	Auto [car] Bus	gefahren [...went]

Die Fahrt [The trip]	hat drei Stunden gedauert [took 3 hours]	und hat mir gut gefallen, weil sie [and I liked it a lot because it]	spannend [exciting] unterhaltsam [fun]	war [was]

In Berlin	habe ich [I...] haben wir [we...]	in einem Hotel	über-nachtet. [...stayed]	Es war günstig/teuer [It was cheap/ expensive] Es war sauber [It was clean]	, aber [but] und [and]	das Personal war [the staff were]	freundlich [friendly] hilfsbereit [helpful] unfreundlich

Das Hotel	war [was]	in der Nähe vom [near] weit vom [far from]	Zentrum [centre] Hauptbahnhof [central station]	Reichstagsgebäude [Reichstag building] Brandenburger Tor [Brandenburg Gate]

Das Beste an dem Ausflug nach Berlin war [The best part of the trip toBerlin was]	die Currywurst, die ich am Alexanderplatz gegessen habe [the currywurst that I ate at Alexanderplatz] das DDR Museum [the GDR museum] die Besichtigung der Berliner Mauer [the visit of the Berlin Wall]

Mir [I] Uns [We]	hat die Reise nach Berlin [the trip to Berlin]	sehr gefallen [enjoyed a lot]	und ich würde [and I would] und wir würden	gerne nächstes Jahr wieder dorthin fahren [go back next year]

Mein kommender Ausflug nach Wien

Heute [Today] Morgen [Tomorrow]	werde ich [I am going to go] werden wir [we are going to go]	mit dem Zug/Bus	nach Wien fahren.	Die Fahrt dauert [the trip takes]	circa zwei Stunden [2 hours]

In Wien [In Vienna]	werde ich [I will...] werden wir [we will...]	in einer Jugendherberge [in a youth hostel] in einem Hotel [in a hotel]	in der Nähe [near]	des Stephansdoms von der Karlskirche	übernachten [...stay]
			neben [next to]	dem Stephansdom der Albertina	

Am ersten Tag [On the first day]	werde ich [I am going to...] werden wir [we are going to...]	am Morgen [in the morning] am Nachmittag [in the afternoon]	einen Spaziergang machen [...go for a walk]	
			Schloss Schönbrunn den Prater	besuchen [...visit]

Am zweiten Tag	werde ich werden wir	den Burggarten besuchen [visit the Burggarten] einen Spaziergang in der Innenstadt machen [walk around the city centre]

Schließlich [Finally]	werde ich werden wir	mit dem Auto / Bus / Zug	nach Hause [home]	fahren
		mit dem Flugzeug [by plane]		fliegen

Ich bin mir sicher, dass der Wochenendtrip nach Wien [I am certain the weekend trip to Vienna will be]	unvergesslich [unforgettable]	sein wird

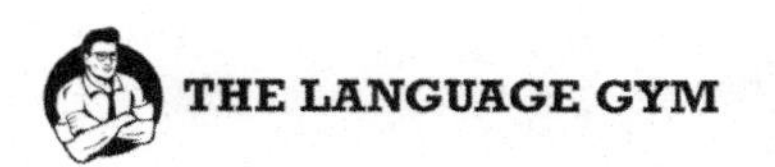

1. Match

ein Schloss	the people were
eine historische Stadt	it's on the coast
sie liegt an der Küste	we stayed
die Reise hat ... gedauert	the journey lasted…
die Leute waren	on the first day
ich bin mir sicher	I liked it a lot
wir haben übernachtet	go back next year
mir hat es gut gefallen	a historic city
es war sauber	the weather was nice
das Wetter war schön	it was clean
am ersten Tag	a castle
noch einmal dorthin fahren	I am certain

2. Complete the words

a. e_n S_hlos_	a castle
b. ic_ h_b_ übern__htet	I stayed
c. d_e L_ute	the people
d. die R_i_e	the journey
e. ic_ m_c_t_	I liked
f. gas_f_e_ndlich	welcoming
g. d_s _e_t_	the best
h. das We__er	the weather
i. d_e Inn_nst_dt	city centre
j. u_ver_essli_h	unforgettable
k. n_b_n	next to

3. Break the flow

a. VorzweiTagenwarenwirinBerlin.

b. BerlinisteinehistorischeStadt.

c. DieFahrtwarziemlichlang.

d. DieFahrthatfastzweiStundengedauert.

e. DieLeutewarensehrfreundlich.

f. DasHotelwarsauber.

g. SchließlichwerdeichmitdemZugnachHausefahren.

h. InWienwerdeichineinerJugendherbergeübernachten.

5. Spot and correct the nonsense sentences

a. Berlin ist eine historische Stadt.

b. Die Fahrt dauerte ein Jahr.

c. Wir haben in einem Hotel übernachtet.

d. Leider war das Wetter gut.

e. Wir haben Sightseeing in meinem Zimmer gemacht.

f. Wir haben Pommes im Dom gegessen.

g. Mein großer Bruder ist ausgegangen.

h. In Berlin werde ich den Eiffelturm besichtigen.

4. Complete with the missing words

a. Vor zwei __________ waren wir in ___________.

b. Die Fahrt dauerte zwei ____________.

c. Berlin ist eine historische _____________.

d. Es liegt im ____________ von Deutschland.

e. Wir haben in einem __________ Hotel übernachtet.

f. Das Hotel war sauber und das Personal nett und ______________. Mein Zimmer ______schön.

g. Das ____________ war gut. Es hat _____ geregnet.

h. Wir haben das _________ _________ und den _________________ besucht.

i. Wir haben ________ an einer Imbissbude gegessen.

j. Wir haben ein Rad gemietet und haben eine ___________ durch das Zentrum gemacht.

k. Abends ist mein großer Bruder _____________.

l. Mir hat die ________ sehr gut gefallen.

Currywurst	Wetter	Tagen	günstigen
Stadt	Berlin	Stunden	Radtour
gast-freundlich	aus-gegangen	Branden-burger Tor	Alexander-platz
nicht	Reise	war	Norden

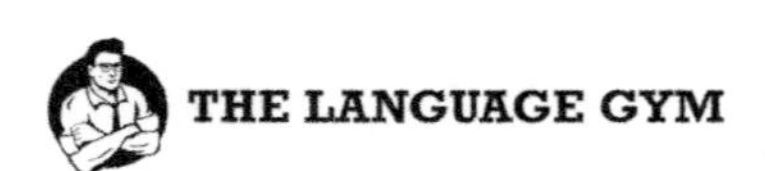

6. Sentence puzzle

a. mit Berlin Vor Woche war ich Familie einer meiner in.

b. Die ziemlich war lang Fahrt.

c. Berlin Wir haben Tage in verbracht zwei.

d. Samstagmorgen Wir angekommen am sind.

e. einem Wir Hotel in übernachtet haben schönen.

f. Das im Hotel Stadtzentrum war.

g. eine Wir besichtigt große haben Kathedrale.

h. Wir besichtigt Schloss auch ein altes haben.

i. typische haben Wir Gerichte probiert viele.

7. Gapped translation

a. Letzte Woche bin ich nach Berlin gefahren.

___________ ___________ *I went to Berlin.*

b. Wir sind sehr früh aufgewacht.

We woke up ________ __________.

c. Die Reise war lang und anstrengend.

The journey was _________ *and* ___________.

d. Wir haben in einem 3-Sterne-Hotel übernachtet.

We stayed in a ________-________ *hotel.*

e. Das Hotel war im Zentrum von Berlin

The hotel was in the _________ *of Berlin.*

f. Wir haben zwei unvergessliche Tage verbracht.

We spent two _________________ ________.

g. Wir haben sehr leckere lokale Gerichte gegessen.

We _________ *very tasty typical* ___________.

h. Wir haben ein sehr schönes Schloss besucht.

We visited a very ____________ ___________.

i. Wir haben eine Radtour durch die Altstadt gemacht.

We did a bike tour of the ___________ *town.*

j. Das Hotelpersonal war sehr gastfreundlich.

The hotel staff was very _______________.

8. Translate into English

a. Wir waren letzten Monat dort.

b. Wir haben zwei unvergessliche Tage verbracht.

c. Wir haben in einer Jugendherberge übernachtet.

d. Wir haben ein Rad gemietet und sind Sightseeing gegangen.

e. Wir haben viele Fotos von alten Gebäuden gemacht.

f. Das Beste war, als wir ein Schloss besucht haben.

g. Zum Glück war es jeden Tag sonnig.

9. Guided translation

a. *I went there last week*	I_____ w____ l___________ W_________ d_____.
b. *I spent three days in Berlin.*	I____ h____ d_____ T______ i__ B_______ v__________.
c. *We travelled by coach.*	W___ s_____ m____ d___ B______ a_____________.
d. *We stayed in a cheap hotel.*	W___ h_____ i__ e_____ g________ H______ ü___________.
e. *The hotel was near the centre.*	D__ H______ w___ i__ d___ N______ d____ I___________.
f. *Every day we went sightseeing.*	W___ h____ j_____ T____ S_________________ g__________.
g. *On the last day I rented a bike.*	A__ l________ T___ h_____ i____ e____ R___ g__________.
h. *We went to see the cathedral.*	W___ h______ e______ K______________ b_____________.
i. *We also visited the castle.*	W___ h_______ a______ d____ S_______ b____________.
j. *It is near the museum*	E__ i___ i__ d____ N_______ v___ M____________.
k. *We met two very nice boys.*	W___ h_____ z___ n_____ J________ k_____________.

(1) Hallo! Ich heiße Mark. Ich bin fünfzehn Jahre alt und komme aus Rosenheim. Mir gefällt meine Stadt, weil sie klein ist. Es gibt außerdem viele Angebote für junge Leute. In meiner Nachbarschaft gibt es nette Restaurants und eine Bibliothek.

(2) Vor einer Woche war ich in Berlin mit meinen Eltern. Wir sind mit dem Flugzeug geflogen, weil es sonst zu lange gedauert hätte. Der Flug hat circa eine Stunde gedauert. Wir sind mit dem Auto nach Müchen gefahren und dann weiter nach Berlin geflogen. Der Flug war kurz, aber die Autofahrt war langweilig. In Berlin haben wir in einem kleinen, zentral gelegenen Hotel übernachtet. Das Hotelpersonal war sehr hilfsbereit.

(3) Jeden Tag bin ich früh aufgestanden. Dann habe ich im Hotel gefrühstückt und bin im Stadtzentrum spazieren gegangen. Einmal habe ich Currywurst mit Pommes zu Mittag gegessen. Das war sehr lecker. Dann habe ich eine Führung durch das Reichstagsgebäude gemacht. Das war sehr interessant. Die Führung bei Checkpoint Charlie hat mir am besten gefallen. Ich habe sehr viel über die deutsche Wiedervereinigung (*reunification*) gelernt. Meine Eltern waren auch begeistert, da sie sich sehr für Geschichte interessieren.

(4) Machnmal allerdings finde ich meine Eltern etwas langweilig. Deshalb bin ich einmal alleine Königsberger Klopse essen gegangen. Das war eine tolle kulinarische Erfahrung. Außerdem habe ich ein sehr nettes Mädchen getroffen. Ihr Name ist Anja. Sie ist sportlich, intelligent und sehr witzig. Wir haben den ganzen Nachmittag geplaudert und schließlich Telefonnummern ausgetauscht. Noch immer schreiben wir uns WhatsApp-Nachrichten.

(5) Der Wochenendtrip nach Berlin hat mir sehr gut gefallen und ich will unbedingt noch einmal hinfahren, vor allem um Anja wiederzusehen.

(Mark, 15 Jahre. Rosenheim)

10. Find the German equivalent in parts 1 and 2 of Mark's text

a. because it is small

b. there are many things to do

c. a week ago

d. we travelled by plane

e. about an hour

f. we stayed

g. the hotel staff were very helpful

11. Complete the statements below based on the content of Parts 3 & 4

a. Every day Mark got up ___________.

b. After breakfast he went ______________ in town.

c. One day he ate _____________ for lunch.

d. He did a guided tour of both the ________________ and the _________________.

e. I learned a lot about the German ____________.

f. His parents didn't have _____________with him.

g. Mark and Anja ___________ phone numbers.

12. Tick the words/phrases contained in part 4 and 5 and cross out the ones that aren't

a. however	f. exciting
b. boring	g. finally
c. experience	h. still
d. her name is	i. we called each other
e. culinary	j. absolutely

13. Answer the following questions about Mark's whole text

a. Why did Mark take a plane to Berlin?

b. Where was their hotel located?

c. What did he think of Currywurst?

d. Why did his parents enjoy Checkpoint Charlie?

e. What does Mark sometimes think of his parents?

f. What is Anja like?

g. What did they do all afternoon?

14. Complete the table

English	German
tomorrow	
	das hat lange gedauert
	wir werden reisen
by car	
	mit dem Flugzeug
	ich werde übernachten
we are going to stay	
	das Beste wird sein
on the first day	
	am zweiten Tag
	wir werden besuchen
	wir werden Sightseeing machen
we are going to try	

15. Complete with a suitable word

a. Morgen werde ich nach Stuttgart ______________.

b. Ich werde mit meinem ____________ dorthin fahren.

c. Wir werden mit dem _____________ fahren.

d. Wir werden in einem _________ übernachten.

e. Zum Frühstück werde ich ____________________ essen.

f. Wir werden ein ____________ mieten.

g. Wir werden alle historischen ____________ der Stadt besuchen.

h. Ich werde viele ___________ machen.

i. Am ersten Tag wollen wir das Porsche Museum ____________.

j. Am zweiten Tag werden wir durch die Altstadt __________________.

16. Slalom translation

e.g. We are going to spend two days in Berlin.

a. It is the capital of Germany.

b. Maybe we are going to rent a bike.

c. The hotel is centrally located.

d. The journey takes more than an hour.

e. We are going to stay in a cheap hotel.

f. I am going to go for a walk in the old town.

g. My brother is going to take many pictures.

h. I will try a typical dish of the region.

i. I think the trip will be exciting.

Wir werden	werde	**Tage**	von	mieten.
Es ist	**zwei**	typisches	günstigen Hotel	Region probieren.
Vielleicht	dass	einem	spazieren	sein wird.
Das	werden in	in der Innenstadt	**in Berlin**	eine Stunde.
Mein	werden wir	die Reise	mehr als	gehen.
Ich glaube,	Fahrt	dauert	sehr spannend	**verbringen.**
Ich werde	Hotel	ein	Rad	Fotos machen.
Wir	ein	wird	zentral	übernachten.
Die	die	ist	viele	gelegen.
Ich	Bruder	Hauptstadt	Gericht aus der	Deutschland.

17. Multiple choice: choose the correct translation

	1	2	3
a. Ich werde übernachten.	I am going to stay.	I am going to go.	I am going to leave.
b. Wir werden ausgehen.	We are going to try.	We are going to go out.	We are going to rent.
c. Wir werden fahren.	We are going to go.	We are going to visit.	We are going to return.
d. Ich werde mich amüsieren.	I am going to divert.	I am going to travel.	I am going to have fun.
e. Ich werde mich entspannen.	I am going to sleep.	I am going to relax.	I am going to disco.
f. Er wird probieren.	He is going to try.	He is going to probe.	He is going to eat.
g. Sie wird kochen.	She is going to buy.	She is going to cook.	She is going to sell.
h. Ich werde mieten.	I am going to buy.	I am going to rent.	I am going to try.

18. Complete with the correct option

a. Ich werde Currywurst ___________.

b. Ich werde einen Spaziergang durch den Rosensteinpark ____________.

c. Ich werde die St. Nikolaus-Kathedrale ____________.

d. Ich werde ein Rad ____________.

e. Ich werde Souvenirs ____________.

f. Ich werde Sightseeing in der Altstadt ___________.

g. Ich werde in einem günstigen Hotel __________.

h. Ich werde mit dem Auto ___________.

i. Mein Bruder wird abends ___________.

j. Meine Mutter wird bummeln ____________.

k. Meine Eltern werden viele Fotos ____________.

l. Wir werden durch den chinesischen Garten spazieren _______________

gehen	übernachten	kaufen	ausgehen
machen	mieten	besuchen	machen
gehen	essen	fahren	machen

19. Complete the table

Perfect Tense	Future Tense
Ich bin mit dem Auto gefahren.	
	Ich werde essen.
Ich habe in einem Hotel übernachtet.	
	Wo werdet ihr hinfahren?
Was hast du gemacht?	
	Mein Bruder wird ausgehen.
Meine Mama hat Souvenirs gekauft.	
	Mein Papa wird viele Fotos machen.
Mein Bruder und ich haben Kleidung gekauft.	
	Wir werden uns sonnen.
Meine Eltern haben Museen besucht.	

(1) Hallo! Ich heiße Eva und komme aus Bremen, lebe aber in Mainz. Letztes Jahr bin ich mit meiner besten Freundin Emma nach Wien gefahren. Wir sind mit dem Zug über München und Salzburg gefahren. Insgesamt hat die Fahrt achteinhalb Stunden gedauert. Glücklicherweise konnten wir beide auf der Fahrt schlafen.

(2) In Wien haben wir in einer Jugendherberge übernachtet, die fünf Minuten vom Stephansdom entfernt war. Am ersten Tag haben wir morgens einen Spaziergang im ersten Bezirk gemacht. Wir haben den Stephansdom besucht, dann haben wir uns die Geschäfte am Graben und die Ausgrabungen (*excavations*) am Michaelaplatz angesehen. Nachmittags haben wir im berühmten Restaurant Figlmüller ein Schnitzel gegessen. Das war sehr lecker.

(3) Am zweiten Tag waren wir in der Albertina und haben uns die Sammlung Batliner, die Werke von Picasso und Monet enthält, angesehen. Paul Signacs „Venedig, die rosa Wolke" hat mir am besten gefallen. Am Nachmittag sind wir dann mit der U-Bahn zum Schloss Schönbrunn gefahren und haben einen langen Spaziergang im Schlosspark gemacht.

(4) Die Reise nach Wien war einzigartig. Wien ist ohne Zweifel meine Lieblingsstadt in Österreich. Deshalb werde ich nächstes Wochenende wieder hinfahren. Am ersten Tag werde ich einen Spaziergang durch den Prater machen und nachmittags eine Führung durch die Wiener Hofburg mit anschließendem Spaziergang durch den Burggarten. Abends werde ich im Rathauskeller zu Abend essen. Das wird bestimmt lecker.

(5) Am zweiten Tag will ich ins Kunsthistorische Museum gehen und anschließend im Café Leopold im Museumsquartier zu Mittag essen. Vielleicht sehe ich mir am Abend noch ein Musical im Raimundtheater an. Mal sehen (*we'll see*).

(6) Ich freue mich schon sehr auf mein Wochenende in Wien, weil es so viel Kultur zu entdecken gibt und das Essen der Hammer (*amazing*) ist.

(Eva, 18 Jahre. Mainz)

20. Answer the following questions about Parts 1 to 3 of Eva's text

a. Where does Eva live?

b. Who is Emma?

c. How did they travel to Vienna?

d. How long did the journey take and what where they fortunately able to do?

e. Where in Vienna did they stay?

f. What did they do in the morning and afternoon on the first day?

g. Which art collection did they view in the Albertina and which painting did Eva enjoy the most?

h. What did they do in Schönbrunn?

21. Complete the translation of Part 4

The trip to __________ was unique. Without a ________, Vienna is my ______________city in Austria. Therefore, next ______________ I am going to _____ there __________. On the __________ day, I am going to go for a _________ through the Prater and in the ________________, I will do a guided _________ of the Wiener Hofburg, followed by a _______ through the Burggarten. In the _______________, I am __________ to __________ in the Rathauskeller. Surely, the food is going to be ______________.

22. Find the German equivalent in the text

a. altogether	j. in the afternoon
b. fortunately	k. guided tour
c. a youth hostel	l. I am going to return
d. tasty	m. to dine
e. works	n. definitely
f. included	o. subsequently
g. underground train	p. maybe
h. walk	q. to discover
i. therefore	r. the food

23. Complete the text below choosing from the options provided

Hallo! Ich heiße Anton. Ich _________ aus Dresden, das im Osten von Deutschland liegt, lebe allerdings in Hannover. Letztes _________ war ich mit meinem _________ Tom in Bayern auf ________. Bayern _________ im Süden von Deutschland. Bayern ist traumhaft schön. Wir ________ mit dem Zug ___________. Ich reise gerne mit dem Zug. Wenn ich mit dem ________ reise, wird mir sehr oft übel. Die Zugfahrt hat circa fünf __________ gedauert. Wir sind direkt ________ München gefahren.

Freund	Urlaub	liegt	Jahr	Stunden
sind	komme	gefahren	Auto	nach

24. Complete the text below with a suitable verb in the perfect tense.

Letzes Jahr _____ ich nach Wien ______________. Ich ______ mit dem Flugzeug ______________. Der Flug _______ eineinhalb Stunden ____________. In Wien _______ ich in einem billigen Hotel ________________.

In Wien _______ ich mir viele tolle Sehenswürdigkeiten _________________.

Am ersten Tag _____ ich in der Innenstadt spazieren ______________. Ich _______ viele Fotos ______________.

Am zweiten Tag _________ ich Schnitzel in einem tollen Restaurant _____________.

Weil es sehr heiß war, ___________ ich mir ein Eis (*ice cream*) _________________. Das war sehr lecker. Wien ist einfach super!

25. Gapped translation

a. Letztes J_ _ _ war ich in W_ _ _ auf U_ _ _ _ _. — *Last year I went on holiday to Vienna.*

b. Mir h_ _ die Busf_ _ _ _ nicht g_ _ _ _ _ _ _ _ ... — *I didn't like the journey by coach...*

c. ..., aber d_ _ Zugf_ _ _ _ war t_ _ _. — *...but the train trip was great.*

d. A_ e_ _ _ _ _ T_ _ b_ _ i_ _ f_ _ _ a_ _ _ _ _ _ _ _ _ _ _ _. — *On the first day I got up early.*

e. I_ W_ _ _ war d_ _ W_ _ _ _ _ g_ _. — *In Vienna the weather was good.*

f. E_ h_ _ nur ei_ _ _ T_ _ ge_e_ _ _ _ . — *It only rained on one day.*

g. W_ _ h_ _ _ _ den Z_ _ n_ _ _ W_ _ _ g_ _ _ _ _ _ _ _. — *We took the train to Vienna.*

h. Meine E_ _ _ _ _ sind nicht e_ _ _ _ _ _ _ _ _ gegangen. — *My parents didn't go shopping.*

i. A_ Ab_ _ _ ha_e_ w_ _ e_ _ M_ _ _ _ _ _ _ g_ _ _ _ _ _. — *In the evening we saw a musical.*

j. D_ _ Beste w_ _ d_ _ Sc_ _ _ _ _ _ _ _. — *The best thing was the Schnitzel.*

k. A_ ersten Tag habe ich e_ _ nettes Mäd_ _ _ _ kennengelernt. — *One the first day I met a nice girl.*

26. Translate into German

a. last year

b. we went on holiday

c. to Bavaria

d. in the south of Germany

e. it is a beautiful city

f. in the city

g. we travelled

h. by train

i. we rented a bike

j. we stayed

k. in a cheap hotel

l. in a youth hostel

m. in the city centre.

n. we took the bus

o. we went for a walk

p. near

(1) Ich heiße Robert und wohne in London. Normalerweise fahre ich mit meiner Familie nach Mallorca auf Urlaub. Mallorca gefällt uns sehr gut, weil das Wetter immer schön ist. Wir fliegen mit dem Flugzeug nach Palma und dann nehmen wir ein Taxi nach Puerto Pollensa. Wir fahren immer dorthin, weil die Leute nett sind und das Essen phänomenal ist. In Puerto Pollensa kann man den alten Yachthafen besichtigen und tolle Restaurants besuchen.

(2) Letzten Monat sind wir nach Bath auf Urlaub gefahren. Bath liegt im Südwesten von England. Wir sind mit dem Zug gefahren und die Fahrt hat drei Stunden gedauert. Wir haben drei Nächte in einem Hotel nahe der Innenstadt übernachtet. Am ersten Tag haben wir uns die römischen Bäder angesehen und einen Spaziergang in der Altstadt gemacht. Die alten Gebäude gefallen mir sehr gut. Am zweiten Tag haben wir eine Tour am Fluss gemacht. Bath ist wirklich eine faszinierende Stadt.

(3) Nächstes Jahr würde ich gerne nach Jena fahren. Jena ist bekannt für seine Optik- und Feinmechanikindustrie. Ich interessiere mich sehr für Mikroskope und will deshalb das Optische Museum dort besuchen. Wir werden im Scala Turm Hotel übernachten, von wo aus man einen perfekten Ausblick auf die Stadt hat.

(4) Am ersten Tag werden wir den Botanischen Garten und die Goethe-Gedenkstätte besuchen. Goethe war einer der bekanntesten deutschen Dichter, der unter anderem das Werk „Faust" geschrieben hat. Am Nachmittag wollen wir ins Zeiss-Planetarium gehen, um das älteste Planetarium der Welt mit seiner einzigartigen Kuppel (*dome*) anzusehen. Am zweiten Tag wollen wir uns dann auch noch Schillers Gartenhaus ansehen, um zu erfahren, wie der berühmte deutsche Dichter mit seiner Familie im 18. Jahrhundert gelebt hat. Wir freuen uns schon sehr auf Jena, weil die Stadt viel für Kultur- und Wissenschaftsinteressierte bietet. Ich kann es kaum erwarten, mit meiner Familie hinzufahren. **(Robert, 19 Jahre. London)**

27. Find the German equivalent

a. because the weather is always lovely
b. we take a plane
c. the old marina
d. near
e. we stayed for three nights
f. old town
g. the Roman baths
h. the old buildings
i. on the second day
j. fascinating
k. a perfect view
l. interested in microscopes
m. one of the most famous German poets
n. I cannot wait

28. Answer in English

a. Why does Robert like Mallorca?
b. Why do Robert and his family like Puerto Pollensa?
c. Where in Bath did Robert stay?
d. What did they do in Bath on the 2nd day?
e. When is he going to go to Jena?
f. What is Jena famous for and why is this of interest to Robert?
g. What does the hotel offer?
h. What does Robert want to visit in the morning of his the first day?
i. What are two special features of the Zeiss planetarium?

29. Translate the following into English

a. …, weil die Leute nett sind. (P.1)
b. im Südwesten von Englands (P.2)
c. nahe der Innenstadt (P.2)
d. eine faszinierende Stadt (P.2)
e. ich interessiere mich für... (P.3)
f. einen perfekten Ausblick (P.4)
g. Goethe-Gedenkstätte (P.4)
h. unter anderem (P.4)
i. um zu erfahren (P.4)
j. ich kann es kaum erwarten (P.4)

30. Spot and correct the mistakes with the verbs. HINT: not all the verbs are wrong

a. Gestern waren ich auf Mallorca auf Urlaub.

b. Meine Eltern haben Ausflüge gemacht.

c. Mein kleiner Bruder hast gar nichts gemacht.

d. Wir werden mit dem Auto fahren.

e. Meine Eltern hast Fahrräder gemietet.

f. Ich hat einen Spaziergang im Stadtzentrum gemacht.

g. Meine Mama wird Souvenirs kaufen.

h. Ich wird an den Strand gehen.

i. Sie wird sich sonnen.

j. Wir war in der Innenstadt.

k. Meine Brüder hatten eine tolle Zeit.

l. Er wird typische Gerichte probieren.

m. Ich hast viele Fotos gemacht.

n. Mein Papa war sehr zufrieden.

31. Complete with *ich, du, er/sie/es, wir, ihr, sie.*

a. (__________) waren in der Stadt einkaufen. (me+my friends)

b. Wirst (__________) mit dem Auto fahren oder nimmst (__________) den Bus?

c. (__________) war letztes Wochenende mit meinem Freund Martin in Wien.

d. Habt (__________) das Kunsthistorische Museum besucht? Es ist sehr interessant.

e. Meine Freunde sind sehr nett. (__________) laden mich immer auf einen Milchshake ein.

f. Meine Schwester hat viele Ausflüge gemacht. (__________) liebt es, neue Orte zu erkunden.

g. Mein Bruder liebt den Strand. (__________) fährt jeden Sommer nach Mallorca.

32. Translate the following texts into German

1. My name is Franz and I am from Melk, in the east of Austria. Normally I go on holiday to the Wörthersee, in the south of Austria. I like it a lot, but it sometimes rains. Last year I went on holiday to Mallorca, which is a Balearic island, with my best friend Karl. Karl is very tall and funny. We went to Mallorca by plane and we stayed in a youth hostel. In Palma, the capital of Mallorca, we went for a walk in the town centre and we bought souvenirs. One day we went to an art gallery. It was an exciting trip and I would love to go back again.

2. My name is Johann and I am from Bamberg, in the south of Germany. Normally I go on holiday to Sylt, which is an island in the North Sea. I like it a lot because the people are very nice. Last year I went on holiday to Rügen, which is an island in the Baltic sea, with my girlfriend Tina. Tina is clever and hard-working. We went to Rügen by coach and we stayed in a cheap hotel. We saw the Seebrücke and went to the beach. One day we went to the Rügen Gallery. It was a fun trip and we would like to go back again next year.

3. My name is Sandra and I am from Aachen, in the west of Germany. Normally I go on holiday to Portugal. I like it a lot because the weather is good and the food is delicious. Last year I went on holiday to Tyrol, in the west of Austria, with my best friend Anna. Anna is strong and very kind. We went to Tyrol by plane and we stayed in a luxury hotel. We saw the Goldene Dach and we also visited the old town. The best thing was the people and the food. It was an interesting trip and I would like to go back again some day.

Question Skills Unit 15

1. Match questions and answers

Wo bist du hingefahren?	Mit dem Auto.
Wie bist du angereist?	In einem bekannten türkischen Restaurant.
Wie war die Fahrt?	Es war meistens warm.
Wo hast du übernachtet?	Ich habe Sightseeing gemacht.
Wo warst du essen?	Die Leute waren sehr hilfsbereit.
Was hast du in Berlin gemacht?	Nach Berlin.
Welche Sehenswürdigkeiten hast du besichtigt?	Die Fahrt war lang und langweilig.
	Ja, das würde ich gerne.
Wie war das Wetter?	Ich habe das Brandenburger Tor und Checkpoint Charlie besichtigt.
Was hat dir an Berlin am besten gefallen?	
Wie waren die Leute?	Das Beste war die Currywurst.
Willst du noch einmal hinfahren?	In einer sehr guten Jugendherberge.

2. Sentence puzzle: rewrite the sentences in the correct order

a. gefahren du letzten Sommer Wohin auf Urlaub bist? *Where did you go on holiday last summer?*

b. waren Wie die in Leute Berlin? *What were the people in Berlin like?*

c. Wie das im war Urlaub Wetter? *What was the weather like during the holidays?*

d. besten hat dir am an der Stadt Was gefallen? *What did you like bestabout the city?*

e. hinfahren Warum gerne würdest du noch einmal? *Why would you like to go back there?*

f. historischen Welche besucht Orte hast du? *Which historic places did you visit?*

g. gemacht Was Abend hast du am? *What did you do in the evening?*

h. wirst du Sommer nächsten Was machen? *What are you going to do next summer?*

i. Mit du wirst reisen wem? *Who are you going to travel with?*

3. Guided translation

a. W___ b____ d___ l_______ W___________ h__________? *Where did you go last weekend?*

b. W____ b____ d__ h_______________? *How did you travel?*

c. M_____ w_____ b____ d__ h_______________? *Who did you travel with?*

d. W____ l_____ w______ d___ d______? *How long did you stay?*

e. W____ w____ d____ F__________? *How did the trip go?*

f. W___ h_____ d___ ü_______________? *Where did you stay?*

g. W____ h______ d__ a__ A__________ g__________? *What did you do in the evening?*

h. W________ O_______ h______ d___ b___________? *What places did you visit?*

i. W____ w____ d____ W___________? *What was the weather like?*

j. W____ h____ d____ a___ b_______ g____________? *What did you like best?*

4. Write a question for each of the answers below

Questions	Answer
a.	Ich werde mit dem Zug fahren.
b.	Ich werde zwei Wochen bleiben.
c.	Es war sehr warm.
d.	Ja, die Reise war super.
e.	Ich war wandern und klettern.
f.	Ich bin mit meiner Familie gefahren.
g.	Meine Eltern waren Sightseeing.
h.	Wir haben uns alte Bauten angesehen.
i.	Wir haben in einem Luxushotel übernachet.
j.	Das Hotel war in der Innenstadt.

5. Spot and correct the mistakes in the German sentences

a. Wann bist du nach Deutschland gereist? *How did you go to Germany?*

b. Wie bist du gereist? *Who did you travel with?*

c. Wie war das Haus? *How was the trip?*

d. Wo haben wir übernachtet? *Where did you stay?*

e. Welche Sehenswürdigkeiten hat sie gesehen? *What places did he visit?*

f. Warum hat es dir gefallen? *Why did you not like it?*

g. Was hast du am Morgen gemacht? *What did you do in the evening?*

h. Würdest du gerne das Schloss besuchen? *Would you like to go back there again?*

6. Translate into German

a. Where did you go?

b. Who did you go with?

c. How long did you stay there?

d. Where did you stay?

e. What was the hotel like?

f. What did you do in the mornings?

g. What did you do in the evenings?

h. What did your parents do?

i. Would you like to go back there again?

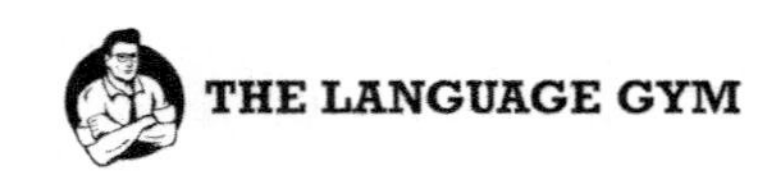

Printed in Great Britain
by Amazon